To: Norman

With dearest wishes & love
for Xmas 84.

Lesley Jim Fiona Cameron

GW00707253

WHAT SHELL IS THAT?

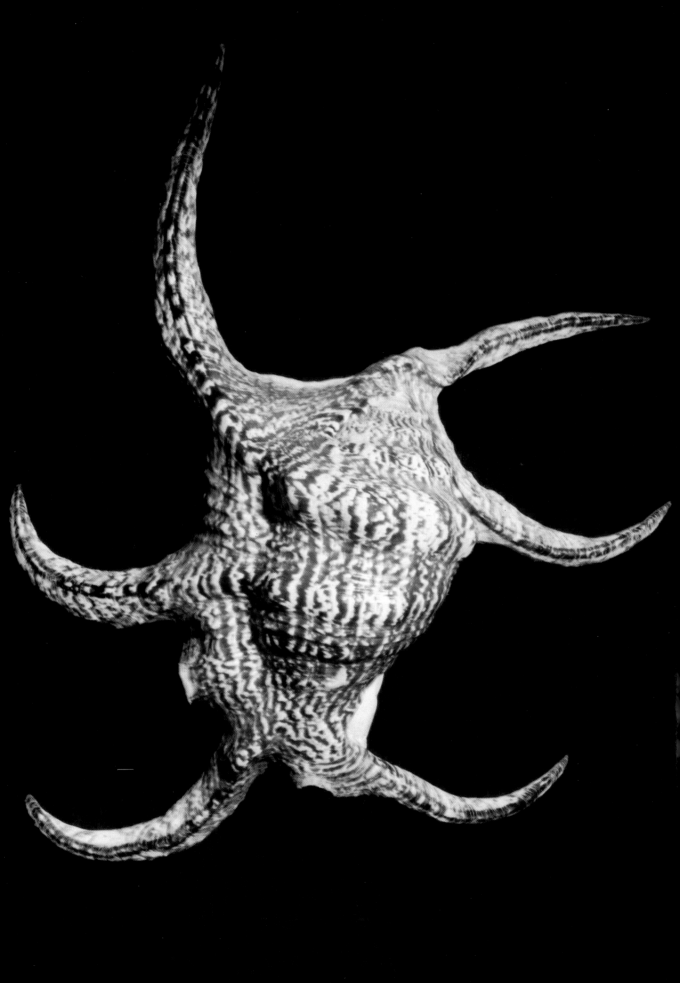

WHAT SHELL IS THAT?

Neville Coleman

Sydney · Auckland · London · New York

Published by Lansdowne Press
176 South Creek Road, Dee Why West,
NSW, Australia 2099
First published 1975
2nd Edition 1981
Reprinted 1983
© Neville Coleman
Produced in Australia by the Publisher
Typeset in Australia
Printed in Hong Kong

National Library of Australia
Cataloguing-in-Publication Data
Coleman, Neville
    What shell is that?
    Rev. ed.
    Previous ed., Sydney, Hamlyn, 1975.
    Includes indexes
    ISBN 0 7018 1550 7
    1. Molluscs — Australia. I. Title.
594'.047

Contents

Acknowledgements

The photographs in this book are from the files of the Australasian Marine Photographic Index. The Index contains colour transparencies of living animals and plants, cross-referenced against identified specimens housed in museums and scientific institutes. It also covers related marine activities.

As Curator of the Index, it is my hope that one day the marine flora and fauna of Australia may be identified alive; there will then no longer be any necessity for large collections of animals to be made just for the purposes of identification. If we are able to find methods of protecting our seas and husbanding the animals and plants that are in them, people must be made aware of their existence. It is for this purpose that the Index was created.

Although the project has world recognition and is being used by many overseas museums and scientific institutes, as well as most major museums in Australia, it cannot survive without the co-operation of groups and individuals. The following institutions, companies and individuals have aided the Index and assisted in the compilation and updating of this book. Their foresight, interest and assistance will enable the Index to continue its programme of advancing the knowledge of living Australian marine organisms.

Sea Australia Productions Pty Ltd, The Australian Museum, The National Museum of Victoria, The Queensland Museum, The Western Australian Museum. Dr W. Ponder, Mrs S. Slacksmith, Mr P. Colman, Mr I. Loch and Dr W. Rudman for the identification of specimens, constructive criticism and advice on nomenclature. The C.S.I.R.O. Science and Industry Endowment Fund for contributions towards the Australian Coastal Marine Expedition. (1969-73). Dr B. Wilson for unrivalled help and comradeship while the expedition was in Western Australia. Mr Keith Gillet and Mr Allan Power for advice during the early stages of my photography. The Australian Rope Manufacturers for donations of their excellent products.

I would especially like to thank Mr Bob Burn, Honorary Associate of the National Museum of Victoria and the trustees of that institution, whose continued encouragement throughout many years has been instrumental in bringing to press this first major colour reference to the Australian opisthobranch fauna. This is especially significant as only a mere handful of the profusely common multicoloured nudibranchs have ever been published in colour from well over a thousand species thought to exist.

Steve Parish, wildlife photogapher, and Jim Tobin (USA), both friends for being. Karen Handley and Deborah FitzGerald for the typing and index, and to all the collectors, photographers, naturalists, trawlermen and divers who have in many ways enabled Australasian Marine Photographic Index Explorer programmes to continue their unrivalled endeavours.

Neville Coleman
(I.A.P.)
Curator

Abbreviations

N.S.W.	New South Wales
Qld.	Queensland
N.T.	Northern Territory
northern W.A.	northern Western Australia
W.A.	Western Australia
S.A.	South Australia
Vic.	Victoria
Tas.	Tasmania

For sight beyond the light

Explanation

During the six years since this book was first published there have been many changes to the nomenclature of molluscs. Many groups have been studied more thoroughly, resulting in the publication of more updated scientific papers allowing modern corrections to be added to this text.

The knowledge of shell distributions has also been expanded. Some of the species are now known to be new to science and subsequently undescribed, eg. no. 180, Coleman's Phyllodesmium, *Phyllodesmium* sp. A major revision of changes to over 250 species now makes "What Shell is That?" the largest and most up to date full colour visual identification guide compiled on shells of the South Pacific.

Photographic details
Cameras: Hasselblad — 50 mm lens, Rollei Marine — 80 mm lens — no. 3 diopters, Nikon — 55 mm Micronikkor + 105 mm Micronikkor, Nikonos — 35 mm + close up tube.
Flashes: Metz — 108 — 302B — 402
Film: Kodachrome 64 ASA, Ektachome 64 ASA

Introduction

Throughout the years the ever increasing popularity of shell collecting and its allied studies has led to a great deal of excellent literature being made available.

Although many of these books cover almost every aspect of the mollusc, from anatomy through to nomenclature and descriptive identification, each has been based on a similar pattern, that of scientific systematics. Each family of shells is pictured together in order of priority according to its ancient lineage.

In the past this has been sufficient, the majority of collectors were concerned only with the shell of the mollusc, a study called Conchology.

Today a much younger science known as Malacology is blooming. This study includes all the features of the mollusc, both living and dead, together with its ecology and natural history. This has led to a new awareness of looking at shells as living animals.

It seems incredible that these soft bodied architects of nature can combine salt water and their own body fluids to produce structures of so many intricate and delicate shapes, patterns and colours. They bring unceasing amazement to all who behold them and often the animals themselves are even more striking in colour and form than the shells they produce.

Because publishers normally only cater to known markets, most of the shells pictured in books are of similar species and are made up of those which are popular and have aesthetic appeal to both collectors and the public. In this regard *What Shell is That?* also contains many of these species, but it has gone beyond the normal mode of shell books and reproduced shells and animals the like which has never before been attempted. Besides close-up studies of the shells themselves there are hundreds of living animals from almost every class. The shells are presented where they live, in their single or combined habitats. Much of the information concerning ecology, collecting natural history and conservation is unique to this publication.

There are no hard and fast rules which can be laid down in regard to where shells live, where they are found, how big they grow, or their colours.

As new information comes to hand past knowledge may be added to or deleted. Names, geographical distribution, types of food, habits, size, colour and availability are all subject to change. The examples shown within this book are therefore merely guidelines.

Figuring over 750 species each shell has a family name, common name and scientific name, together with the author and the date his description was published.

Because of past complex problems involved with the naming procedures of many Australian shells there is still much confusion as to correct identities.

It is not the purpose of this book to become involved in a purely professional field but rather to make available a little knowledge gleaned from the molluscs themselves. For the pursuit of knowledge is a pastime in which all may benefit, from the youngest to the oldest, amateur or professional.

Within these covers are facts, photographs and observations, the accumulated results of ten years study. Important as they may be in their own context they will never be as meaningful as when the book is first opened by a reader. From that moment on, each figure and fact will be shared, and to share, is the ultimate achievement.

Neville Coleman

Part I
Mud and Mangroves

Mud and Mangroves

2

The first section deals with molluscs which inhabit areas of mangrove swamps, mud and muddy sand rubble flats, both intertidally and in shallow waters.

Mangrove swamps are very rich in nutritional output and their existence is imperative if the overall food chain balance of the estuaries and nursery areas is to be maintained. Although the shells found in these areas are not always colourful or attractive they are nevertheless extremely interesting for many are unique to this habitat and live in no other.

A mangrove swamp is where the land and the sea have compromised, animals and plants from both environments have adjusted to the various degrees of change, allowing life to be co-existent. Mangrove trees can resist quite large percentages of salinity and although their roots and lower trunks are intermittently covered by salt water they flourish in areas where other trees would die. Some species have adopted special methods of combating the soft oozy oxygen depleted mud and send their roots up through the surface of the mud to help in respiration. These roots are termed pneumatophores.

Numbers of mud and mangrove molluscs have also adapted to a half life on land and sea. Many can extract the oxygen from sea water and also breathe air. Different species have evolved in different geographical areas but in the main their living and feeding habits are similar. The very existence of vast acres of cultured oysters depends largely on the presence of muddy estuarine mangrove swamps which stabilize their growth.

Lower down towards the sublittoral the mangroves give way to mud flats, rubble banks, shore reefs and sea grass flats. These areas are also very rich in species although they are not as restricted to habitat as much as the mangrove molluscs.

Some molluscs are detritus feeders taking in mouthfuls of mud and sifting out the organic matter. Others are filter feeders siphoning in the water and feeding on all the small planktonic animals and plants contained therein. The latter species are mostly bivalves and live below the surface of the mud. The cockles and lanterns, tellins and wedges, all in turn being preyed upon by sand snails, dog whelks and murex. These are eaten by crabs and fish, and so on, finally ending up as a proportion of the average human diet. Molluscs are only a small part of the overall life to be found in these areas and even though a complete record of these is beyond the scope of this book it is hoped that those included will give the reader an inside glimpse into an important world that is more than just mud and mosquitoes.

3

4

3
AKERIDAE
Papery Bubble Shell
Akera soluta
Gmelin, 1791

This delicate little bubble shell seems to be very cyclic in its appearance. For many years it will be of rare occurrence, then there will be an upsurge in population and shells may be found en masse. *A. soluta* lives on muddy sand flats intertidally down to 10 metres and feeds mostly on other small molluscs, ingesting them whole. Range: N.S.W. to southern W.A. Size: 25 mm. Periodically common.

4
AMPHIBOLIDAE
Fragile Air Breather
Salinator fragilis
Lamarck, 1822

Larger and more delicate than its nearest relative *S. solida, S. fragilis* can be identified by its dark concentric bands. The shell is extremely common on muddy intertidal flats, and seems to prefer areas where there is a certain amount of fresh water run off or drainage. During high tides the shell stays burrowed beneath the mud. It mates in summer. Range: Qld., N.S.W., Vic., Tas., S.A., W.A. Size: 12 mm. Common.

5

5
AMPHIBOLIDAE
Solid Air Breather
Salinator solida
von Martens, 1878

These shells appear at low tide from out of muddy sand habitats in many southern estuaries. Their eggs are cemented with sand and laid in small collar shaped girdles. Range: Qld., N.S.W., Vic., Tas., S.A., W.A. Size: 9 mm. Extremely common in some areas.

6
ANOMIIDAE
Jingle Shell
Anomia descripta
Iredale, 1936

Separate valves of these varicoloured translucent shells are of frequent occurrence on mud flats and beaches, particularly those in estuaries. They live from low tide level to over 10 metres subtidally and frequent several habitats. In a live state they are prolific on muddy flats where they form clumps either attached to other shells or to each other. Also found on muddy reefs or rubble bottoms. Range: N.S.W. to W.A. Size: 50 mm. Common.

6

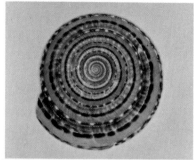

7
ARCHITECTONICIDAE
Perspective Sundial
Architectonica perspectiva
Linnaeus, 1758

Found from low tide level down to 40 metres *A. perspectiva* is one of the most common sundial shells. Growing to 50 mm. it is the largest species in Australia and is usually found in areas of muddy sand. Range: N.S.W. to northern W.A. Size: 50 mm. Common.

8
ARCIDAE
Mud Ark
Anadara trapezia
Deshayes, 1839

A well-known edible species. These shells are commonly collected amongst mud and weed on intertidal flats in N.S.W. estuaries where they are usually located below the surface of the mud. They have a bright red animal. Range: Qld., N.S.W. southern W.A. Size: 70 mm.

9
BULLIDAE
Quoy's Bubble Shell
Bulla quoyii
Gray, 1843

This species is very prolific on tidal mud flats and also in shallow areas below tide level. Inveterate burrowers, they are usually a little difficult to locate alive, especially underwater. Dead shells wash up on tidelines by the hundreds in areas adjacent to their habitat. They are carnivorous and feed on other small molluscs. Range: N.S.W., Vic., Tas., S.A., Size: 35 mm. Common.

8

7

9

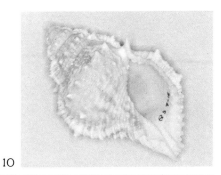

10

10
BURSIDAE
Frog Shell
Bufonaria rana
Linnaeus, 1758

Often difficult to find alive, this
species lives in muddy sand below
tide level. Good specimens can be
acquired by tideline collecting as
dead shells are washed up frequently
on northern beaches. Range: Qld. to
northern W.A. Size: 50 mm.
Common.

11

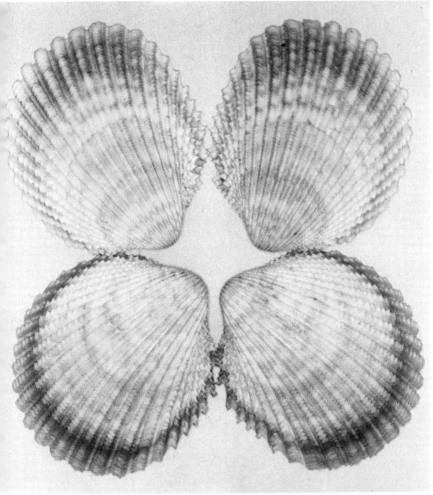

11
CARDIIDAE
Flavum Heart Cockle
Acrosterigma flava
Linnaeus, 1758

Fairly common in muddy sand on the
intertidal flats of the Queensland
mainland, these shells live in
extensive colonies below tide level to
around 10 metres. They have a
brown periostracum and are quite
edible. Range: Qld. to northern W.A.
Size: 80 mm. Common.

12
CARDIIDAE
Half Cockle
Fragum hemicardium
Linnaeus, 1758

These shells live in muddy sand both
intertidally or subtidally. Generally
this species is whitish in colour but
some specimens are a yellowish
colour with red flecks. Range: Qld.
Size: 30 mm. Very common in some
areas.

12

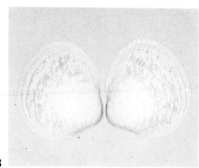

13

13
CARDIIDAE
Rackett's Strawberry Cockle
Fulvia racketti
Donovan, 1825

Common along the southern Australian coastline this shell inhabits sand and sandy mud flats from low tide level to beyond 20 metres. After rough weather hundreds of these shells can be found washed up on beaches. Most of these have a yellow appearance, but this is only the skin or periostracum of the shell. When removed their base colour is white with varied amounts of red patterning. Range: N.S.W., Vic., S.A., Size: 35 mm. Common.

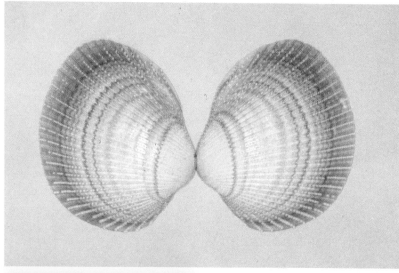

14

14
CARDIIDAE
Hairy Cockle
Plagiocardium setosum
Redfield, 1846

Fairly restricted to areas of muddy sand along the northern N.S.W. and Qld. coast, *V. setosum* has a brown hairy periostracum and grows to a little over 50 mm. Range: N.S.W. to northern W.A. Size: approx. 50 mm. Common.

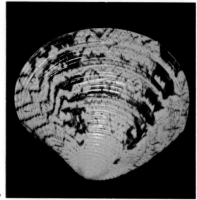

15

15
CIRCIDAE
Circular Tapestry Shell
Circe trigona
Reeve, 1863

Very common on intertidal mud flats in Qld., this shell is also found in mud below tide level. The shell pattern varies but the internal colouring is dark purple. Range: N.S.W. to Qld. Size: 50 mm. Common.

16
CLAVAGELLIDAE
Australian Watering Pot
Brechites vaginiferus australis
Chenu, 1843

This sub-species occurs in muddy rubble flats intertidally along the north-west coast of Australia, but also inhabits coarse shell sand areas on the offshore islands. The shell begins life as a small bivalve, the elongated tube and complex posterior siphoral appendages are constructed as it grows and it is often difficult to remove the shell from the substrate. Range: W.A. Size: 200 mm. Moderately common in some localities.

16

17

17
CONIDAE
Sting Ray Cone
Conus trigonus
Reeve, 1848

A much sought after shell uncommonly collected over its restricted range. It lives on intertidal mud flats and feeds mostly on worms. The eggs are white, typically cone shaped, and are laid on solid objects during early summer. Range: northern W.A. to N.T. Size: 65 mm. Uncommon.

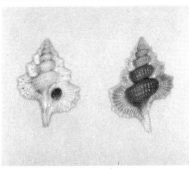

18

18
CYMATIIDAE
Little Kookaburra Shell
Gyrineum jucundum
A. Adams, 1854

This little shell is also much sought after by enthusiastic collectors. It can be taken occasionally on mud banks at extreme low tides, or dredged in mud at depths exceeding 12 metres. It has a sparsely haired periostracum. Range: Qld. to W.A. Size: 25 mm. Common in some areas.

19
CYPRAEIDAE
Pyriform Cowry
Cypraea pyriformis
Gray, 1824

C. pyriformis enjoys a mud flat habitat and is not a common mollusc. It lays its eggs in late spring or in summer and these are usually deposited in an upturned bivalve shell or beneath rocks. The female sits on the eggs until they hatch. The shells are subject to flaws such as growth marks and heal breaks. Range: Qld. to northern W.A. Size: 30 mm. Uncommon.

19

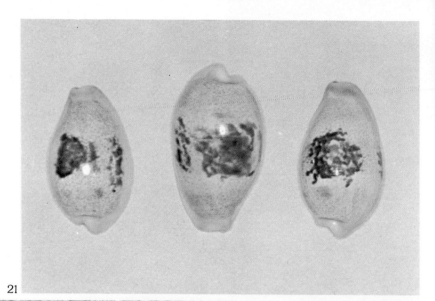

21

20 & 21
CYPRAEIDAE
Blotched Green Cowry
Cypraea subviridis
Reeve, 1835

Common on mud flats and muddy reef *C. subviridis* can be found intertidally around sponges, soft corals or under rocks or shells. Eggs are laid in summer and the female sits on these until they hatch. If disturbed she will leave the egg mass, returning only if re-positioned. Range: Qld. to W.A. Size: 40 mm. Common.

22
DENDRODORIDIDAE
Wart-Backed Nudibranch
Dendrodoris tuberculosa
Quoy & Gaimard, 1833

Although quite a large sized species, it is not often observed in Australian waters. The large wart-like tubercules on the back make it an easily identified mollusc even without a shell. Found on intertidal mud flats and muddy reef in Western Australia. Range: Qld. to W.A. Size: 170 mm. Uncommon.

22

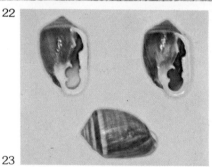

23

24

24
ELLOBIIDAE
Judas Ear Shell
Ellobium aurisjudae
Linnaeus, 1758

This air breathing shell lives in mangrove swamps. For an ear shell, it is particularly long and narrow, and has a dark yellow periostracum covering a white shell. Range: Qld. to northern W.A. Size: 50 mm. Seldom found alive.

23
ELLOBIIDAE
Angular Ear Shell
Cassidula angulifera
Petit, 1841

This small dark brown shell lives in the upper reaches of mangrove swamps. It is an air breather and like its cousins has no operculum or trap-door to protect itself. Members of its family have enlarged teeth on the lip which prevent predators entering the aperture or harming the mollusc, short of crushing the shell. Range: Qld. to northern W.A. Size: 25 mm.

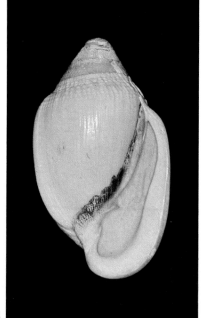

25
ELLOBIIDAE
Midas Ear Shell
Ellobium aurismidae
Linnaeus, 1758

This is the largest species of shell in this family. An air breather, it lives intertidally amongst mangroves in the far north of Australia. Although the name is similar to *E. aurisjudae*, the shell is entirely different being much broader and having a dark brown periostracum. Range: northern Qld. to northern W.A. Size: 76 mm.

25

26
ELLOBIIDAE
Southern Mangrove Air Breather
Ophicardelus ornatus
Ferussac, 1821

A very common little shell, well distributed throughout the mangroves and mud banks of its range. One of the largest of the few air breathing marine molluscs in southern waters. Range: N.S.W., Vic., Tas., Size: 12 mm. Common.

26

27
ELLOBIIDAE
Rugate Ear Shell
Cassidula rugata
Menke, 1843

Not as common as its relative *C. angulifera*, this shell inhabits intertidal areas of mangrove swamp usually just below the high tide zone. It is reputed to grow larger than *C. angulifera* but all shells found by the author have been smaller. Range: Qld. to W.A. Size: 20 mm. Moderately common.

28
ELLOBIIDAE
Scarab Ear Shell
Pythia scarabaeus
Linnaeus, 1758

P. scarabaeus lives intertidally in mangroves or brackish water swamps. As with other members of its family it is able to live in or out of the water and requires only a minimum of dampness. Its eggs are laid close to the water on branches and trunks of mangrove trees. Range: northern Qld. to N.T. Size: 25 mm. Moderately common.

27

28

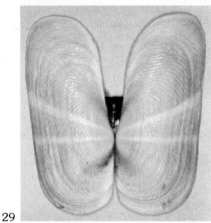

29

29
SOLECURTIDAE
Sulcate Sunset Shell
Solecurtus sulcatus
Dunker, 1861

Not often found alive, these shells live subtidally in sandy mud and are usually burrowed to depths exceeding 200 mm. They have a light brown periostracum. Range: Qld. to N.T. Size: 65 mm. Moderately common.

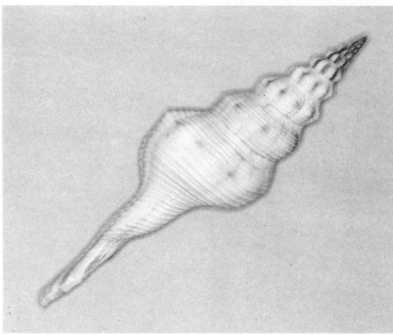

30

30
FASCIOLARIIDAE
Distaff Spindle
Fusinus colus
Linnaeus, 1758

A pretty, delicate species found on intertidal mud banks from Qld. to W.A. It is readily distinguishable from other members of its family. The animal is bright red in colour and feeds on small bivalves. Not very common above the low tide level, specimens can be trawled or dredged in shallow waters. Range: Qld. to W.A. Size: 115 mm. Uncommon.

31
EUCRASSATELLIDAE
Cuming's Crasatella
Eucrassatella cumingii
A. Adams, 1854

A large heavily ribbed species with a dark periostracum, *E. cumingii* inhabits intertidal areas of muddy sand. Range: northern N.S.W. and Qld. Size: grows to nearly 76 mm. Very common.

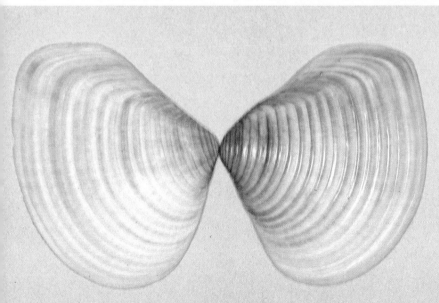

32
ISOGNOMONTIDAE
Mauve Pearl Shell
Melina ephippium
Linnaeus, 1758

Common throughout mangrove swamps and upper tidal inlets, throughout its range. Similar to a pearl shell in shape it is easily distinguished by its hinge teeth and beautiful pinky mauve interior. Range: northern N.S.W. to northern W.A. Size: 140 mm. Common.

31   32

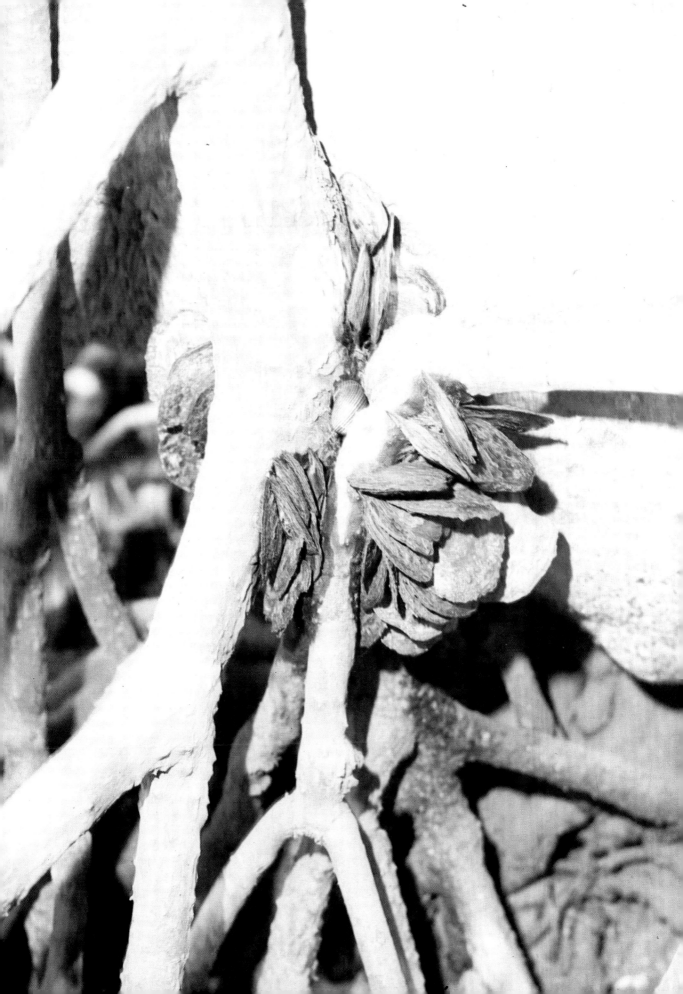

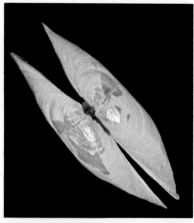

33
LATERNULIDAE
Creccina Lantern Shell
Laternula creccina
Reeve, 1860

This thin white bivalve lives several inches below the surface in mud banks. It has a long white siphon which is forced up through the mud to the surface. The siphon takes in water which supplies the mollusc below with food and oxygen. Range: N.S.W., Vic., Tas., S.A., W.A. Size: 65 mm.

33

34
LITTORINIDAE
Mangrove Australwink
Littorina scabra
Linnaeus, 1758

Commonly observed on the upper branches and leaves of mangrove trees, *L. scabra,* like others of its genus, seems to prefer a dry habitat rather than a wet one. Scientists have suggested that this species could be evolving into a terrestrial mode of life. The most colourful of our australwinks, specimens can be found in reds, yellows, browns and various patterned combinations. The female returns to the intertidal level after mating to bear her living young. The juvenile shells spend some time in this marine environment before moving up onto the trunks and branches. Range: Qld. to northern W.A. Size: 25 mm. Common.

34

35
MACTRIDAE
Scoop Trough Shell
Lutraria rhynchaena
Jonas, 1884

Unless dug for in muddy sand flats below low tide level this shell is not collected alive. Valves often wash ashore on estuarine beaches and are covered by a brown periostracum. Divers sometimes find dead shells in tide channels. Range: N.S.W. to southern W.A. Size: 100 mm. Common.

36
MELONGENIDAE
False Trumpet Shell
Syrinx aruanus
Linnaeus, 1758

One of the largest univalves in Australia. *S. aruanus* is found commonly on seldom visited mud flats. It also inhabits deeper water down to at least 60 metres. The animal is bright yellow in colour and the females lay a white column of sectioned egg capsules cemented together and attached to substrate or any suitable solid object. They are most voracious, feeding mostly on other molluscs. The large foot of the animal is quite edible as evidenced by extensive shell remains in Aboriginal middens. The Aborigines also used whole shells with the whorls cut out as water carriers. Range: W.A. and Qld. Size: to 600 mm. Common.

35

36

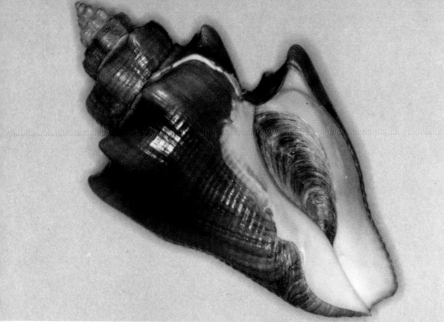

37

37
MELONGENIDAE
Northern Volema
Volema cochlidium
Linnaeus, 1758

This shell lives on intertidal mud flats
and is fairly gregarious. Because of
this and its size, some localities have
been extensively collected, resulting
in extreme reductions in populations
in isolated areas. In life it is covered
with a thick periostracum which
has to be removed before the rich
colour of the shell can be appreciated.
Range: northern W.A., N.T., northern
Qld. Size: up to 120 mm. Common
to some areas of W.A. and N.T.

38

38
MITRIDAE
Wilson's Mitre
Scabricola barrywilsoni
J. Cate, 1968

This rare species can be found
intertidally on mud flats throughout
its range. Although the majority of
specimens are collected in a dead
condition, recently several have been
found alive. Range: northern W.A. to
N.T. Size: 40 mm. Rare.

39
COSTELLARIIDAE
Coffee and Rum Mitre
Vexillum caffrum
Linnaeus, 1758

In Australia this species is found on
the north Qld. coast where it lives in
semi-sand mud flats. It is not
commonly found alive and can be
superficially confused with a similar
species *V. vulpecula* (Linnaeus, 1758).
Range: northern Qld. Size: 44mm.
Uncommon.

40
MITRIDAE
Strange's Mitre
Cancilla strangei
Angas, 1867

A very rare species in shallow waters.
It has only been taken alive on a few
occasions. The author has recorded
specimens living on a subtidal muddy
bottom amongst detritus and
mussels. When alive the shell has a
mauve protoconch but this fades with
time. The animal is white with black
spots. Range: Qld., N.S.W., Vic., Tas.
Size: 25 mm. Common on the
continental shelf.

41
MURICIDAE
Spine-Winged Murex
Pterochelus acanthopterus
Lamarck, 1816

Without doubt *P. acanthopterus* is the
most well distributed muricid in
Australia. Found in every state except
Tas. it has many variations of form,
colour and habitat. The largest and
most perfect specimens live
intertidally in W.A. reaching a size of
over 100 mm. Strangely enough, in
the same vicinity as these giants live
dwarf forms which mate only with
other dwarfs and produce their own
peculiar midget egg capsules. An
attempt is being made to show some
logical reason for these two
extremes. Eggs are laid in early
summer months, usually in an empty
bivalve shell. Food is generally
bivalves or tube worms. Some shells
have been located as deep as 150
metres although most available
specimens range from low tide to 50
metres. A very popular shell amongst
collectors, good specimens are none
the less considered uncommon.
Range: all States except Tas. Size: up
to 100 mm.

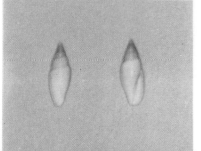

39

40

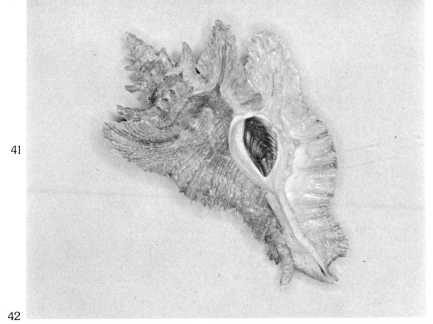

41

42

42
MURICIDAE
Centre-Horned Murex
Chicoreus axicomis
Lamarck, 1822

Found on intertidal rubble mud flats in the extreme north of Australia, this shell is often covered with a red sponge. It has an orange animal almost identical to *C. banksii* and lives on small bivalves, including chamas and spondulus. It is trawled regularly off the Qld. coast in depths ranging from 10 to 30 metres, the deeper water shells which live on muddy or rubble bottoms are also prone to encrustation by orange sponge. Range: Qld., N.T., W.A. Size: 76 mm. Moderately common.

43
MURICIDAE
Burnt Murex
Chicoreus brunneus
Link, 1807

A common species of murex shell along the Qld. mainland and offshore Barrier Reef islands, *C. brunneus* displays beautiful foliated varices. Specimens that live in muddy areas develop larger varice extensions than those living on coral reefs. Also the coral reef forms are extremely hard to clean because of the marine growths adhering to their varices. The shells are normally black with a distinctive pink aperture. Occasionally in some areas, the aperture may be orange or even yellow. Their food consists mainly of bivalves, preference being shown for chama shells. The murex have no difficulty in drilling through the thick shells of their prey taking up to three days to consume the animal inside. Eggs are laid in September, usually underneath ledges and coral rock. Range: Qld. to N.T. Size: 95 mm. Common.

43

44
MURICIDAE
Two Fork Murex
Chicoreus cervicornis
Lamarck, 1822

Fairly common on intertidal mud flats in N.T. and northern Qld., this shell also inhabits the same type of areas in northern W.A., but is considered uncommon there. During pearling operations in northern Australia, divers found numbers of these shells attached to the sides of pearl shells. Egg capsules were also laid on pearl shells. Recent deep water dredging by the W.A. Museum from the HMAS *Diamantina* off Rottnest Island has revealed *C. cervicornis* living at depths of 200 metres. Range: N.T., northern Qld., northern W.A. Size: 50 mm. Common.

45

45
MURICIDAE
Staghorn Murex
Chicoreus cornucervi
Roeding, 1798

Fairly common on intertidal mud flats in some areas of northern W.A., this shell is also found on offshore islands and ranges through the N.T. to Qld. Not all shells are restricted to an intertidal existence as specimens have been found living in deep water at several localities. The variceal extensions, from which *C. cornucervi* gets its common name, serve the species well in regard to self preservation. These extensions become covered with algae and other marine organisms. This, combined with the mud and their habit of seeking the protection of solid objects, makes their discovery a little difficult for beginners. Eggs are laid in the summer and food consists mainly of bivalves. Range: northern W.A., N.T. to Qld. Size: 112 mm. Common.

44

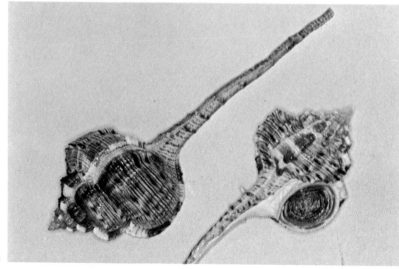

46
MURICIDAE
Snipes Head Murex
Haustellum haustellum
Linnaeus, 1758

Although reasonably common in its habitat, *H. haustellum* is not collected very often in Australian waters. They live in a sandy mud habitat and seem to prefer areas adjacent to river mouths. Range: Qld. to northern W.A. Size: 101 mm. Uncommon.

46

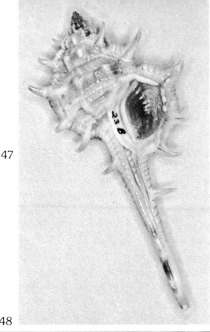

47

47
MURICIDAE
Macgillivray's Murex
Murex macgillivrayi
Dohrn, 1862

One of the most common *Murex* species, this shell is found on intertidal sand banks in northern W.A. and N.T. It is also dredged and trawled to 60 metres of water off the Qld. coast on a mud or sandy mud bottom. Eggs are laid in communal masses, sometimes 10 to 20 shells laying at once. The egg mass may be comprised of many thousands of individual capsules and measure well over 400 mm in length. Contained within the mass are tunnels and compartments housing

the female shells. Feeding mainly on small bivalves, these shells grow to 80 mm. Range: Qld. to northern W.A. Size: up to 80 mm. Common.

48
MURICIDAE
Mangrove Murex
Naquetia capucinus
Lamarck, 1822

This extremely interesting species of murex shell is confined entirely to an intertidal habitat in the northern mangrove swamps. Under a permanent shade canopy of branches, its dirty brown shell coated with mud blends almost perfectly with its surroundings. Food consists of various species of boring molluscs (teredos) and worms inhabiting the dead logs, stumps and branches within the mangroves. Mud worms are also eaten. Mating takes place in December, the larger females sometimes having as many as 5 smaller males attached to their shells. Eggs are laid in singular white capsules deep in the shelly tubes of dead teredos or inside hollow logs or sticks. Predators are mainly fish. Range: Qld. to northern W.A. Size: 76 mm. Uncommon.

49
MURICIDAE
Secund Murex
Homolocantha secunda
Lamarck, 1822

This beautiful little murex which lives completely covered in mud, is one of the most difficult species to distinguish from its habitat. It takes the searcher many hours of field practice and know-how before its secret can be discovered. Occasional specimens are found in weedy areas and also under stones and dead coral. They feed on worms and their eggs are laid in September, October. The capsules are laid in the base of empty worm shell tubes, several hard translucent ovals containing yellow eggs. There is evidence that the female sits on the eggs till hatching. The only natural predators observed have been fish. Range: northern W.A. to N.T. Size: 40 mm. Uncommon.

48

49

50

51

50
MURICIDAE
Stainforth's Murex
Hexaplex stainforthi
Reeve, 1842

The delicate fronds of *H. stainforthi* harbour many unsightly growths. This is especially noticeable in larger adult shells and in many cases these are not worth collecting as they can never be cleaned effectively. As in all collecting only perfect specimens should be sought. The older or coraline covered shells must be left for breeding. Eggs are laid in summer months and, as with many other muricids, any available substrate will do, even the backs of their fellows. Food is obtained by boring holes through the shells of bivalves and feeding on the animal within. Range: central north-west Australian coast. Size: 76 mm. Common.

51
MYTILIDAE
Hairy Mussel
Trichomya hirsuta
Lamarck, 1819

Vast matted beds of these shells are found in tidal estuaries from Qld. to W.A. Although present at low tide level they are far more extensive subtidally. They have a thick brown periostracum and make up a large part of the diets of many marine animals. Although quite edible they are not as popular for human consumption as the black mussel *M. planulatus*. They can be found in clumps on mudflats, muddy bottoms or on rocky reefs usually in silty areas. Range: Qld. to W.A. Size: 50 mm. Common.

52
NASSARIIDAE
Unicolor Dog Whelk
Nassarius dorsatus
Roeding, 1798

Besides being one of the largest dog whelks, *Z. dorsatus* is also one of the smoothest as it has no granules, ribs or beads on its shell surface. This species lives intertidally on muddy sand flats and is a scavenger. Range: Qld. to northern W.A. Size: 35 mm. Common.

53

54

55

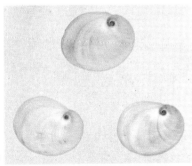

56

57

58

53
NASSARIIDAE
Burchard's Dog Whelk
Nassarius burchardi
Dunker, 1849

Very common on tidal estuary muddy sand flats. *N. burchardi* is a conspicuous feeder on carrion and will often completely cover a fisherman's bait in the shallows. Range: Qld. to Vic. Size: 7 mm. Common.

54
NASSARIIDAE
Mangrove Dog Whelk
Nassarius melanioides
Reeve, 1853

With their black colouring and hideaway habits, *N. melanioides* is not an easy shell to locate. Occurring deep in mangrove swamps in Qld., live specimens can be found inside rotten logs. Range: Qld. to N.T. Size: 25 mm. Fairly rare.

55
NASSARIIDAE
Poor Dog Whelk
Nassarius pauperatus
Lamarck, 1822

This species has a thin yellow periostracum and feeds on small bivalves. It is common on tidal estuary mud flats but like most dog whelks it is extremely variable over its distribution. Range: Vic., Tas. Size: 12 mm. Common.

56
NASSARIIDAE
Ribbed Dog Whelk
Nassarius pullus
Linnaeus, 1758

Living on intertidal mud and sand flats, this species feeds mainly on small bivalves and by scavenging. Range: N.S.W. to Qld. Size: it grows to 12 mm. Common.

57
NATACIDAE
Zoned Sand Snail
Sinum zonale
Quoy & Gaimard, 1833

Moderately common on intertidal mud or muddy sand flats, these molluscs also occur below tide level. The shell is much smaller than the animal and is almost covered by the mantle lobes. It is a carnivore and preys on other small molluscs. Range: N.S.W., Vic., S.A., W.A. Size: grows to 25 mm. Moderately common.

58
NERITIDAE
Mud Nerite
Neritina crepidularia
Lamarck, 1822

Because of its unlikely habitat, *N. crepidularia* is not a well-known species. Its colour blends with the rotten logs and mud of mangrove swamps so well that it takes a very keen eye to distinguish the shells in their environment. Range. Qld., N.T., northern W.A. Size: grows to 16 mm. Uncommon.

59

59
NERITIDAE
Lined Nerite
Nerita lineata
Gmelin, 1791

One of the largest species of nerites, N. lineata lives attached to the roots of tropical mangrove trees. Preferring an area close to and above the high tide level they feed on minute algae scraped from the middle zone mangrove roots to which they migrate, usually at night. Dead shells are favoured by the small hermit crabs inhabiting the mangroves. Range: Qld. to northern W.A. Size: to 38 mm. Common.

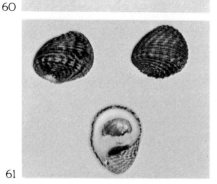

60

60
NERITIDAE
Necklace Nerite
Neritina oualaniensis
Lesson, 1830

An abundant little nerite which lives in colonies on mud flats in northern Australia. It is extremely variable in colour and design. Range: N.S.W. to W.A. Size: grows to 9 mm. Common.

61

61
NERITIDAE
Spired Nerite
Nerita planospira
Anton, 1839

Living on muddy sand, rock and rubble flats of mainland Qld., *N. planospira* is a fairly distinctive species. Live specimens have a brown periostracum, often coated with mud, which effectively adds to their camouflage. Range: Qld. Size: 25 mm. Common.

62
ONCHIDIIDAE
Common Mangrove Slug
Onchidium daemelii
Semper, 1882

To most collectors O. daemelii does not exist. Even if noticed at all it may only earn a passing scuff with a shoe as the collector scurries through the mud to get at the species on the low water. Living high up on the mangrove flats O. daemelii is usually found in small communities. Each slug lives in its own particular hole in the mud. As the tide recedes they emerge and crawl around looking for food which is found lower down on the still wet mud flats. As the tide turns they return to their own hole. This homing sense is not fully understood, even by the experts. Range: N.S.W. Size: 38 mm. Uncommon.

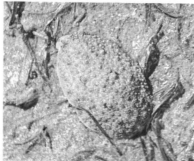

63   62

63
OSTREIDAE
Mud Oyster
Ostraea angasi
Sowerby, 1871

The shells of this very large oyster were used in the days of early settlement for the manufacture of lime for building. Once common on mud flats in most southern estuaries, these shells were almost wiped out by over-commercialisation in the early 1900s. Nowadays divers collect quite a number from bays and inlets along the east and west coasts. Certain places in Sydney Harbour have sparse colonies of these shells, although pollution renders them inedible. In natural habitat these oysters lie on their larger flat surface, normally thought to be the top. Range: N.S.W., Vic., Tas., S.A., W.A. Size: grows to over 150 mm.

64

64
OSTREIDAE
Commercial Oyster
Saccostrea commercialis
Iredale, 1939

Used extensively for food by the Aboriginals for many thousands of years, the commercial oyster has not lost any of its popularity today and it is cultured throughout most of the suitable estuaries within its range. Normally living in a variety of habitats it seems to favour areas of mangroves, mud flats and rocky reefs. In fact mangrove sticks are still favoured in some areas for catching spat. Range: Vic. to Qld. Size: 80 mm. Common.

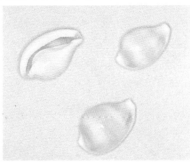

65
OVULIDAE
Banded Ovulid
Margovula bimaculata
Adams, 1854

Usually found on intertidal mud or sand flats, this species is associated with the same alcyonarian host as *M. pyriformis*. Eggs are laid on the host in summer and have planktonic larvae. Range: Qld. Size: 20 mm. Moderately common.

66   65

66
OVULIDAE
Cavanagh's Ovulid
Globovula cavanaghi
Iredale, 1931

Fairly common amongst alcyonarian corals growing intertidally on mud flats throughout their range, their mantles blend in quite well with their host's colours. Specimens found by the author which were living in Botany Bay, N.S.W. 5 years ago, were located on soft corals at a depth of 10 metres. Here the molluscs were feeding on an entirely different genus of alcyonarian which was blue in colour. Mostly nocturnal feeders the shells hide away in daylight hours amongst the wavy fronds of their host. Range: N.S.W., Qld., N.T., northern W.A. Size: 15 mm. Fairly common.

67

68

69

67
OVULIDAE
Punctate Ovulid
Pseudosimnia punctata
Duclos, 1831

Although this species does not live directly on mud flats, its host soft corals do. Found on small spiky alcyonarians this little allied cowry was considered a rarity until its habitat was discovered several years ago. Over zealous collectors who damage the host animals, the young and eggs of this little cowry, might well be the cause of their becoming uncommon in the future. Range: Qld. to northern W.A. Size: 9 mm.

68, 69
OVULIDAE
Pyriform Ovulid
Margovula pyriformis
Sowerby, 1828

Living in the same mud flat area as its cowry namesake *M. pyriformis* is nevertheless quite distinguishable. Although it roams at will, its host is a small whitish-grey alcyonarian which can raise or lower itself below the surface of the mud. If the hosts are dug out, the food, eggs and young of this mollusc are also sacrificed. This practice, along with many others is a selfish unwarranted act of vandalism, and must be treated with abhorrence. Range: N.S.W. to Qld. Size: 15 mm.

70
PECTINIDAE
Leopard Scallop
Chlamys leopardus
Reeve, 1853

Found on muddy sand flats intertidally in Qld., this shell is also trawled in depth down to 40 metres. Quite a beautiful scallop it is subject to attacks by marine boring animals which leave discoloured holes in the surface of the shell. Range: Qld. Size: 76 mm. Common.

70

72   71

73

71
PHENACOLEPADIDAE
Black Mud Limpet
Phenacolepas cinnamomea
Gould, 1846

Although fairly common in its habitat, this shell is not collected very often. It

lives subtidally in estuarine conditions and can be found beneath rocks or rubble on muddy bottoms to depths of 2 metres. Range: N.S.W. Size: 12 mm. Common.

72
PHILINIDAE
Angas's Philine
Philine angasi
Crosse and Fischer, 1865

This white shield-shaped slug spends most of its time ploughing through the soft silt of mud flats looking for other small shells upon which it feeds. Its shell is concealed in the mantle folds and is similar to a frail, widened bubble shell. These animals are very common and many a collector has cursed their presence when looking for more coveted species. The tracks they leave in the muddy sand are similar to those of other burrowing molluscs. Growing to 50 mm the animal lays thousands of tiny eggs in a soft balloon-like egg capsule usually in summer. Range: N.S.W., Vic., S.A., Tas., southern W.A. Size: grows to 50 mm.

73
PHOLADIDAE
Angel's Wings
Pholas australasiae
Sowerby, 1849

One of the burrowing bivalves, *P. australasiae* inhabits the solidified shallow water mud flats of estuaries mostly just beyond low tide level. After storms or rough weather numbers are cast up on the beaches. The collector wanting the best specimens should be waiting on the spot, otherwise the seagulls damage the delicate shells while feeding on the animal within. Range: N.S.W., Vic., Size: 101 mm. Common.

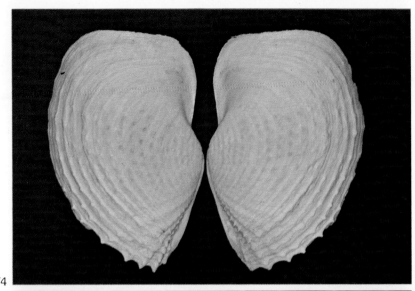

74

74
PHOLADIDAE
Broad Angel's Wings
Pholas latissima
Sowerby, 1849

To collect this species alive usually takes a bit of hard digging on the extreme low water mark of Queensland's northern beaches. The mollusc is a dirty grey colour with black marks and seems almost too big for the shell. Range: Qld. to N.T. Size: 60 mm. Moderately common.

75
PINNIDAE
Bicoloured Pinna Shell
Pinna bicolor
Gmelin, 1791

Sometimes called a razor clam, this species lives almost completely buried in mud flats. All those who have walked with bare feet on the protruding edges of this shell probably have their own names for it! Being bivalves they feed by filtering micro organisms from the sea water. Some specimens harbour a small commensal shrimp which spends its whole life cycle within the protection of its host's valves. Range: Qld. to northern W.A. Size: 200 mm.

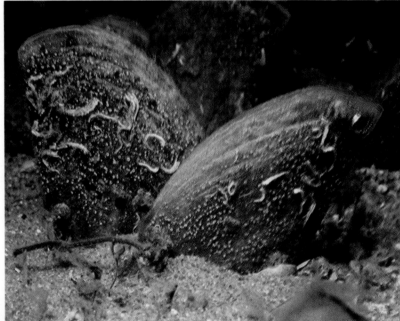

75

76
PLACUNIDAE
Window Pane Shell
Placuna placenta
Linnaeus, 1758

Almost translucent even when alive these shells have been used for centuries in eastern civilisations for window panes. Hence their common name. They live on mud flats where they can be collected at low tide once the art of finding them is mastered. Their life cycle is very similar to other semi-sedentary bivalves. Range: Qld., N.T., northern W.A. Size 100 mm.

76

77

78

77
POTAMIDIDAE
Blunt Creeper
Cerithidea anticipata
Iredale, 1929

A thin shell in comparison with most of the other mangrove whelks. A common characteristic in adults is an expanded lip which is typical of many surface mud dwellers. This species lives on mud flats and occasionally can be seen on the roots, trunks and lower branches of mangrove trees. The majority of adult specimens are decollate which gives the shells their seemingly imperfect shape. Range: Qld. to W.A. Size: 44 mm.

78
POTAMIDIDAE
Australian Mud Whelk
Velacumantus australis
Quoy & Gaimard, 1834

Extremely common, this little shell inhabits mud flats, estuaries and enclosed marine lagoons in southern Australia. Most colonies of this species are important intermediate hosts in the life cycle of the minute blood fluke *Austrobilharzia* sp. The larvae of this parasitic flatworm emerge from their host during the summer months and usually burrow into the legs of wading birds to enter their bloodstream and so begin another generation of worms. Huge concentrations of these larvae may be present in some of the still back-water lagoons. Humans wading in these waters in summer are subject to attacks by these larvae. Although the parasite is unable to live in a human host it nevertheless makes its presence felt by way of a skin complaint called *schistosome dermatitus* or 'swimmer's itch'. Range: Qld. to W.A. Size: grows to approx. 38 mm. Common.

79

79
POTAMIDIDAE
Hercules Club Shell
Pyrazus ebeninus
Bruguière, 1792

A very common species in mangrove swamps and mud flats throughout eastern Australia. Although not considered edible by today's standards, evidence of ancient feasts still exists in Aboriginal middens along the east coast which display huge mounds of these shells. This species can live for quite a lengthy time out of water. Range: Qld., N.S.W., Tas., Vic. Size: grows to 101 mm. Common.

80
POTAMIDIDAE
Sulcate Mud Creeper
Terebralia sulcata
Born, 1778

Thick robust shell inhabiting the surface mud of tropical mangrove swamps. Easily recognisable by the thick apertural lip which crosses the anterior canal. Range: Qld. to northern W.A. Size: 56 mm. Common.

80

81
POTAMIDIDAE
Telescope Mud Creeper
Telescopium telescopium
Linnaeus, 1758

The largest of all the mud creepers found in Australia, it inhabits mangrove areas. The animal is not often noticed in the field for it is shy to any movement and quickly retreats into its shell when approached. Range: Qld. to northern W.A. Size: 101 mm. Common.

82
PTERIIDAE
Southern Pearl Shell
Pinctadá fucata
Gould, 1850

Occurring in estuaries from N.S.W. to Qld. these shells seem to prefer a muddy environment and are usually found attached to sea grasses or on clumps of dead shells. They live from low tide level to 30 metres. Range: N.S.W., Qld. Size: grow to 85 mm. Common.

83
PYRAMIDELLIDAE
Ventricose Pyramid Shell
Pyramidella ventricosa
Guerin, 1831

These small carnivorous molluscs live on muddy intertidal rubble flats and are usually associated with some soft bodied invertebrate upon which they feed. The particular host or hosts of this species have not yet been recorded. Range: Qld. to N.T. Size: 25 mm. Moderately common.

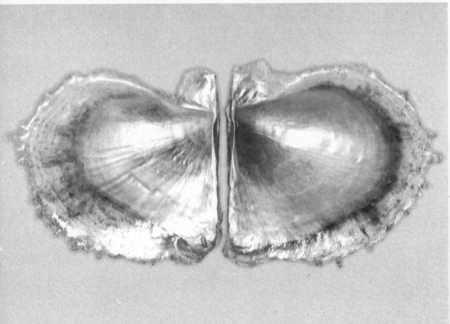

82

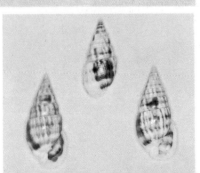

83

84

85

84, 85
SPONDYLIDAE
Long-Spined Thorny Oyster
Spondylus wrightianus
Crosse, 1872

The ivory white of the shell set off by a red splashed umbo and delicate spines, almost too fragile to touch, make this species one of nature's wonders and certainly yours, if you find a good one. As with so many shells the finding is only the beginning. A field specimen of *S. wrightianus* may take many hours of delicate manipulation before all the marine growths adhering to its spines are removed. They live on intertidal mud flats but can also be trawled in deep water. Range: Qld. to northern W.A. Size: 70 mm.

86
STROMBIDAE
Black Mouth Stromb
Strombus aratrum
Roeding, 1798

S. aratrum live on intertidal muddy sand banks and rubble patches and are fairly common along the Qld. coast. Because of marine growths on the dorsum they are not always easy to distinguish from their surroundings. They also inhabit the mainland islands and coral cays of the Great Barrier Reef. In these areas divers have found specimens down to 20 metres living on algae covered rubble. Like all strombs they are herbivores. In many specimens the apertures are deep red gold with black ventral surface and lip. These forms are very much sought after by collectors. Range: Qld. Size: 76 mm. Common.

86

87

87
STROMBIDAE
Campbell's Stromb
Strombus campbelli
Griffith & Pidgeon, 1834

An extremely prolific species living on intertidal mud flats, *S. campbelli* can be found in an amazing variety of designs and colours. In certain areas on the northern Queensland coast it is not uncommon to find pink, mauve or lemon coloured shells. This species is not entirely restricted to an intertidal habitat and is regularly trawled to depths of 50 metres. Range: N)S.W. to northern W.A. Size: 70 mm. Common.

88
STROMBIDAE
Partridge Wing Stromb
Strombus carnarium
Linnaeus, 1758

Restricted to the north-eastern coast of Australia, this solid little shell is found on mainland mud flats where it is often well camouflaged by marine algae growths. On occasions the aperture of older shells may have a silver or gold-like glaze. The reasons for this are not fully understood but may be caused through some element in local water conditions. Range: north-eastern Australia. Size: 50 mm.

88

89
STROMBIDAE
Sail Stromb
Strombus epidromis
Linnaeus, 1758

Although not a common species in Australia this stromb is very easily identified. Usually found on muddy sand flats at low tide although some specimens have been taken in deeper water. Range: Qld. to northern W.A. Size: 76 mm. Uncommon.

89

90
STROMBIDAE
Orr's Stromb
Strombus urceus orrae
Abbott, 1960

This subspecies is a herbivore and is very common on coastal muddy sand flats. The shell varies in colour pattern and shape throughout its known range. Range: northern W.A. to N.T. Size: 45 mm. Common.

90

91

91
TRIGONIIDAE
Common Brooch Shell
Neotrigonia margaritacea
Lamarck, 1804

The family Trigoniidae lives only in Australia but is well known amongst collectors and naturalists. Their beautiful external colourings and iridescent, nacreous internal lustre also tempt many a tourist into purchasing one or more. The common name arose from the popular practice of wearing these as an ornament. They live at various depths to 80 metres below tide level, usually in sand or sandy mud. Shallow water forms seem to prefer areas where the water movement is regular, such as in off points or in channels. Some specimens which can be found living on top of the sand in Westernport Bay, Vic. have shells covered in a red encrusting sponge. This sponge is recorded to have stinging properties to which some people are allergic. Range: N.S.W., Vic., Tas. Size: 35 mm. Common.

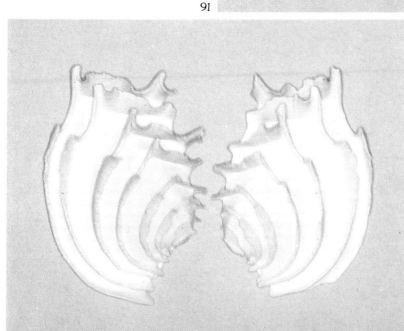

92
VENERIDAE
Frilled Venus
Bassina disjecta
Perry, 1811

Not usually found intertidally, paired shells are occasionally found washed up on shore. Living below the surface in muddy sand banks these shells can be collected by dredging or diving. Because of their delicate fluted shells they are very popular amongst collectors. Range: N.S.W., Vic., Tas., S.A. Size: 64 mm. Common.

93
VENERIDAE
Chemnitz's Cockle
Periglypta chemnitzi
Hanley, 1844

The largest southern venus shell, *P. chemnitzi* inhabits subtidal mud and weed beds in sheltered estuaries. Although usually buried deep in the mud, specimens are occasionally found exposed. Like most burrowing bivalves they are able to move around at will by means of expansion and retraction of their foot. Range: N.S.W. to W.A. Size: 100 mm. Moderately common.

93

94

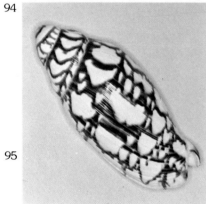

95

94
VOLUTIDAE
Baler Shell
Melo amphora
Solander, 1786

M. amphora is the largest representative of the Volutidae family. Its common name was derived from early settlers who noticed the shell being used by Aboriginals and Torres Strait Islanders for bailing out their dugouts. Since then the letter 'i' has been dropped resulting in the word as we know it today. Very prolific on coastal mud flats it is also trawled in deep water on the continental slope. A voracious predator on other shells it also will feed on juveniles of its own species. Eggs are laid at the beginning of summer, they are then deserted and the young shells emerge within several months. The beauty and large size of this shell have made it very popular with collectors and the tourist trade. Range: southern Qld. and northern W.A. Size: grows to approx. 560 mm. Common.

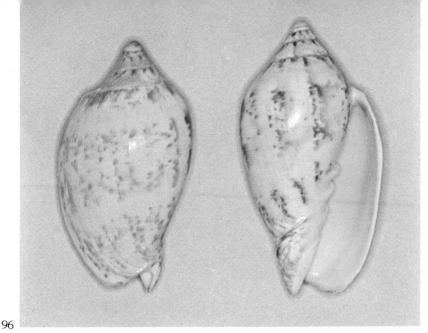

96

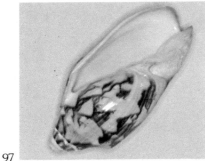

97

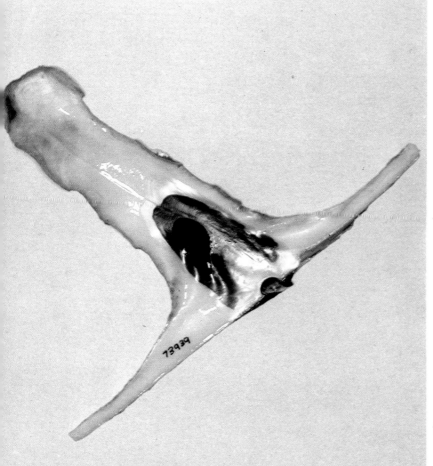

73939

98

95
VOLUTIDAE
Bednall's Volute
Volutoconus bednalli
Brazier, 1878

Occasionally found intertidally or in shallow water sea grass beds on mud, *V. bednalli* is brought up by pearl shell divers working between 10 and 20 metres. In recent years with the advent of prawners working in northern Australia, shells have been taken to 100 metres. Range: Qld. to northern W.A. Size: 100 mm. Uncommon.

96
VOLUTIDAE
Mud Volute
Aulica flavicans
Gmelin, 1791

An interesting shell, *A. flavicans* is one of the few volutes which lives intertidally in mud. Many specimens have been located in recent years from Darwin and the northern offshore islands. Quite variable in form and colour, it is mostly collected at night. As with its relatives, food consists mainly of other molluscs. Range: N.T., northern Qld. Size: 100 mm.

97
VOLUTIDAE
Bat Volute
Cymbiola vespertilio
Linnaeus, 1758

Found intertidally in muddy sand, *C. vespertilio* has only recently been recorded in Australia. Range: As yet it is restricted to N.T. Size 50 mm. Uncommon.

98
VULSELLIDAE
White Hammer Oyster
Malleus albus
Lamarck, 1819

This strangely shaped bivalve is by far the most impressive of its group. It is a filter feeder and lives on mud flats or muddy sand flats. Range: Qld., N.T., northern W.A. Size: 150 mm.

Part 2
Rocky reefs

Rocky reefs

Rocky reefs occur all round Australia. In some southern rock platform areas, molluscs have figured as samples in many publications to show how intertidal animals are restricted to various zones. These zones are usually the result of several factors and depend on the molluscs' retention of moisture in the duration between high and low tide, food supply and exposure to the elements. As the majority of molluscs can move around freely some species may alter their zone a little depending on the seasons.

Below tide level these zones are not so defined and some species may be found from 3 metres of water down to 300 metres. Others are restricted because of food supply, oxygen saturation of the water, or by the number of predators.

On the northern rocky reefs shells may overlap several other habitats and species may be found on mud, rocky reef or coral reef. Quite often in this case each habitat will have evolved a particular form, which in many cases can be separated from the same species living under different conditions.

The shells that live within the scope of this section often have their own specific micro habitat. Bivalves may live attached to reefs by a byssus while others are glued to the substrate by hardened secretions. The univalves are capable of considerable movement and can roam at will, living on the exposed surface of rocks, beneath rocks or on algae attached to rocks. They occur under caves, ledges and amongst other marine growths. The univalves are usually robust of structure and can be herbivores, carnivores, or both. Most species are either male or female and the latter lays eggs. These eggs may be attached to the substrate, retained within the body till hatching, or released into the water to join the drifting plankton. Because of the shelter and food provided by this habitat the number of species within it is extensive.

Most of these shells have a wide distribution and specimens are reasonably accessible to collectors, although some species below tide level on deep reefs may be fairly difficult to obtain.

It must always be remembered when collecting in these areas that all rocks, whether above or below tide level, should be returned to their previous positions. Those left overturned in the intertidal zone will mean death by exposure to the sun for all sedentary forms of life beneath that rock. Below tide level a rock left overturned is quickly depleted of all living organisms by schools of predatory fish. Shells may seem common enough today but if their habitat is destroyed it will be a long time before the area is repopulated, if ever.

101

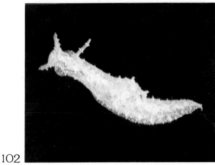

102

103

101
AEOLIDIIDAE
Fusiform Berghia
Berghia fusiformis
Baba, 1949

This specimen was found in shallow water at Cockburn Sound, W.A. It is fairly common to see this species moving around in the open over algae covered rocks in search of the small coelentrates upon which it feeds. Range: Qld. to W.A. Size: 30 mm. Common.

102
APLYSIIDAE
Long-Tailed Sea Hare
Stylocheilus longicaudus
Quoy & Gaimard, 1824

Always found amongst algae upon which it feeds, this beautiful little sea hare has no internal shell. Its foot is very narrow in width, and specially adapted for crawling on sea weeds and grasses. Fairly common in warm temperate areas. Range: specimens have been recorded from N.S.W. to W.A. Size: 70 mm. Moderately common.

103
APLYSIIDAE
Little Sea Hare
Aplysia parvula
Mörch, 1863

This species is quite common along the shores of southern Australia where it is found on algae below tide level. When disturbed, or if moving in another area, some sea hares can swim for quite considerable distances. This is accomplished by alternate undulations of the body and mantle flaps. Range: N.S.W. to W.A. Size: 100 mm. Common.

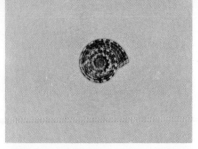

104

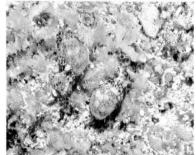

105

106

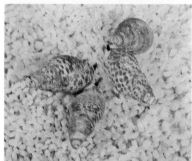

107

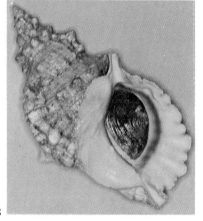

108

104
ARCHITECTONICIDAE
Variegated Sundial
Heliacus variegata
Gmelin, 1791

Often found feeding on zoanthids, this species occurs in several habitats according to its host and inhabits intertidal areas down to 5 metres. It has a very unusual operculum similar to a solid, spirally lined cone. Range: N.S.W. to W.A. Size: 15 mm. Moderately common.

105
HAMINOEIDAE
Cymbal Bubble Shell
Haminoea cymbalum
Quoy & Gaimard, 1833

Living in low tide pools amongst algae and sand, this little bubble shell is not an easy shell to find, even when you know where to look. These specimens were recorded in northern W.A. Range: Qld. to W.A. Size: approx. 9 mm in length. Locally common.

106
BUCCINIDAE
Red Mouthed Buccinid
Cantharus erythrostoma
Reeve, 1846

Commonly found under stones and on reef in W.A., this species lives from intertidal level to 3 metres. It has a fairly thick periostracum and has two main colour variations, dark brown and orange. Range: N.T. to W.A. Size: 30 mm. Common.

107
BUCCINIDAE
Lineated Cominella
Cominella lineolata
Lamarck, 1809

Widely distributed along the southern coast, this species is found on intertidal reefs and is very common. Shells are pictured with a communal egg mass which is laid in early summer. Range: N.S.W., Vic., Tas., S.A., W.A. Size: 25 mm. Common.

108, 109
BURSIDAE
Red Mouthed Frog Shell
Tutufa bufo
Roeding, 1798

Shells of this species, inhabited by hermit crabs, are quite commonly brought up in craypots from depths down to 120 metres off the southern mainland shores. However, shells taken live are few and far between. In N.S.W. they live on subtidal reefs at the base of sea cliffs at depths of 30 to 40 metres. Females are larger than males. Egg capsules are laid in late summer. These are clear transparent tubes, 25 mm in height and filled with yellow eggs. The capsules are attached to flat substratum and the female broods them until hatching takes place. Range: N.S.W. to W.A. Size: 200 mm. Common.

109

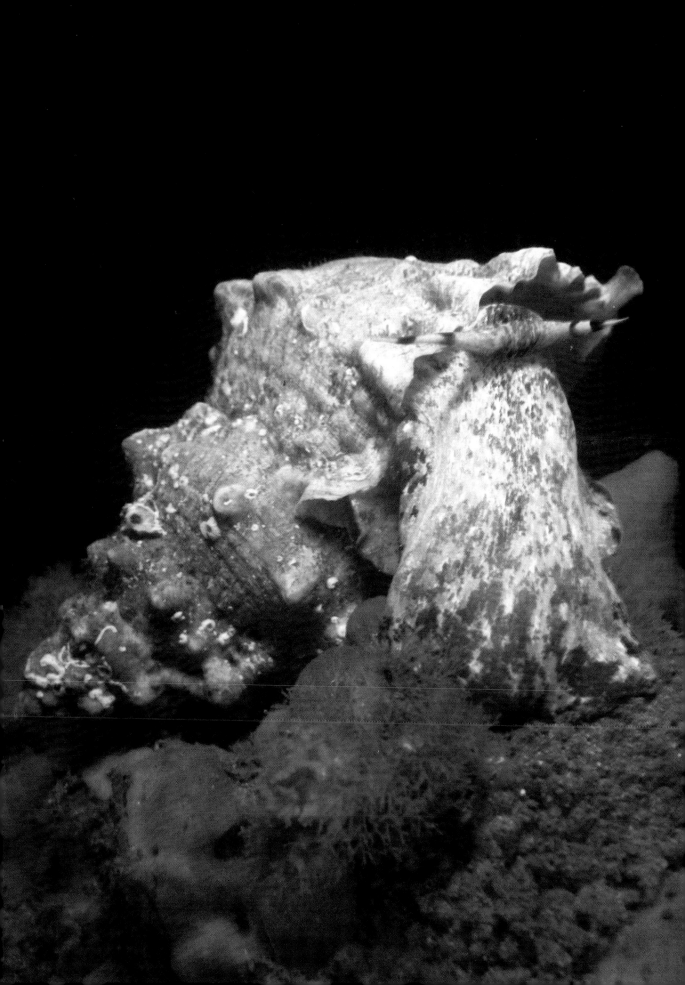

110

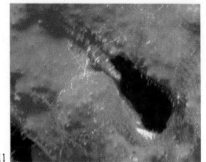

111

110
CALYPTRAEIDAE
Shelf Limpet
Sigapatella calyptraeformis
Lamarck, 1822

Frequently found in beach drift, this shell lives mostly below tide level. It inhabits areas of reef and rubble and is usually attached to small stones or other shells at depths of between 2 to 20 metres. Range: N.S.W., Vic., Tas., S.A., W.A. Size: 25 mm. Moderately common.

111
CERITHIIDAE
Little Sponge Creeper
Ataxocerithium serotinum
A. Adams, 1855

A fairly common shell washed up on beaches; its habitat has only been discovered within the last few years. The first living specimens taken by divers were found in Botany Bay, N.S.W. on orange finger sponges. These sponges grow to almost a metre in height and are found on reefs in approximately 10 to 20 metres. Range: N.S.W. Size: 15 mm. Common.

112

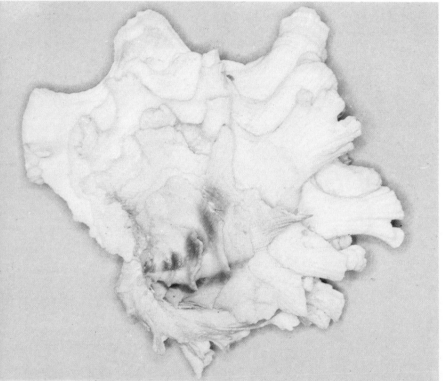

112
CHAMIDAE
Leafy Chama
Chama lazarus
Linnaeus, 1758

A quite distinctive species, *C. lazarus* is taken on intertidal rocky rubble flats in the open or beneath rocks. It is also found in deeper water and the larger specimens are often heavily encrusted with marine life. This figured specimen is from Dampier, W.A. Range: Qld. to W.A. Size: grows to 120 mm. Moderately common.

113
CHITONIDAE
Spiny Chiton
Acanthopleura spinosa
Bruguiere, 1792

Very common on rocky shore reefs throughout its range. This large spectacular chiton usually inhabits cracks and crevices during the day where it hides away from the heat of the sun. In darkness, or early morning, it can be seen moving around and feeding on algae scraped from the rock surfaces. Range: Qld. to northern W.A. Size: up to 100 mm. Common.

113

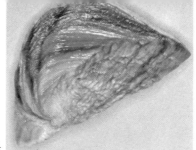

114

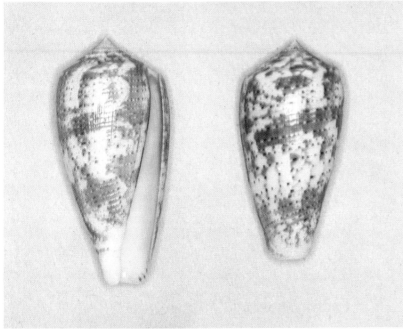

115

114
CLEIDOTHAERIDAE
White Cleidothaerus
Cleidothaerus albida
Lamarck, 1819

Although its name suggests that this shell is always white, this is not so. Quite often shells are pink or even shades of orange. This remarkable species lives attached to reef from a metre or so below tide level down to 40 metres. They are filter feeders and have a brilliant pink nacreous interior. The shell is comprised of three individual pieces, the base, which is the largest part and usually fixed firmly to the reef, the lid or movable valve and a small twig-like structure which is located in the hinge muscle. Large specimens are often bored by marine organisms and therefore not suitable for collectors. Range: N.S.W. to southern W.A. Size: 76 mm. Fairly common.

115
CONIDAE
Agate Cone
Conus achatinus
Gmelin, 1791

Occurring beneath rocks on tidal muddy reef, this shell has a thin opaque periostracum. Its colours are quite varied, and because of this, beginners may have difficulty with identification. Range: Qld. to W.A. Size: 70 mm. Common.

116

117

116
CONIDAE
Anemone Cone
Conus anemone
Lamarck, 1810

Very common along the whole south-west coast, *C. anemone* comes in a host of colours and patterns. It is usually found under stones on reef, sand or rubble substrate and has been recorded as a minor stinger. Egg capsules are laid on the underside of rocks in summer and on occasions numbers of females will join in communal egg laying. The pictured specimen is from Vic., taken in 25 metres on muddy reef. Range. N.S.W. to southern W.A. Size: 50 mm. Common.

117
CONIDAE
Kermadec Cone
Conus kermadecensis
Iredale, 1913

Originally named from shells found in the Kermadec Islands off New Zealand, specimens have since been trawled in 200 metres off southern Qld. The author also recorded this species living at the base of sea cliffs on reefs off Cronulla, N.S.W. in 26 metres. Range: N.S.W. to Qld. Size: 50 mm. Uncommon.

118

119

120

121

118
CONIDAE
Klem's Cone
Conus klemae
Cotton, 1953

One of the most beautiful of the southern cones, *C. klemae* inhabits intertidal rock platforms amongst algae. Also found under stones and rubble down to 20 metres. A much sought after species. Range: extends from S.A. to southern W.A. Size: grows to 70 mm. Uncommon.

119
CONIDAE
Mud Cone
Conus luteus
Sowerby, 1833

Well named, *C. luteus* lives beneath rocks on intertidal muddy reef. The animal is bright orange and the shell has a thin brown periostracum. It mostly feeds on worms and other small invertebrates. Range: Qld. to N.T. Size: 50 mm. Uncommon.

120
CONIDAE
Supreme Cone
Conus monachus
Linnaeus, 1758

Recorded as being a fish eater *C. monachus* should be considered as dangerous. It lives under stones and coral on reefs. Range: Qld. to southern W.A. Size: 60 mm. Common.

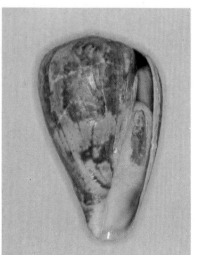

122

122
CONIDAE
Papal Cone
Conus papilliferus
Sowerby, 1834

A small southern species, *C. papilliferus* is generally found under rocks on tide platforms and to depths of 10 metres on reef. Eggs are laid on the underside of rocks in autumn. Feeds almost exclusively on worms. Range: N.S.W. Size: to 45 mm. Common in some areas.

121
CONIDAE
New Holland Cone
Conus novaehollandiae
A. Adams, 1854

Extremely common, this cone is found on rocky mainland reefs intertidally in W.A. Mostly located beneath rocks or dead coral slabs it is most variable in colour and approaches the southern *C. anemone* in many aspects. Range: W.A. Size: 40 mm. Common.

123

124

123
CONIDAE
Rawhide Cone
Conus peronianus
Iredale, 1931

Although generally found in N.S.W., this species ranges into Qld. and lives on intertidal reef under stones and ledges. It feeds on worms and is collected by divers to depths of 30 metres. More prolific below low tide level, eggs are generally laid on the underside of rocks and communal egg laying is common. Range: N.S.W. to Qld. Size: 60 mm. Fairly common in N.S.W.

124
CONIDAE
Tender Cone
Conus tenellus
Dillwyn, 1817

Restricted to a small area on the central Qld. coast, *C. tenellus* lives intertidally beneath rocks on a muddy reef or rubble habitat. A rather distinctive species, it has a very thin periostracum and feeds on worms. Range: Qld. Size: 50 mm. Uncommon.

125
CONIDAE
Victoria's Cone
Conus victoriae
Reeve, 1843

This species lives under stones and amongst rubble rock. Its colours and forms are extremely variable, leading some collectors to confuse them with other species, mostly less common ones. Range: northern W.A. to N.T. Size: 75 mm. Very common.

126
CALYPTRAEIDAE
Slipper Limpet
Crepidula aculeata
Gmelin, 1791

A very common shell in beach drift, the slipper limpet lives attached to substrate under rocks from low tide level to beyond a depth of 13 metres. In deeper water they can be found in colonies on the sides of caves usually covered by an encrusting red sponge. The sexes are separate, males being smaller and sometimes attached to the shell of the larger female. After fertilization the eggs are incubated and protected beneath the shell of the female until hatching. Range: N.S.W., Qld., W.A. Size: 19 mm. Common.

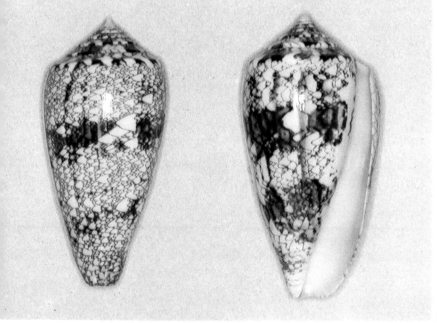

125

126

127

128

129

130

127
CUTHONIDAE
Colman's Eolid
Cuthona colmani
Burn, 1961

Although the first specimens were found by Mr Phillip Colman of the Australian Museum at low tide level at Long Reef, N.S.W., those pictured came from 25 metres. A very small nudibranch, it feeds on hydroids and may spend its whole life on a single colony. Egg girdles are laid in summer close to or on the host hydroid and are white in colour. Range: N.S.W., Vic. Size: 4 mm. Rare.

128
CYMATIIDAE
Australian Triton
Ranella australasia
Perry, 1811

Usually a deep chocolate brown shell with a velvet yellow periostracum, colour and shape vary with distribution and depth. Occasionally pure white forms are encountered. Adult shells are almost always eroded on the spire and the species is also subject to boring attacks by marine organisms. Transparent finger-like capsules with yellow eggs are laid in winter, generally beneath rocks or on the ceilings of caves or ledges. Range: N.S.W. to S.A. Size: 80 mm. Common.

129
CYMATIIDAE
Bass's Triton
Sassia bassi
Angas, 1869

A rather rare little triton, specimens are occasionally found on intertidal reef. They have been dredged in rubble at 20 metres and divers have also come across a specimen on submerged reef. They live in exposed positions and adult shells are usually heavily encrusted or eroded. Range: Vic., Tas. Size: 25 mm. Uncommon.

130
CYMATIIDAE
Exarate Triton
Septa exarata
Reeve, 1844

Like many of the Cymatium family, this species can be found in a variety of habitats. To the average collector the majority are located on shore reef mostly in exposed positions or hidden in holes or ledges. This mollusc feeds on ascidians. Eggs are laid below tide level in a circular nest during autumn, and the female broods these until hatching occurs. Sometimes this shell is a little difficult to find alive as it blends so well with its surroundings. Range: Qld. to S.A. Size: 50 mm. Reasonably common.

131
CYMATIIDAE
Cut Throat Triton
Ranularia gutternia
Roeding, 1798

Living amongst rubble, coral or rocky reef, *R. gutternia* is found in the littoral zone usually in the open, but is also trawled in deeper water. The anterior canal varies in length depending on the shell's environment. Those living on a muddy bottom subtidally have extremely long canals. This is also a very prominent feature in many species of the genus *Septa*. Figured specimen was taken at Exmouth, W.A. in surf conditions on rocky reef. This hostile environment was no doubt responsible for the shell's extra short anterior canal. Range: Qld. to W.A. Size: 60 mm. Uncommon.

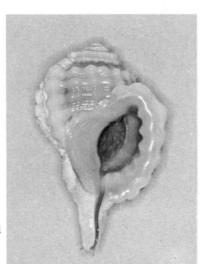

131

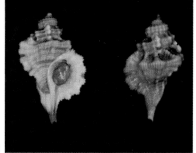

132

133

134

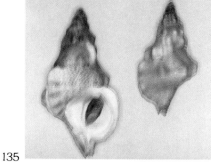

135

132
CYMATIIDAE
Wide-Lipped Triton
Turritriton labiosus
Wood, 1828

This shell has a varied habitat and as well as being found on rocky reef it inhabits areas of rubble in deep water. Specimens have been recorded from just below tide level down to 20 metres. Range: N.S.W., Qld., W.A. Size: grows to 30 mm. Uncommon.

133
CYMATIIDAE
Lesueur's Triton
Cymatiella lesueuri
Iredale, 1929

A small southern species, *C. lesueuri* is fairly common in Vic. and grows to 25 mm. It lives on intertidal reef under stones and also subtidally to at least 20 metres. Food consists mainly of small compound ascidians. Range: Vic., Tas., S.A. Size: 20 mm. Common.

134
CYMATIIDAE
Calloused Triton
Ranularia muricina
Roeding, 1798

Easily recognisable by a thickly calloused columella, they live exposed on intertidal reef down to several metres. Range: from Qld. to W.A. Size: 60 mm. Common in some areas.

135
CYMATIIDAE
Parkinson's Triton
Sassia parkinsoniana
Perry, 1811

Although these shells are found on intertidal reef they are more common below tide level, the best specimens being located in muddy estuaries. They live in an exposed position and have been observed feeding on the egg capsules of cuttles. They will also scavenge on dead or decaying animal tissue. Mating takes place in the winter months, the males being smaller than the females. Two major colour variations exist, the orange form being the less common. Range: N.S.W., Vic., Tas. Size: 45 mm. Common.

136
CYMATIIDAE
Hairy Whelk
Septa parthenopea
von Salis, 1793

This very common species of cymatium is easily recognisable by the dense, hairy periostracum or skin covering the shell. It can be found in a variety of habitats from mud flats and rocky reefs at low tide down to 40 metres. Densest populations seem to be in estuaries from 2 to 5 metres. For many years they have been one of several molluscs regarded as destructive pests in commercial oyster beds. Range: from southern Qld. throughout N.S.W., Vic., Tas., S.A. and southern W.A. Size: grow to 101 mm. Common.

136

137

137
CYMATIIDAE
Purple Mouthed Kookaburra Shell
Gyrineum pusillum
Broderip, 1832

G. pusillum lives under rocks and dead coral at low tide. Not always easily recognisable in their natural habitat, they feed on small brown compound ascidians and seem to prefer a sandy mud environment. Range: N.S.W. to Qld. Size: 25 mm. Fairly uncommon.

138
CYMATIIDAE
Red Whelk
Charonia lampas rubicunda
Perry, 1881

The largest of the southern Cymatiums, deep water specimens of *C. l. rubicunda* grow in excess of 304 mm. Smaller specimens are commonly found on intertidal reefs throughout the range. Their food consists mainly of echinoderms (sea stars and sea urchins), although they will also scavenge on other dead marine life. Colours are variable, brown forms being the most common. Range: N.S.W., Vic., S.A., W.A. Size: see above. Fairly common.

138

139

139
CYMATIIDAE
Spengler's Triton
Cabestana spengleri
Perry, 1811

These shells live on intertidal coastal reefs down to 26 metres in all southern Australian States including south Qld. Quite often they can be observed in beds of cunjevoi, *Pyura stolonifera* at low tide. This ascidian is the main food for *C. spengleri* in the majority of low tide and shallow water localities. The females lay their eggs in circular cellulose nests in September, which they protect until the young shells hatch. Should the egg mass be left unattended, predators soon dispose of them. Range: southern Australia. Size: to 177 mm. Common.

140

140
CYMATIIDAE
Subdistorted Triton
Sassia subdistorta
Lamarck, 1822

Although numbers of this species can be found as beach shells, specimens taken live are uncommon. They live below tide level to depth of 50 metres on reef and in semi rubble. Shells can be taken by divers working between 5 and 25 metres in Vic. and S.A. Range: N.S.W., Vic., Tas., S.A. Size: 60 mm. Uncommon.

141
CYMATIIDAE
Flag Triton
Argobuccinum pustulosum tumidum
Dunker, 1862

Recorded from Vic., S.A. and Tas., it is by far the most common in the latter State. They live on rocky reef around the edges of boulders under rocks and in exposed positions. Found intertidally, specimens have been observed to be more prevalent below tide level between 5 and 10 metres. Live shells have a thick velvet periostracum and older shells display eroded spires. Range: Vic., S.A., Tas. Size: 100 mm. Moderately common.

141

142

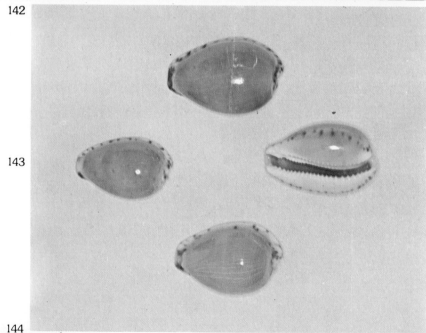

143

144

142
CYMATIIDAE
Tabulate Triton
Cabestana tabulata
Menke, 1843

C. tabulata lives intertidally on rocky reef down to at least 40 metres on muddy rubble. Often confused with *C. spengleri* it has a much thicker furry periostracum in life and its spiral costae are more finely beaded and wider apart. Range: N.S.W. to southern W.A. Size: 100 mm. Common.

143
CYPRAEIDAE
Slim Cowry
Cypraea angustata
Gmelin, 1791

One of the species peculiar to southern waters, *C. angustata* is nevertheless fairly common beneath rocks on extreme low tides in southern N.S.W., Vic., Tas., and S.A. They are also collected by divers down to 10 metres. Eggs are laid in summer, and upon hatching, the young stay beneath the foot of the female until such time as instinct depicts they crawl away and fend for themselves. Many southern cowries share this type of direct reproduction. Range: southern N.S.W., Vic., Tas., S.A. Size: 30 mm. Common.

144
CYPRAEIDAE
Arabian Cowry
Cypraea arabica
Linnaeus, 1758

A medium sized species of around 50 mm, these cowries are well distributed throughout the tropical seas of the world, and even in Australia they have an extensive range. Living under rocks and coral, in caves, crevices and under ledges, they seem to cover a wide expanse of reefy habitats and, more often than not, are found in pairs. Although taken by diving down to 10 metres they tend to be more abundant at low tide level. Range: N.S.W. to Qld., N.T., W.A. Size: around 50 mm. Common.

145

146

145
CYPRAEIDAE
Compton's Cowry
Cypraea comptoni
Gray, 1847

Found in all the southern States, *C. comptoni* lives under stones in holes and crevices, in wharf piles and sometimes in sponges. Fairly common on intertidal reef, more specimens seem to be taken snorkelling in shallow water beyond low tide. Shells have been taken by scuba divers down to 20 metres. Range: N.S.W., Vic., Tas., S.A., southern W.A. Size: 25 mm. Common.

146
CYPRAEIDAE
Cylindrical Cowry
Cypraea cylindrica
Born, 1778

Similar to most cowry shells, *C. cylindrica* lives under stones and dead coral on reefs and mud flats. More common in northern·W.A. and N.T., the figured specimens are from Darwin. Range: from Qld. to northern W.A. Size: 35 mm. Common.

147
CYPRAEIDAE
Sloping Cowry
Cypraea declivis
Sowerby, 1870

Endemic to Australia, *C. declivis* lives beneath stones along the south-west coast between Vic. and S.A. Not as common as other species in these States, this shell seems to be more prevalent in Tas. where it can be found from low tide level down to 20 metres. Range: Vic., S.A., Tas. Size: 25 mm. Moderately common.

147

148
CYPRAEIDAE
Erroneus Cowry
Cypraea errones
Linnaeus, 1758

Very common intertidally, it lives under rocks and dead coral on mainland and offshore reefs. Eggs are laid on the underside of rocks in early summer. Range: N.S.W. to northern W.A. Size: 35 mm. Common.

149   148

149
CYPRAEIDAE
Friend's Cowry
Cypraea friendii
Gray, 1831

One of Australia's largest and most popular species of cowry, this shell is endemic to south-west Australia. Like other members of its genus, *C. friendii* is almost always associated with sponges, upon which it feeds. Eggs are laid in November, usually in sponges. The female sits on the eggs until they hatch. The young are bright orange and hide away in cavities and holes in sponges. Diving is the most modern method of collecting these shells as they live below tide level. Range: south-west Australia. Size: 101 mm. Fairly common.

151   150

153   152

150
CYPRAEIDAE
Slender Cowry
Cypraea gracilis
Gaskoin, 1849

Usually red mantled cowries are ones to be admired and sought, for these types are normally uncommon. This isn't the case with *C. gracilis,* for although it has a red mantle, the shell itself is extremely common. Found under stones and coral rock, the shells lay their eggs in autumn. Range: N.S.W. to northern W.A. Size: 25 mm. Common.

151
CYPRAEIDAE
The Stage Cowry
Cypraea histrio
Gmelin, 1791

Inhabiting limestone ledges and the underside of rocks in the intertidal zone, *C. histrio* is common in some areas. It is quite a solid chunky shell and is popular amongst collectors. Range: northern W.A. to N.T. Size: 80 mm. Common.

152
CYPRAEIDAE
Lined Margin Cowry
Cypraea labrolineata
Gaskoin, 1848

C. labrolineata lives on intertidal reefs. Specimens have been taken as far south as Sydney at low tide and by diving, the latter shells being found in 25 metres on reef. Range: N.S.W. to northern W.A. Size: 25 mm. Uncommon.

153
CYPRAEIDAE
Margin Cowry
Cypraea marginata
Gaskoin, 1848

Another uncommon highly regarded shell, *C. marginata* lives on offshore reefs. Several geographical forms have been recorded; the specimen pictured came from the Fremantle area of W.A. Basically a diver's shell this species was rediscovered in craypots off Geraldton, W.A., nearly 100 years after the unique original was named. Range: S.A. to central W.A. Size: Males are generally smaller than females which grow to a size of 70 mm. Uncommon.

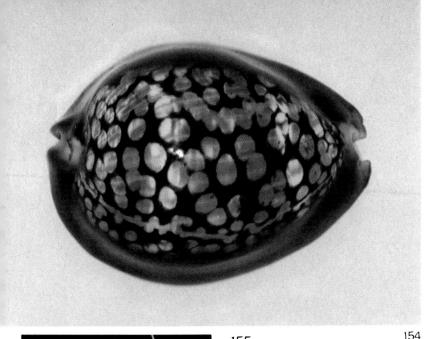

154
CYPRAEIDAE
Chocolate Cowry
Cypraea mauritiana
Linnaeus, 1758

Fairly common on mainland islands in northern Australia, this species frequents volcanic rocks on the exposed seaward faces. Here they live intertidally in the shade of caves and ledges. The surf pounding on these rocks creates good supplies of oxygen, a situation most of the larger cowries prefer. They feed on algae scraped from the rocks, the darkness of their shells blending in with their habitat. Specimens of *C. mauritiana* have recently been reported from Lord Howe Island, N.S.W. Range: N.S.W., Qld. to northern W.A. Size: 120 mm. Moderately common.

154

156
CYPRAEIDAE
Peppered Cowry
Cypraea piperita
Gray, 1825

Common over most of its range, *C. piperita* lives intertidally on reef down to 10 metres. Usually found under stones, it is a fairly variable shell in colour and pattern. Eggs are laid in summer and the female sits on them until they hatch. Range: N.S.W., Vic., Tas., S.A., southern W.A. Size: 25 mm. Common.

55

155
CYPRAEIDAE
Military Cowry
Cypraea milaris
Gmelin, 1791

C. milaris is fairly uncommon and occurs beneath stones and dead coral on mud flats and reefs. Range: N.S.W. to W.A. Size: 45 mm. Uncommon.

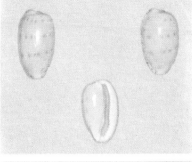
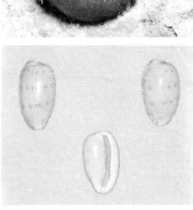

56

157
CYPRAEIDAE
Flea-Spotted Cowry
Cypraea pulicaria
Reeve, 1846

Restricted in range, this species lives under stones intertidally or in moderately shallow water. Although fairly common in some areas it is not easily found in others. Range: southern W.A. Size: 20 mm. Common.

57

58

158
CYPRAEIDAE
Four Spot Cowry
Cypraea quadrimaculata
Gray, 1824

This shell is found under rocks and dead coral. In some areas it is found in the same vicinity as *C. cylindrica*. Range: Qld. to northern W.A. Size: 30 mm. Uncommon.

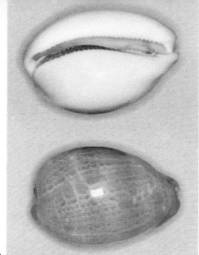

160   **159**

159
CYPRAEIDAE
Reeve's Cowry
Cypraea reevei
Sowerby, 1832

A very ancient type of cowry, *C. reevei* lives under rocks below tide level. Specimens are also taken in caves and ledges where there is excessive water movement. Not an easy shell to find, live shells are still considered to be fairly uncommon. Range: S.A. to southern W.A. Size: 40 mm. Uncommon.

160 CYPRAEIDAE
Rossell's Cowry
Cypraea rosselli
Cotton, 1948

This photograph, the result of many months searching, was the first to be published of this species in natural habitat. *C. rosselli* is by far the rarest of the south W.A. cowries and as its habitat is in very deep water it will probably remain that way for some time. The eggs are laid in sponges and the female sits on them until hatching. As with other cowries of this genus the young shells have an orange animal. Also taken in craypots and by trawling, northern forms are mostly larger than southern ones. Range: central W.A. to southern W.A. Size: 60 mm. Rare.

16

162
CYPRAEIDAE
Tapering Cowry
Cypraea teres
Gmelin, 1791

Collectors find this species fairly elusive although specimens are found beneath rocks and coral at low tide. Range: N.S.W. to W.A. Size: 40 mm. Uncommon.

161

161
CYPRAEIDAE
Saul's Cowry
Cypraea saulae
Gaskoin, 1843

Found intertidally on rocky reef, coral reef and amongst muddy rubble, this species is not a commonly encountered shell. Eggs are laid in early summer, usually beneath a rock or dead shell. Range: Qld. to W.A. Size: 30 mm. Uncommon.

162

163
CYPRAEIDAE
Black Cowry
Cypraea friendii thersites
Gaskoin, 1849

C. f. thersites have been badly exploited by divers and collectors. Recently these shells have been protected during their breeding season with a daily limit of 5 during open season. By proclaiming limits on this species the S.A. Fisheries Dept. have shown that molluscs as well as other marine species must be fished in a sensible manner. Range: S.A. Size: 90 mm. Common.

164
CYPRAEIDAE
Much Desired Cowry
Cypraea venusta
Sowerby, 1846

Until the recent popularity in skin diving, this shell was considered a very rare species. It lives on and in limestone reefs between depths of 3 and 200 metres. There are a number of different variants and forms, some of which still bring high prices. The animal feeds on encrusting sponge, and eggs are usually laid in the shells of dead bivalves or gastropods. Range: central W.A. to southern W.A. Size: 80 mm. Uncommon.

164

165

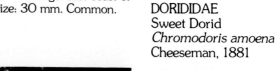
166

165
CYPRAEIDAE
Green Cowry
Cypraea xanthodon
Sowerby, 1832

Extremely common in some areas along the Qld. coast, *C. xanthodon* is restricted to the east coast of Australia. Usually found beneath rocks and dead coral they tend to be more prolific on the mainland islands off central Qld. However, specimens have been recorded as far south as Botany Bay, N.S.W., living in 10 metres of water. Range: east coast of Australia. Size: 30 mm. Common.

166
DENDRODORIDIDAE
Elongate Dorid
Dendrodoris elongata
Baba, 1936

Found beneath rocks on intertidal reef, this nudibranch does not appear to be a common species. It is unusual in having its gills at an extremely posterior position on its body. Range: northern W.A. Size: 60 mm. Uncommon.

167
DORIDIDAE
Sweet Dorid
Chromodoris amoena
Cheeseman, 1881

Fairly common on open reef or algae, this species lives from low tide down to 30 metres. It lays pink egg rings, usually in winter. Range: N.S.W. to S.A. Size: 35 mm. Common.

168

167

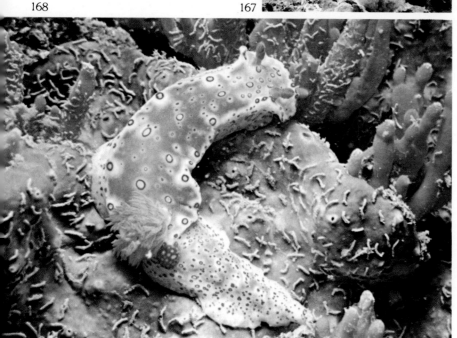

168
DORIDIDAE
Short Tailed Ceratosoma
Ceratosoma brevicaudatum
Abraham, 1876

One of the most common species of the southern nudibranchs. Its colours and size in many localities are extremely variable. The largest specimens observed by the author have been in Port Lincoln, S.A. and Cockburn Sound in W.A. Range: N.S.W. to W.A. Size: 150 mm. Common.

169
DORIDIDAE
Golden Dorid
Neodoris chrysoderma
Angas, 1864

Strictly a diver's species in N.S.W., this mollusc lives on reefs in Jervis Bay at depths of between 15 and 40 metres. Range: N.S.W. to southern W.A. Size: 40 mm. Common.

169

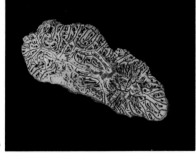

170

171

170
DORIDIDAE
Fine-Lined Nudibranch
Halgerda graphica
Basedow & Hedley, 1905

This mollusc lives below tide level usually in caves where it feeds on sponges. Relatively common in Cockburn Sound, W.A., it frequents depths of around 5 to 10 metres. Range: S.A. to W.A. Size: 50 mm. Common.

171
DORIDIDAE
Painted Dorid
Hypselodoris sp.

Common in Cockburn Sound, W.A. where, during summer, numbers crawl around in the open on limestone reefs from low tide level down to 5 metres. Range: Qld. to W.A. Size: 35 mm. Common.

175
DORIDIDAE
Victoria Dorid
Chromodoris victoriae
Burn, 1957

With its unique colour pattern, *C. victoriae* is easily recognisable in the field. It can be found in Tasmania to depths of 15 metres under rocks. Range: Vic., Tas. Size: 30 mm. Uncommon.

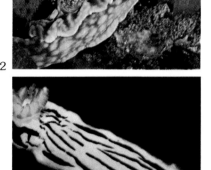

172

172
DORIDIDAE
Magnificent Nudibranch
Miamira magnifica
Eliot, 1910

A rather uncommon species, this nudibranch lives below tide level on open reef between 15 and 30 metres. Range: eastern Aust. Size: 76 mm. Uncommon.

173

173
DORIDIDAE
Wavy Dorid
Chromodoris maritima
Baba, 1949

C. maritima lives on algae covered broken limestone reefs in W.A. where it roams freely amongst the nooks and crannies between 2 and 6 metres. Range: Qld. to northern W.A. Size: 50 mm. Uncommon.

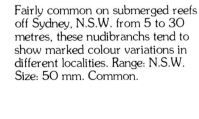

174

174
DORIDIDAE
Splendid Dorid
Chromodoris splendida
Angas, 1864

Fairly common on submerged reefs off Sydney, N.S.W. from 5 to 30 metres, these nudibranchs tend to show marked colour variations in different localities. Range: N.S.W. Size: 50 mm. Common.

175

176

177

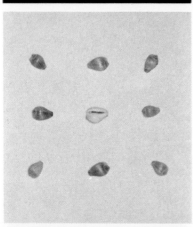

178

179

176
DORIDIDAE
West Australian Dorid
Chromodoris westraliensis
O'Donoghue, 1924

Common subspecies found in W.A., this mollusc can be seen in the open on reef from low tide down to 30 metres. It lives in a number of habitats and has several colour variations. Range: W.A. Size: 50 mm. Common.

177
DORIDIDAE
Youngbleuth's Dorid
Chromodoris youngbleuthi
Kay & Young, 1969

An absolutely magnificent species which is found in Cockburn Sound, W.A., to depths of 15 metres. It lives on limestone reef in the open and mates in winter. Range: Qld. to W.A. Size: 65 mm. Not uncommon.

178
ERATOIDAE
Gem Cowry
Erato gemma
Bavay, 1917

Restricted to an intertidal habitat, *E. gemma* can be found beneath stones and coral slabs and are usually associated with encrusting compound ascidians. They live in mainland areas and also on the Great Barrier Reef. Range: N.S.W. to W.A. Size: 3 to 4 mm. Moderately common.

179
FACELINIDAE
West Australian Eolid
Austraeolis westralis
Burn, 1966

Extremely spectacular in its form and colour, *A. westralis* lives on open reef in Cockburn Sound, W.A. to depths of 5 metres. Range: W.A. Size: 35 mm. At certain times of the year it can be quite common.

180

180
GLAUCIDAE
Coleman's Phyllodesmium
Phyllodesmium sp.

Specimens are occasionally found
feeding on alcyonarian sea whips in
Exmouth Gulf. The specimen figured
was taken at a depth of 5 metres.
Range: N.S.W. to W.A. Size: 25 mm.
Uncommon.

181
FASCIOLARIIDAE
Belcher's Latirus
Latirus belcheri
Reeve, 1847

Fairly common on subtidal and
intertidal shore reefs of the north-
west coast. Usually found in holes or
cracks in the reef, specimens are also
taken beneath rocks and dead coral.
Range: W.A. Size: 70 mm. Common.

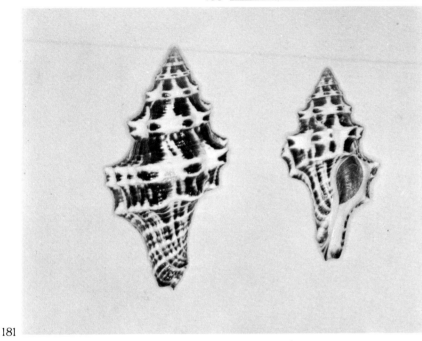

181

182
FASCIOLARIIDAE
Tessellate Spindle Shell
Fusinus tessellatus
Sowerby, 1880

F. tessellatus inhabits rocky reef areas
and lives from low tide level down to
several metres where it is more
prevalent. Not considered to be a
common shell, more specimens
would be found if the molluscs
weren't so well camouflaged. Range:
southern W.A. Size: 50 mm.
Moderately common.

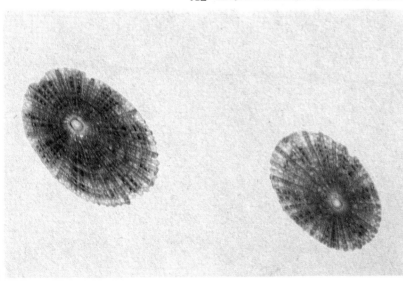

182

183
FISSURELLIDAE
Giant Keyhole Limpet
Diodora lineata
Sowerby, 1835

The largest of the keyhole limpets,
D. lineata lives beneath rocks on
rocky reefs. In deeper water it lives
in a similar habitat although in
some areas many large specimens
may be found under ledges, in
caves and crevices. Its food is
basically algae which it grazes from
surrounding rocks. Range: Vic. to
Qld. Size: 50 mm. Common.

183

184

185

184, 185
FISSURELLIDAE
Duck-Billed Limpet
Scutus antipodes
Montfort, 1810

Found beneath stones intertidally, these molluscs also live subtidally to 20 metres. The animal is vivid black and quite agile. It is a herbivore and rather slimy to touch. Range: Qld. to Tas. Size: 80 mm. Common.

186
FISSURELLIDAE
Juke's Keyhole Limpet
Diodora jukesi
Reeve, 1851

One of the most exquisite of all the keyhole limpets, D. jukesi can be found living under rocks on intertidal reefs. Low tide specimens may be covered in disfiguring marine growths but shells from deeper water display extensive delicate sculpture and are usually perfect specimens. Range: Qld. to W.A. Size: 25 mm. Common.

187
FISSURELLIDAE
Black Keyhole Limpet
Amblychilepas nigrita
Sowerby, 1834

Quite a common shell which lives beneath rocks both intertidally and subtidally in southern Australia. The shell reaches a length of 12 mm but the animal itself is much larger. It is a herbivore. Range: Qld., N.S.W., Vic., Tas., S.A., W.A. Size: 12 mm. Common.

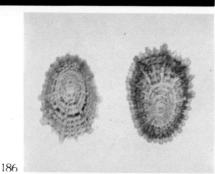

186

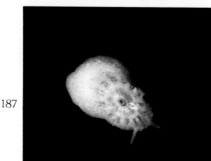

187

188

190   189

188
GONIODORIDIDAE
Pellucid Okenia
Okenia pellucida
Burn, 1966

Another cyclic species this nudibranch lives on the polyzoan *Zoobotryon pellucidus* a common fouling organism on wharf piles and boat bottoms. *O. pellucida* appears in winter when the *Zoobotryon pellucidus* blooms and when it goes the nudibranch is no longer found. Range: N.S.W. to W.A. Size: 25 mm. Common.

189
HALIOTIDAE
Brazier's Ear Shell
Haliotis brazeri
Angas, 1869

Not common, even as a beach shell, the animal itself was unknown until the author located a live mollusc at 30 metres off the southern N.S.W. coast in 1969. Range: N.S.W. Size: 30 mm. Uncommon.

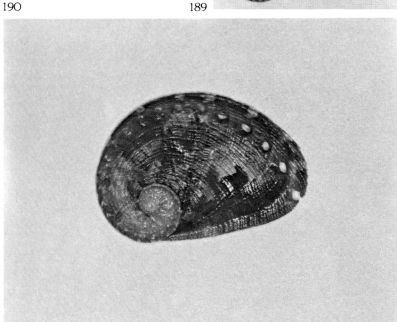

190
HALIOTIDAE
Scarlet-Rayed Ear Shell
Haliotis coccoradiata
Reeve, 1846

A small brilliantly coloured species, *H. coccoradiata* lives beneath rocks on reef. It is often confused with juveniles of the warty ear shell and for this reason has contributed to the downfall of some fisheries projects on abalone growth studies. Range: N.S.W. to Vic. Size: 65 mm. Common.

191
HALIOTIDAE
Circular Ear Shell
Haliotis cyclobates
Peron, 1816

An easily recognised species, they inhabit reefy areas, and occasionally specimens may be found clinging to the sides of razor clams (Pinnas). Not common over their entire range, shells are more easily located in S.A. and W.A. Range: Vic. to southern W.A. Size: 50 mm. Uncommon.

191

192
HALIOTIDAE
Elegant Ear Shell
Haliotis elegans
Philippi, 1899

This species lives below tide level
under caves, ledges and limestone
rocks. Although good dead
specimens are collected, a live animal
is exceedingly rare. Range: restricted
to southern W.A. Size: sometimes
exceeds 115 mm. Uncommon.

193
HALIOTIDAE
Emma's Ear Shell
Haliotis emmae
Reeve, 1846

Living on intertidal reef down to 10
metres, *H. emmae* usually inhabits
the under surface of large rocks.
They live in small hollowed out
pockets, mainly at the edge of the
rock. Not easily seen underwater for
the marine growths on their backs
blend into their surroundings. Range:
Vic., Tas., S.A. Size: 100 mm.
Uncommon.

194

195

194
HALIOTIDAE
Hargrave's Ear Shell
Haliotis hargravesi
Cox, 1869

One of the rarest Australian ear shells it was only after many years of searching that the author finally discovered live specimens off northern New South Wales in 1977. Since then several other specimens have been found by enthusiastic divers. However, due to its small size and deep water habitat, the species may never become common. Range: N.S.W. Size: 30 mm. Rare.

195
HALIOTIDAE
Smooth Ear Shell
Haliotis laevigata
Donovan, 1808

Also a major commercial species in Australia, *H. laevigata* is known amongst divers as the green lip abalone and is very good eating. This name relates to the mantle and side of the foot which are light green. It lives under shallow ledges along the sides of smooth boulders or in gutters or faults in the reef. Range: Vic., Tas., S.A., southern W.A. Size: grows to just over 200 mm. Common.

196
HALIOTIDAE
Roe's Ear Shell
Haliotis roei
Gray, 1826

In W.A. this shell is fished commercially. It lives in holes on the tops of limestone reefs, and seems to prefer areas of excessive water movement although in the two other States it can inhabit deeper water. Range: Vic., S.A., W.A. Size: 50 mm. Common.

196

69

197
HALIOTIDAE
Warty Ear Shell
Haliotis ruber
Leach, 1814

Living on reef from low tide level down to at least 50 metres, this species inhabits crevices, ledges and caves. Specimens have been recorded from deep water off southern Qld. but apparently it is not common there, being at the end of its northern geographical range. One of the largest Australian abalone, its food consists of drift algae or algae scraped off the surrounding reef surfaces, a preference being shown for red algae. Besides man, its predators include stingrays, crayfish (crabs and fish when it is juvenile), and sharks. Range: Qld., N.S.W., Vic., Tas., S.A., W.A. Size: 200 mm. Common.

198
HALIOTIDAE
Ridged Ear Shell
Haliotis scalaris
Leach, 1814

Not a common shell, although diving collectors have increased the numbers available. It is found on subtidal reef along the coast, and is a nocturnal algae feeder. It is one of the most difficult species of the family to prepare for a cabinet specimen. Range: south-west coast of W.A. Size: 100 mm. Uncommon.

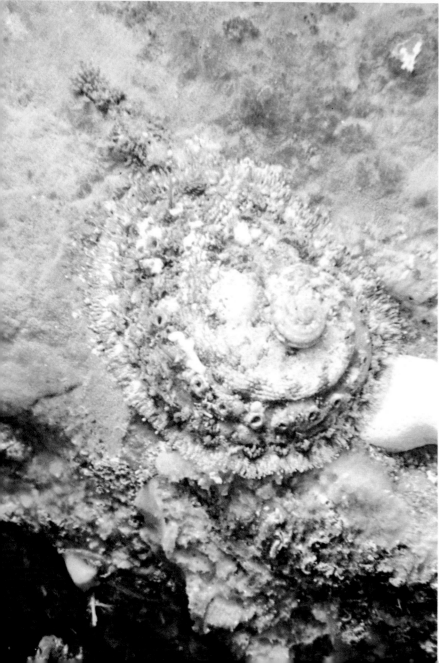

200   199

199
HALIOTIDAE
Variable Ear Shell
Haliotis varia
Linnaeus, 1758

Very common under rocks on intertidal reefs, this little species can be found in many colours. It feeds on algae scraped from the rock surface, usually at night. Range: Qld. to W.A. Size: 45 mm. Common.

200
CALYPTRAEIDAE
Cup & Saucer Limpet
Cheilea equestris
Linnaeus, 1758

Not often seen in collections or in the field. The female shell pictured is comprised of two basic parts: the bottom part or saucer is attached very firmly to the substrate usually beneath boulders or dead coral. The lid or inverted cup to which the animal is attached fits neatly into the saucer below its protective rim. Juvenile shells begin as typical limpets and it is quite some time before the young females begin to build a saucer. Sexual dimorphism is very marked within this species, the males being much smaller. Male shells have not been observed to build saucers, but are often found attached to the top of the female shells. Eggs are laid within the female's shell and brooded until they hatch as free swimming larvae. Range: N.S.W. to northern W.A. Size: 50 mm. Uncommon.

201

201
LAMELLARIIDAE
Australian Lamellarid
Marseniopsis australis
Basedow, 1905

A very conspicuous mollusc, this *M. australis* was recorded in Vic. waters. Usually found beneath large rocks, it is carnivorous and feeds copiously on small white encrusting compound ascidians. Range: N.S.W., Vic., S.A., southern W.A. Size: 50 mm. Uncommon.

202

202
LAMELLARIIDAE
Wilson's Lamellarid
Mystaconcha wilsoni
Smith, 1886

Very striking in colour and pattern, *M. wilsoni* inhabits rocky reef areas from low tide to 30 metres. A near relative of the hard shelled cowry family, it feeds on sponges and has a very thin internal shell shaped somewhat like a moon snail. Range: N.S.W., Vic., S.A. Size: 76 mm. Common.

203
LIMIDAE
Nimbifer File Shell
Lima nimbifer
Iredale, 1924

This very common species lives from low tide level down to 10 metres on reef, beneath rocks or in sponges, usually attached by a byssus. Range: N.S.W., Vic., Tas. Size: 50 mm. Common.

203

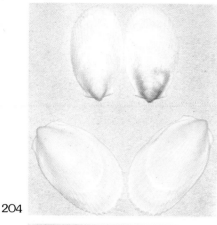

204

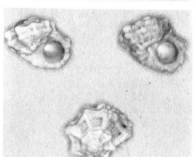

205

204
LIMIDAE
Strange's File Shell
Limatula strangei
Sowerby, 1872

Easily recognised common species washed up by the thousands along the south coast. The shells inhabit reef areas from low tide to 20 metres where they live under rocks and are free swimming. The animal's delicate tentacular filamentous mantle extensions protrude all around the gaping shell, except at the hinge. Range: Qld., N.S.W., Vic., Tas., S.A., W.A. Size: 35 mm. Common.

205
LIOTIIDAE
Wheel Shell
Liotina peronii
Kiener, 1839

This beautifully sculptured species can be found under or on rocks and dead coral at low tide. It feeds by grazing minute algae from the rock surface. Range: Qld. to northern W.A. Size: 19 mm. Common.

206
LITTORINIDAE
Striped Mouth Conniwink
Bembicium nanum
Lamarck, 1822

Common in pools on reef platforms, these shells feed on algae and are often found in small groups. Their spires are nearly always eroded though their dark zebra-like stripes make them easily identifiable. Range: N.S.W. to W.A. Size: 12 mm. Common.

207
LITTORINIDAE
Blue Australwink
Littorina unifasciata
Gray, 1826

Living mostly in crevices or hollows in reef above high water mark, these prolific little shells occur in an area commonly known as the splash zone. They form clusters consisting of a few individuals to groups of several dozen. Juvenile specimens may be found at the high water mark and seem to need a greater degree of moisture than the adults. Range: Qld. to W.A. Size: 15 mm. Common.

207   206

08

208
LORICIDAE
Caterpillar Chiton
Lorica volvox
Reeve, 1847

Usually found below tide level, this species lives beneath rocks down to 30 metres. It is quite a large chiton. Range: from N.S.W. to S.A. Size: 76 mm. Common.

209
MAGILIDAE
Strawberry Coral Shell
Rhombothais arbutum
Woolacott, 1954

Although specimens of this shell can be found on various beaches in central and northern N.S.W., live specimens are fairly uncommon. Mostly found in shallow water below tide level, they feed on the small encrusting coral *Cylicia* sp. Females are larger than males. Eggs are laid in small clear capsules which are brooded within the shell until hatching, usually towards the end of winter. Animals are orange in colour with white flecks. Range: N.S.W. Size: 16 mm. Uncommon.

09

210
MAGILIDAE
Elaborate Coral Shell
Liniaxis elaborata
H. & A. Adams, 1863

Living from 3 metres subtidally down to 40 metres this rather uncommon species can be found associated with the large green solitary corals frequenting shallow waters. After the egg capsules are laid they are retained within the body cavity until the young emerge as free swimming veligers. Range: S.A., southern W.A. Size: 20 mm. Uncommon.

211
MAGILIDAE
Little Southern Coral Shell
Liniaxis sertata
Hedley, 1902

For many years after its discovery, *L. sertata* was known only from a few shells dredged in deep water. Worn dead shells were found on beaches but 63 years passed before their natural habitat was discovered. Living at the base of the soft coral *Capnella* sp. these little shells are usually found in colonies. Females are larger than the males. Eggs are laid in capsules and brooded within the shell. Occasionally found living on the gorgonoid coral *Mopsella ellisi* in depths of around 30 metres, these shells tend to be smaller than the former. Range: N.S.W. to Vic. Size: 20 mm. Fairly uncommon.

212
MARGINELLIDAE
Angas's Margin Shell
Cysticus angasi
Crosse, 1870

These extremely small shells live in colonies below tide level at depths of around 5 metres on the polyzoan *Scutacella* sp. although the shells themselves are translucent pink, the colours of the animals within tend to give them a striped appearance. Range: N.S.W., Tas. to W.A. Size: 2 mm. Uncommon.

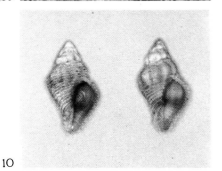

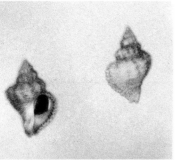

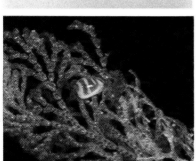

10

213

214

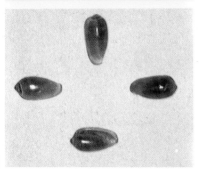

215

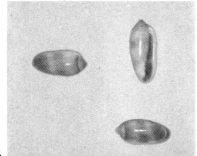

216

217

218

213
MARGINELLIDAE
Cymbol Margin Shell
Microginella cymbalum
Tate, 1878

M. cymbalum usually lives beneath rocks and feeds on encrusting bryozoan. The animal has a black foot and mantle with an orange siphon and tentacles. Range: Vic., Tas., S.A., W.A. Size: 7 mm. Moderately common.

214
MARGINELLIDAE
Minute Margin Shell
Microginella minutissima
Tenison-Woods, 1876

These little shells are not easy to locate unless their habitat is known. They live subtidally at depths of between 15 and 25 metres and feed on polyzoans. The host polyzoan in Vic. is *Amathia biseriata,* while in W.A. they are encountered on other species. Their whole life cycle is spent on the host colonies, eggs being laid in summer. Specimen featured here is from Cockburn Sound, W.A. Range: Vic. to W.A. Size: 3 to 4 mm. Common at specific localities.

215
MARGINELLIDAE
Fly-like Margin Shell
Austroginella muscaria
Lamarck, 1822

A pretty striped brown species, these shells live beneath rocks on reef. They have a rather colourful animal. Range: N.S.W., Vic., Tas., S.A. Size: 12 mm. Common.

216
MARGINELLIDAE
Flesh Coloured Margin Shell
Volvarina philippinarum
Redfield, 1848

Living beneath stones and dead coral in northern W.A., these shells seem to prefer areas of silty mud. Not always easy to locate, sometimes two may be found in close proximity to each other. Range: W.A. Size: 18 mm. Uncommon.

217
TETHYIDAE
Australian Melibe
Melibe australis
Angas, 1864

M. australis lives on red algae, usually below tide level. It has been recorded in Tas. at depths of 5 to 15 metres. This family of nudibranchs nearly all live on algae and have huge circular mouthparts. Range: N.S.W. to southern W.A. Size: 20 mm. Not uncommon.

218
COSTELLARIIDAE
Australian Mitre
Vexillum australe
Swainson, 1820

This strikingly coloured little mitre lives in the open on intertidal reef and also under stones. Range: Vic., Tas., S.A. Size: 30 mm. Common.

219

:21   220

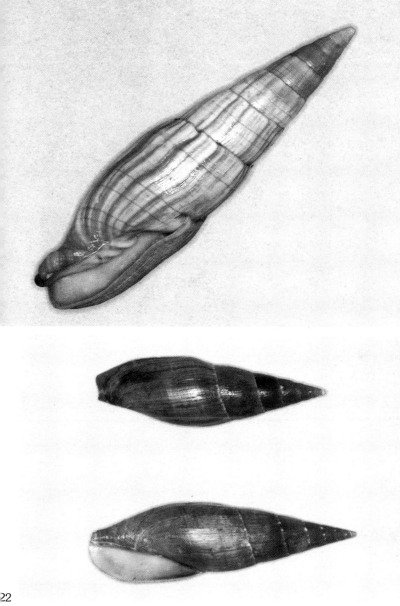

22

219
MITRIDAE
Steel Mitre
Mitra chalybeia
Reeve, 1844

On tidal and subtidal rocky reef, specimens can be found under stones, in crevices or crawling in caves. Range: W.A. Size: 60 mm. Fairly common.

220
MITRIDAE
Cook's Mitre
Mitra cookii
Sowerby, 1874

Occasionally found under stones on reef intertidally, this species mostly occurs below tide level. Eggs are laid in winter months either under rocks or in bivalve shells. Range: N.S.W. to Qld. Size: 30 mm. Uncommon.

221
MITRIDAE
Glabra Mitre
Mitra glabra
Swainson, 1821

Found in sand pockets on reef usually beneath stones. This shell is the largest southern mitre and is easily identifiable by its light brown colour and fine dark brown concentric striae. Range: N.S.W., Vic., Tas., S.A. Size: 100 mm. Moderately common.

222
MITRIDAE
Black Mitre
Mitra carbonaria
Swainson, 1822

Common intertidally to 20 metres, these shells occur under rocks on reef or rubble. Below tide level they live under similar circumstances but also inhabit mussel beds and kelp forests. They feed on worms and seem to prefer sipunculids. Their long proboscis enters the sipunculid from either end and feeds on the internal organs, the empty skin being left. Range: N.S.W., Vic., S.A. Size: 62 mm. Common.

224   223

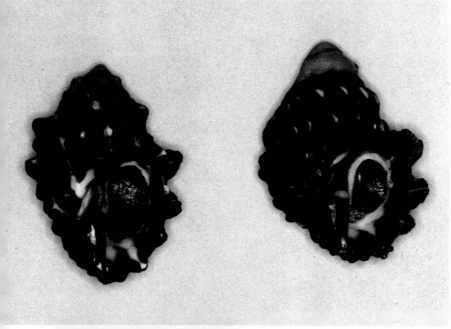

223
MITRIDAE
Badia Mitre
Mitra badia
Reeve, 1844

A dark coloured little mitre, this species is found under stones in sand, on reef, or amongst mussel beds, mostly subtidally. Range: N.S.W., Vic., Tas., S.A. Size: 25 mm. Moderately common.

224
MURICIDAE
Prickly Thaid
Thais distinguenda
Dunker, 1866

Living fairly high in the intertidal zone, these shells feed on oysters and barnacles. They are found in the open and under ledges, with adult shells often being eroded at the spires. Range: Qld. to W.A. Size: 60 mm. Common.

225
MURICIDAE
Double-Sided Aspella
Aspella anceps
Lamarck, 1822

A small chalky white shell, this species inhabits rocky reef, rubble and coral reefs from low tide to at least 30 metres. Quite distinct in form there is only one other shell of this genus represented in Australia. Range: all States except Tas. Size: 10 mm. Fairly common.

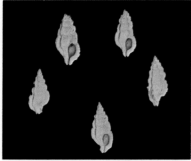

226
MURICIDAE
Angas's Murex
Pterochelus angasi
Crosse, 1863

These small shells live from low tide level down to several hundred metres. Although not considered common over their entire range, live specimens may be found beneath rocks or ledges in reefy areas. Sexual dimorphism exists in this species, the males being almost half the size of the females. During breeding season the smaller males are constantly on the backs of the females. Egg capsules are small and lens shaped, 3 to 4 mm in diameter and laid in small groups on the inside of bivalve shells. Each capsule contains 10 to 15 eggs. Laying takes place in middle winter months and the young hatch within 2 months. Over 24 colour variations and combinations have been recorded from N.S.W. with white being the most prevalent. Range: N.S.W. to W.A. Size: between 10 to 20 mm. Moderately common.

227
MURICIDAE
Bailey's Thaid
Thais baileyana
Tenison Woods, 1881

Specimens are found by diving in shallow water. In this environment the shells are almost always associated with haliotids or abalone. *T. baileyana* sits on the back of an abalone, drills holes through the shell into the mollusc and feeds on the living animal. Although *T. baileyana* may feed on one abalone for many days, the host is very rarely killed. Some abalones have evidence of many attacks but are able to secrete nacre over the holes and close them up. Range: Vic., Tas., S.A. Size: 30 mm. Uncommon.

225

226

227

228

228
MURICIDAE
Bank's Murex
Chicoreus banksii
Sowerby, 1840

As with many species of shells, *C. banksii* can be found in a variety of habitats. It is included here under rocky reefs because this is where the average collector might find them. In northern W.A. the shells live beneath stones and under ledges on muddy shore reef and are considered uncommon. In Qld. they are almost always found below tide level, living amongst rubble between 20 and 30 metres. Shells from Qld. are larger in size and are fairly well encrusted with marine growths. Animals from both forms are similar in colouring, being red or dark orange with small black and white flecks. Eggs are laid in early summer months, usually in valves of bivalves or on dead coral shingle. Range: Qld. to W.A. Size: 76 mm. Common.

229
MURICIDAE
Bednall's Murex
Pterynotus bednalli
Brazier, 1877

A very rare shell for many years, *P. bednalli* is one of the most sought after murex in Australia. Its delicate varices and brilliant colours have at last led to its discovery in moderate quantities. It lives in areas of reef beneath huge stones and deep ledges at low tide level. In some areas shells can also be taken by diving. Range: N.T. to northern W.A. Size: grows to over 100 mm. Uncommon.

230
MURICIDAE
Brazier's Murex
Favartia brazieri
Angas, 1877

Being quite a small species, this shell is fairly difficult to find alive. It lives from low tide level to 300 metres and can be found under rocks or in rubble. Range: every Aust. State except N.T. Size: 8 mm. Fairly uncommon.

229

230

231

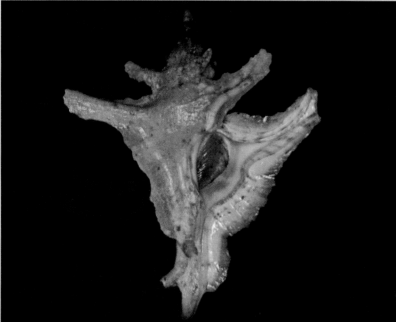

232

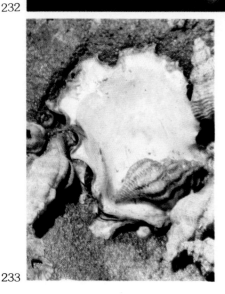

233

234

231
MURICIDAE
Denuded Murex
Chicoreus denudatus
Perry, 1811

This species is very variable in shell characteristics and some of its many forms have been described in the past under different names. It lives from low tide level on rocky reef down to depths of 100 metres on mud. Food is usually restricted to bivalves including oysters, mussels and scallops. Egg capsules are white in colour and are laid beneath rocks, under ledges or in the open on solid substrate. Two main colour forms exist, brown and orange. Natural predators are mainly fish. The best specimens in N.S.W. are found below tide in depths of between 3 and 20 metres, these shells are usually covered in an orange encrusting sponge called *Microciona.* Range: Vic. to Qld. Size: 55 mm. Fairly common.

232
MURICIDAE
Duffuse Murex
Pterochelus duffusi
Iredale, 1936

Living on offshore reefs along the coast the larger forms are occasionally collected by divers working in depths of 20 to 40 metres, also found on fish traps from similar depths. Colour forms include white, pink, brown and orange. Tube worms are a major part of their diet and mating takes place in winter. Range: N.S.W. Size: 65 mm. Uncommon.

233, 234
MURICIDAE
Hanley's Oyster Drill
Bedeva hanleyi
Angas, 1867

Found on intertidal rocky shores, in mangroves and on oyster leases, these little muricids are extremely efficient carnivores. As their common name reveals, oysters are one of their favourite meals and because of this they are a continuous menace to commercial oyster growers. They lay dome shaped egg capsules, similar in shape to *P. angasi,* in the valves of dead oysters. Range: N.S.W. to Qld. Size: 20 mm. Common.

35

236

235
MURICIDAE
Muddy Thaid
Thais luteostoma
Holten, 1802

These shells live high up on intertidal rocks, wharf piles and groins. They feed on oysters and are extremely common in many tropical areas. Range: Qld. to W.A. Size: 60 mm. Common.

236
MURICIDAE
Shouldered Drupa
Morula margariticola
Broderip, 1832

Common intertidal species, it is found towards the high tide level on rocky reefs, usually in the oyster zone. Fairly variable in shape over its distribution. Range: Qld. to W.A. Size: 28 mm. Common.

237
MURICIDAE
Mulberry Shell
Morula marginalba
Blainville, 1832

Found mostly on rocky reefs, these shells live amongst the oyster and barnacle zone on intertidal reef, and are extremely prolific. They are one of the main pests of the commercial oyster beds, and feed on bivalves, univalves and barnacles. Range: N.S.W. to Qld. Size: 30 mm. Common.

237

238

239

240

241

238
MURICIDAE
Cart Rut Shell
Thais orbita
Gmelin, 1791

Extremely common on intertidal reef platforms along the southern coast of Australia, but are also found below tide level to 20 metres. They feed mostly on bivalves and barnacles. Their eggs capsules are deposited in winter; occasionally mass egg laying occurs with up to 15 females depositing capsules under the same rock. Range: Qld. to Vic. Size: 80 mm. Common.

239
MURICIDAE
Penchinatt's Murex
Chicoreus penchinati
Crosse, 1861

This species lives intertidally on rocky reef and subtidally to 20 metres. It can be found under ledges, in caves and beneath rocks where it feeds on a variety of bivalves. Intertidal shells are very often covered in lime encrustations and are useless for specimens. Although the growths can be cleaned off the resulting damage to the shell makes the procedure a time consuming chore. It is better to leave the older shells for breeding and pick only the choice specimens. Range: W.A. to N.T. Size: 70 mm. Moderately common.

240
MURICIDAE
Fimbriate Murex
Muricopsis planiliratus
Reeve, 1845

Fairly common on reef and under stones in Cockburn Sound, W.A. Although often found as a beach shell in Vic. and S.A. it has only recently been taken alive in numbers. Recorded living from low tide level to beyond 30 metres, the shallow water forms feed by drilling small bivalves, mostly mussels. Range: Vic. to southern W.A. Size: 20 mm. Common.

241
MURICIDAE
Rusty Cronia
Cronia pseudamygdala
Hedley, 1903

Very common on intertidal reef down to 10 metres, this shell is a voracious predator on the egg capsules of other molluscs. Range: N.S.W. to Qld. Size: 35 mm. Common.

242
MURICIDAE
Purple Spined Murex
Muricopsis purpurispinus
Ponder, 1972

Only recently discovered, this little muricid is usually found clinging to fish traps brought up from reef off northern N.S.W. in 30 to 40 metres. Specimens are mostly coloured brown to orange. Range: N.S.W. to Qld. Size: 16 mm. Uncommon.

243
MURICIDAE
Robust Typhis
Pterotyphis robustus
Verco, 1895

Another small rare shell, this species was originally recorded from 44 metres off the S.A. coast. For 70 years no other specimens were located and the shell's habitat remained a mystery. Recently the author found several live shells off the W.A. coast living on reef below tide level. Completely covered in coraline algae they are one of the most difficult of all the muricids to find. Range: S.A. to W.A. Size: 12 mm. Rare.

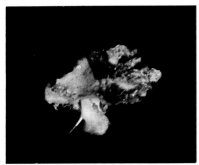

244

244
MURICIDAE
Ruby Murex
Chicoreus rubiginosus
Reeve, 1845

One of the few species of the genus *Chicoreus* which have a wide colour variation. Shells can be black, brown, white, lemon, mauve or orange. In a number of aspects they are very similar to *C. torrefactus* but further studies are needed before accurate status can be placed upon this shell. *C. rubiginosus* are found on muddy intertidal reef beneath rocks and ledges. They feed on oysters and chamas and are heavily encrusted with marine growths. So badly are some shells marked by borers and erosion that their collection is a complete waste of time and effort. These shells should be left to ensure the continuation of future generations. Range: northern W.A. Size: 90 mm. Common.

245
MURICIDAE
Umbilicate Murex
Murexsul umbilicatus
T. Woods, 1876

Heavily over-grown with coraline algae and marine growths, these shells are very difficult to find alive. They live from low tide level down to 20 metres but seem to be more prevalent at 2 to 5 metres exposed on reef. Range: Vic., Tas., S.A. Size: 30 mm. Moderately common.

245

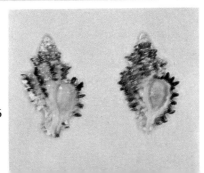

246

247

249

250

251

246
MURICIDAE
Varicoloured Thaid
Pinaxia versicolor
Gray, 1839

Occurring on mainland shores of northern W.A., these shells live on rocky reef usually in the surf zone. Specimens are often badly eroded with many having colour and design almost obliterated. Range: Qld. to W.A. Size: 20 mm. Common at certain localities.

247
MURICIDAE
Wine-Mouthed Lepsiella
Lepsiella vinosa
Lamarck, 1822

An extremely common little shell on rock platforms and reefs along southern Australia. Feeds copiously on bivalves. Range: Vic. to W.A. Size: 25 mm. Common.

248
MYTILIDAE
The Edible Mussel
Mytilus edulis planulatus
Lamarck, 1819

Common on wharf pilings, rock faces and reef, this species is found mostly from mid tide to 5 metres. Sometimes occurring in huge clumps they are well utilised for food in unpolluted areas. Upon opening the mussels small commensal crabs may be found, these are in no way detrimental to the taste or quality of the mussel. Range: N.S.W. to southern W.A. Size: 120 mm. Common.

249
NERITIDAE
White Mouthed Nerite
Nerita albicilla
Linnaeus, 1758

Fairly abundant at mid tide level on intertidal reef, these shells vary in colour from grey to black with white markings. Relatively easy to distinguish from other species; the pustulose columellar plate is an easy identifying characteristic. Range: N.S.W. to W.A. Size: 25 mm. Common.

250
NERITIDAE
Black Nerite
Nerita atramentosa
Reeve, 1855

Common southern Australian nerite, easily recognised by its black colour and white mouth. Some older shells become eroded in various areas, the shell may then be much lighter in colour. This species on intertidal rocks in the upper littoral and feeds on algae. Range: N.S.W., Vic., Tas., S.A., W.A. Size: 25 mm. Common.

251
NERITIDAE
Ribbed Nerite
Nerita costata
Gmelin, 1791

A solid heavily ridged shell, this species inhabits intertidal areas of rocky reef. It feeds on minute algae scraped from the rocks. Range: Qld to northern W.A. Size: 22 mm. Common.

24

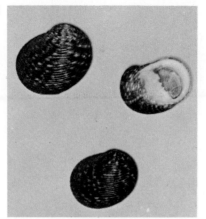

252

252
NERITIDAE
Wavy Nerite
Nerita undata
Linnaeus, 1758

Common on intertidal rocky reefs in Qld., *N. undata* is fairly stable in its colour and patterning. It feeds on algae scraped from rocks and is found mostly in areas of volcanic origin. Range: Qld. Size: 25 mm. Common.

253
OCTOPODIDAE
Australian Octopus
Octopus australis
Hoyle, 1885

A shallow water species, *O. australis* lives on low tide reef platforms in pools and has also been recorded to depths of 20 metres. It feeds on molluscs and crustaceans and often makes its home in the valves of large pinna shells on a sandy bottom. Range: S.A. Size: 300 mm. Common.

254
OCTOPODIDAE
Sydney Octopus
Octopus cyaneus
Gray, 1849

Very abundant around intertidal and submerged reefs, mud and sand flats in southern Australia. Commonly used by fishermen for bait it is also quite palatable when prepared correctly. As with most cephalopods it can alter its colour to that of the terrain it is upon. Although the mollusc grows to over 300 mm, its egg capsules are remarkably small, only 9 mm in length. The female's lair may be under a rock, in a cave, or even inside an old oil drum or tyre. The eggs are usually laid in summer and as the small octopus develop they can be seen through the transparent sides of their capsules. Range: N.S.W. to southern W.A. Size: 300 mm. Common.

254

255
OCTOPODIDAE
Southern Blue Ringed Octopus
Hapalochlaena maculosa
Hoyle, 1883

This small but very well-known mollusc is commonly found on reef under stones or in dead shells, etc., from low tide to 20 metres. When disturbed or touched the fine blue circles upon the animal's body expand into glowing rings of iridescent blue fire. It is during this aggravated state that *H. maculosa* is the most dangerous, for instead of being a small unobtrusive sea creature it is transformed into a brilliantly coloured miniature whose beauty would attract the attention of any would-be fossicker or collector. *H. maculosa* is the most deadly octopus in the world; a single bite incurred could mean death within minutes. Range: southern Qld. to W.A. Size: 100 mm. Common.

256
OCTOPODIDAE
Northern Blue Ringed Octopus
Hapalochlaena lunulata
Quoy & Gaimard, 1832

Like its southern counterpart, this octopus is to be avoided. It has already been credited with one death and is suspect in several other cases. This species grows larger than *H. maculosa* and inhabits the north of Australia. It feeds mostly on small crabs and other molluscs and lives on intertidal reef under stones. Range: Qld. to northern W.A. Size: 150 mm. Common.

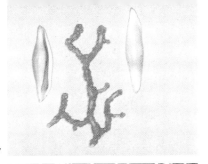

257

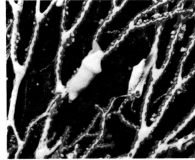

258

259

260

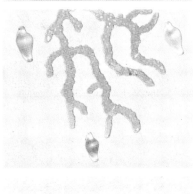

261

262

257
OVULIDAE
Angas's Ovulid
Phenacovolva angasi
Reeve, 1865

A small species found on gorgonian corals, they range in depth from 10 to 40 metres. Colours tend to be translucent and are similar to the gorgonian host. Range: N.S.W. to Qld. Size: 20 mm. Uncommon.

258
OVULIDAE
Semper's Ovulid
Prosimnia semperi semperi
Weinkauff, 1881

Living on gorgonian corals, these little shells were for many years unknown in southern States. In 1963 the author recorded several colour variations living on the gorgonoid *Mopsella ellisi* in depths of 30 metres off Sydney Heads. Since then the species has been found in a number of other localities. The colour of these shells corresponds with the colour of the coral on which they are found. Minute circular transparent egg capsules are laid on their host in summer. Range: N.S.W. to northern W.A. Size: 12 mm. Uncommon.

259
OVULIDAE
Deflexed Ovulid
Cymbula deflexa
Sowerby, 1848

Occasionally found by divers, in association with gorgonians. Feeding scars are quite noticeable on fronds of the host colonies and shells very rarely have their mantles extended during the day. This species is easily distinguished from similar shells by a thick callus on the columella which gives the shell an almost flat base. Range: Qld. to northern W.A. Size: 17 mm. Uncommon.

260
OVULIDAE
Sweet Ovulid
Phenacovolva rosea nectarea
Iredale, 1930

This beautiful little species is associated with either gorgonian corals or soft corals and lives below low tide level. Eggs are laid on its particular host, usually in summer. Often washed up on beaches, they are taken mostly by snorkellers or divers between depths of 2 and 20 metres. Range: N.S.W. to Qld. Size: 30 mm. Uncommon.

261
OVULIDAE
Rosewater's Ovulid
Crenavolva rosewateri
Cate, 1973

This species is a much smaller, squatter shell than its northern relation *C. s. traillii*. It lives amongst gorgonians from 20 to 50 metres, off the coast. Range: N.S.W. Size: 7 mm. Rare.

262
OVULIDAE
Coleman's Ovulid
Aclyvolva sp.

A very rare species found only in one State, it lives in depths down to 70 metres. The author found the figured shells at 60 metres off St. Francis Island, S.A. on gorgonian coral. Range: S.A. Size: 45 mm. Rare.

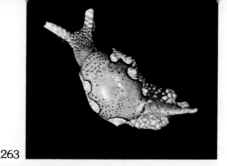

263
OXYNOEIDAE
Green Oxynoe
Oxynoe viridis
Pease, 1861

Only colour film can capture the delicate beauty of this small opisthobranch. Like so many of its relations, the colours are only in the living animal and the shell is quite transparent and very fragile. Found intertidally on green algae on rocky shore reef in W.A. Range: Qld. to W.A. Size: 12 mm. Not uncommon.

264   263

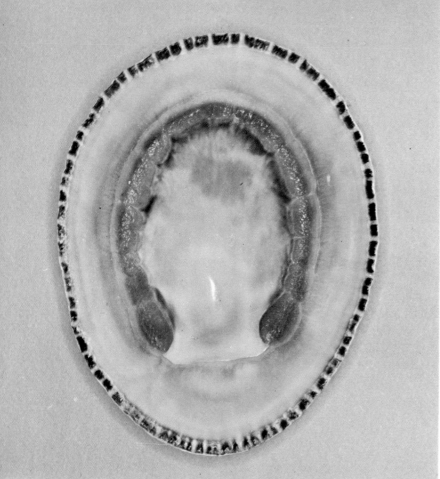

264
PATELLIDAE
Giant Limpet
Patella laticostata
Blainville, 1825

One of two species of large limpets found in southern W.A., they live intertidally on rock platforms usually in the surf zones. Collecting these shells can be hazardous at times as big waves sweep in from the Indian Ocean. The foot of these molluscs is quite edible although a little tough if not prepared correctly. Range: W.A. Size: 100 mm. Common.

265
ACMAEIDAE
Northern Star Limpet
Patelloida saccharina stella
Lesson, 1829

This rather attractive limpet lives on reefy intertidal rocks. Very common in the Hervey Bay area of Qld. Range: Qld. to W.A. Size: 28 mm. Common.

265

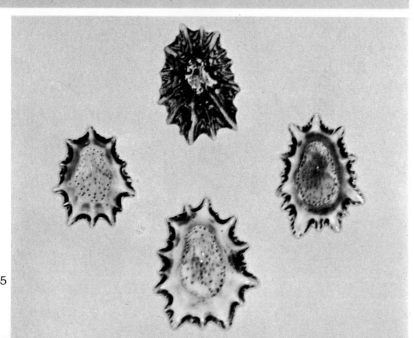

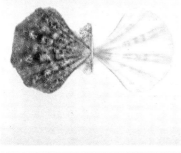

266

267

266
PECTINIDAE
Snake Scallop
Decopecten anguineus
Finlay, 1927

Taken by divers on subtidal rocky and coral reef, *D. anguineus* lives beneath rocks or amongst rubble. Not often collected by hand it frequents depths of 10 to 30 metres. Range: W.A. Size: 25 mm. Uncommon.

267
PECTINIDAE
Doughboy Scallop
Chlamys asperrimus
Lamarck, 1819

This species is found in several states but is only dredged commercially in Tas. and W.A. Specimens living on sandy rubble bottom in deeper water tend to grow larger than those living on reef. Quite often divers will find cup sponges with as many as 8 or 9 live scallops inside. Normally, reef scallops are covered in thick orange sponge. This sponge also has a boarder, a peculiar nudibranch which feeds upon it and is not found anywhere else. Live shells found around Sydney are nearly always attached by their byssus threads to some object. Range: N.S.W., Vic., S.A., Tas., southern W.A. Size: 200 mm. Common.

268
PECTINIDAE
Illuminated Pecten
Semipallium luculentum
Reeve, 1858

These shells occur intertidally, living beneath coral slabs and rocks to which they are generally attached by a byssus. Colours include white, yellow, orange, red and mauve. Range: N.T., W.A. Size: 50 mm. Moderately common in a number of areas.

269
PECTINIDAE
Scaley Scallop
Chlamys lividus
Lamarck, 1819

A delicate frilled species, this shell can be found in a wide variety of colour forms. Juvenile specimens are commonly attached by a byssus to the underside of rocks at low tide level in Qld., N.S.W. and Vic. Larger adults live subtidally and prefer areas of moderate tidal influence. These shells are usually covered with sponge and other marine growths which makes it difficult to distinguish them under water. Range: Qld., N.S.W., Vic., Tas., S.A., W.A. Size: 63 mm. Moderately common.

268

269

270

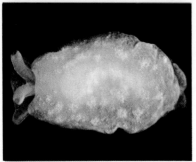

271

272

273

274

275

270
PHYLLIDIIDAE
Quilted Nudibranch
Phyllidia loricata
Bergh, 1873

Specimen pictured is the first record of this species in Australia. They live on intertidal reef beneath stones and are quite firm to touch. Range: N.T. Size: 25 mm. Moderately common.

271
PLEUROBRANCHIDAE
Mediate Side-Gilled Slug
Berthella mediata
Burn, 1962

A small interesting species which lives beneath rocks from low tide level to 5 metres. Range: Vic., S.A., Tas. Size: 20 mm. Uncommon.

272
PLEUROBRANCHIDAE
Peron's Side-Gilled Slug
Pleurobranchus peroni
Cuvier, 1803

This species was first discovered at Lord Howe Island by Julie Booth after whom it was later named. The specimen figured was taken at the Dampier Archipelago off northern W.A., *P. juliae* lives on the hydroid *Solanderia fusca* where it is almost perfectly camouflaged. It lays pink egg girdles on its host's branches during summer. Range: Qld., L.H.I., W.A. Size: 18 mm. Moderately common.

273
PLEUROLIDIIDAE
Julie's Nudibranch
Pleurolidia juliae
Burn, 1966

This species was first discovered at Lord Howe Island by Julie Booth after whom it was later named. The specimen figured was taken at the Dampier Archipelago off northern W.A., *P. juliae* lives exclusively on the hydroid *Solanderia* fusca where it is almost perfectly camouflaged. It lays pink egg girdles on its host's branches during summer. Range: Qld., L.H.I., W.A. Size: 18 mm. Moderatley common.

274
POLYCERIDAE
Conspicuous Polycera
Polycera capensis
Quoy & Gaimard, 1824

Fairly common in depths of 5 to 10 metres in Port Hacking, N.S.W., its appearance is usually restricted to late winter and early summer. It is a carniverous nudibranch feeding mainly on sedentary animals and mollusc eggs. White egg girdles are produced in summer. Range: N.S.W. Size: 50 mm. Cyclically common.

275
PTERIIDAE
Little Zebra Wing Shell
Electroma zebra
Reeve, 1859

Commonly attached to marine growths in clumps, these little shells are usually taken to be juveniles of larger species. They are very delicate, almost translucent, and are taken below tide level to depths in excess of 30 metres. Range: Qld., N.T., W.A., Vic., N.S.W. Size: 25 mm. Common.

277
SEPIIDAE
Giant Cuttle
Sepia apama
Gray, 1849

Common to skin divers around the southern and mid tropical coasts. Its internal shell or cuttle bone is regularly washed ashore on southern beaches. In life this species inhabits caves and ledges during the day in depths of 3 to 30 metres. There is some evidence that cuttles may regularly visit the one cave. They are quite fearless under water and will approach very close to a diver. If attacked or panicked they will emit a cloud of black inky substance into the water and retreat behind it. They have a large parrot-like beak which is situated at the centre of their arms and capable of inflicting a nasty wound. Range: N.S.W. to W.A. Size: may grow to over 1 metre. Common.

276
COLUMBELLIDAE
Ocellate Dove Shell
Pyrene ocellata
Link, 1807

Found beneath stones or dead coral,
these shells are variable in design.
They occur from low tide level to 10
metres with several specimens
usually living under one rock. Range:
Qld. to N.T. Size: 20 mm. Common.

278

278
SEPIIDAE
Harvest Cuttle
Sepia mestus
Gray, 1849

Quite common in estuaries in N.S.W., this species is frequently seen by divers. During the day they hide away under caves and ledges or in weed beds. Diet consists mostly of fish and mating takes place in summer. Eggs are laid in white clusters amongst kelp or soft corals, usually in areas of moderate current. Unlike the octopus, the cuttle does not always stand guard over her eggs. Range: N.S.W., Vic., S.A., Tas. Size: 220 mm. Common.

279
SEPIOLOIDEIDAE
Lined Dumpling Squid
Sepioloidea lineolata
Quoy & Gaimard, 1832

A beautiful species of small squid which lives in shallow waters amongst reef along the southern coast of Australia. It is remarkably swift in movement and like other cephalopod molluscs, the female is maternally minded watching over her eggs until they hatch. Range: N.S.W. to southern W.A. Size: 50 mm. Moderately common.

280
SEPIOLIDAE
Flat Fingered Dumpling Squid
Euprymna stenodactyla
Grant, 1833

A small interesting species, this squid is not often encountered because of its secretive habits. It can be found in tide pools and on open water reefs sheltering beneath rocks or in rubble from low water to 25 metres. Specimens are often brilliantly iridescent in colour. Range: N.S.W. to W.A. Size: grow to a little over 28 mm. Moderatley uncommon.

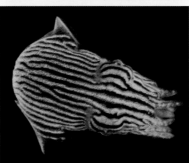

279

280

281

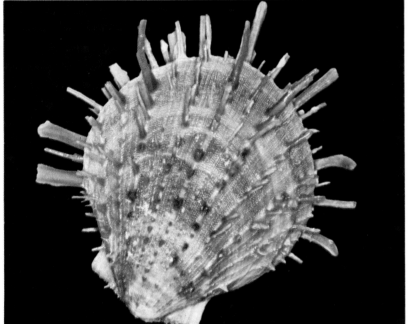

282

281
SIPHONARIIDAE
Van Diemen's Land Siphon Shell
Siphonaria diemenensis
Quoy & Gaimard, 1833

These common inhabitants of intertidal rocky reefs lay white or yellow egg masses in girdles, similar to nudibranchs. Preferring a high littoral habitat their food consists of algae scraped from the surrounding terrain. Range: N.S.W. to W.A. Size: 25 mm. Common.

282
SPONDYLIDAE
Scarlet Thorny Oyster
Spondylus tenellus
Reeve, 1856

Anterior valves or top halves of this shell are often washed ashore on many beaches within its range. However, it is not easy to find a living specimen, for they live below tide level down to many hundreds of metres. Although trawled fairly regularly in some areas, scuba diving provides another method of procuring this species. Camouflaged by marine growths, they are attached to rocks, shells or rubble and experience is needed before shells can be located easily. Range: N.S.W. to southern W.A. Size: 76 mm. Common.

283
EULIMIDAE
Crinoid Stilifer
Curveulima obtusa
Laseron, 1955

Although the majority of stilifers are known to live parasitically on echinoderms little work has been done on recording the species and their various hosts. Indeed a large proportion are known only from dead shells sifted from beach grit. *C. obtusa* has only recently been discovered living on the crinoid feather star *Cenolia trichoptera* in 30 metres of water off Jervis Bay, N.S.W. Range: Qld., N.S.W., Vic., Tas., S.A. Size: 4 mm. Moderately common.

283

284
STOMATELLIDAE
Imbricated False Ear Shell
Stomatella imbricata
Lamarck, 1822

Very common attached to substrate beneath rocks, this species lives from low tide level to 10 metres. The attractive internal lustre of the shell makes it amongst the first to be collected by beginners. Range: Qld. to W.A. Size: 35 mm. Common.

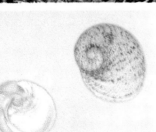

284

93

285

287

288

285
STOMATELLIDAE
False Ear Shell
Stomatelia impertusa
Burrow, 1825

Fairly common under stones at low water. *S. impertusa* is easily distinguished from *Haliotis,* by the lack of holes on the body whorl keel. It is a very agile species and cast off the posterior end of its foot to elude enemies. Range: Qld., N.S.W., Vic, Tas., S.A., W.A. Size: 22 mm. Common.

286
STROMBIDAE
Gouty Spider Shell
Lambis chiragra
Linnaeus, 1758

Although not common on intertidal reef flats on the Great Barrier Reef, specimens have been taken from off Townsville in 3 metres by divers. Living amongst broken coral reef female shells were found to be more than twice the size of male shells. Fairly common in 5 to 10 metres off North West Cape, W.A. living on limestone reef and in sand pockets. Male shells in this area tended to be of similar size to female shells. Range: Qld. to northern W.A. Size: 250 mm. Uncommon.

287
TRIVIIDAE
Pink-Spotted Rice Cowry
Trivia merces
Iredale, 1924

Found beneath rocks and stones from N.S.W. to northern W.A., this little shell is quite common intertidally. Diving regularly turns up specimens from as deep as 15 metres in Tas. and southern W.A. Range: N.S.W., W.A., Tas. Size: 12 mm. Common.

288
TROCHIDAE
Jewelled Top Shell
Calliostoma armillata
Wood, 1828

A very beautiful species of top shell, when found it is remarkably free of marine growths. It lives on submerged reef and rubble to 30 metres. Range: N.S.W. to W.A. Size: 35 mm. Fairly common.

289
LITTORINIDAE
Gold-mouthed Top Shell
Bembicium auratum
Quoy & Gaimard, 1834

One of the most common molluscs found on rocky intertidal shores. These shells are extremely prevalent in sheltered estuarial conditions. They live at mid tide level and usually congregate in groups. Range: Qld., N.S.W., Vic., Tas., S.A. Size: 18 mm. Common.

289

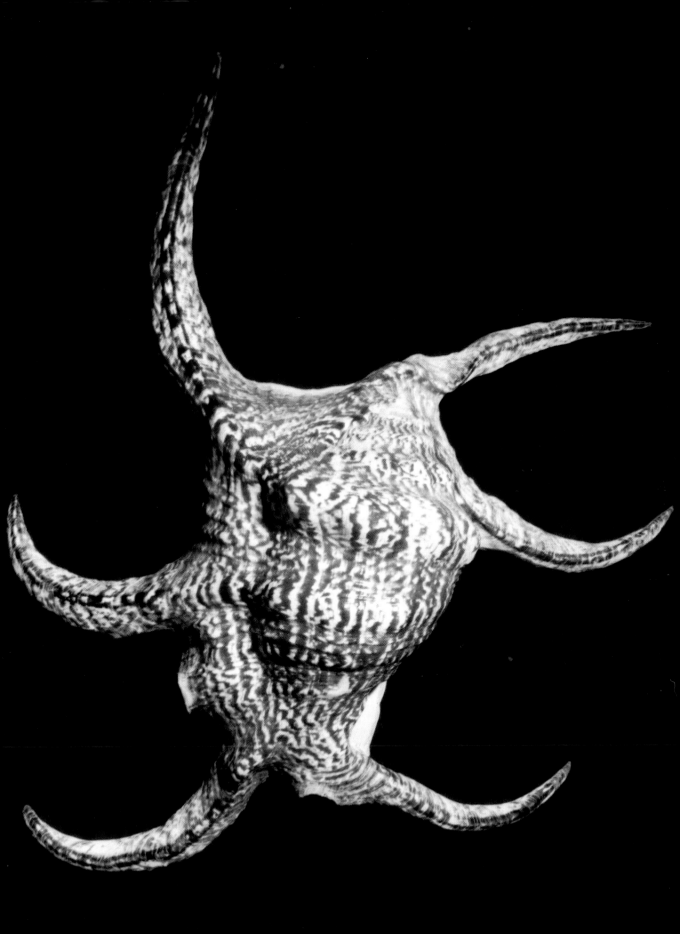

290

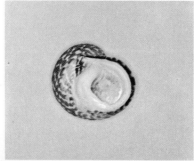

291

292

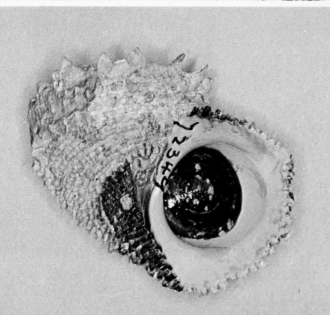

290
TROCHIDAE
Shrewd Trochid
Monilea callifera
Lamarck, 1822

M. callifera lives under rocks intertidally. It has very finely beaded sculpture and its umbilicus is very deep, penetrating to the topmost whorl. Range: N.S.W. to Qld. Size: 15 mm. Fairly common.

291
TROCHIDAE
Wavy Periwinkle
Austrocochlea concamerata
Wood, 1828

Found in similar areas to *A. constricta*, this shell is heavier and squatter in shape and has finer lines with a porcellaneous interior. Quite gregarious by nature. Range: N.S.W. to Qld. Size: 15 mm. Common.

292
TROCHIDAE
Ribbed Periwinkle
Austrocochlea constricta
Lamarck, 1822

Very common on intertidal reefs in N.S.W., these shells are subject to a wide variation in colour patterns. The molluscs are black and grey and have a beautiful pearly internal lustre. A delicacy when boiled in their shell. They are herbivores, feeding on algae. Range: Qld., N.S.W., Vic., Tas., W.A. Size: 19 mm. Common.

293, 294
TURBINIDAE
Purple Banded Dolphin Shell
Angaria tyria
Reeve, 1843

Fairly common on intertidal reef or in weed beds subtidally, this shell is restricted to W.A. Young specimens possess delicate shoulder spines but these are usually eroded on adult specimens. Range: W.A. Size: 70 mm. Common.

293

94

295
LIOTIIDAE
Southern Wheel Shell
Munditia australis
Kiener, 1839

A peculiar little shell, it lives under stones from low tide level to 10 metres. Specimens from Vic. have heavy cancellate sculpture but shells from southern W.A. are much finer in appearance. Range: N.S.W. to southern W.A. Size: 14 mm. Common.

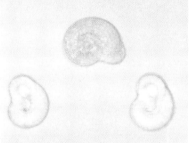

295

296
PHASIAELLIDAE
Australian Pheasant Shell
Phasianella australis
Gmelin, 1791

The largest of the pheasant shells, *P. australis* lives amongst algae on reefs mainly below low tide level. It displays an amazing array of colours and patterns and is preyed upon by quite a lot of fish and other molluscs, particularly volutes. Range: Vic., Tas., S.A., southern W.A. Size: 60 mm. Common.

296

297
TURBINIDAE
Squat Turban
Turbo cinereus
Born, 1778

Found on intertidal rocks. These shells seem to be common only in certain areas, and are herbivores. Range: Qld. to N.T. Size: 30 mm. Common.

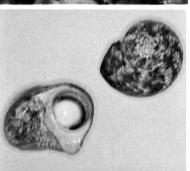

297

299

299
TURBINIDAE
Military Turban
Turbo militaris
Reeve, 1848

Common in some rocky shore areas of northern N.S.W. and southern Qld., this shell has been taken alive as far south as Sydney by diving. Living from low tide level to 5 metres, specimens from some areas may have short protruding spines growing from the body whorl. Range: N.S.W. to Qld. Size: 100 mm. Common.

300
TURBINIDAE
Cap Trochid Shell
Astralium pileola
Reeve, 1842

Common on intertidal reef flats amongst brown algae. The shell is usually coated with algae and older specimens show signs of erosion. Strictly herbivores. Range: central north coast of W.A. Size: 60 mm. Common.

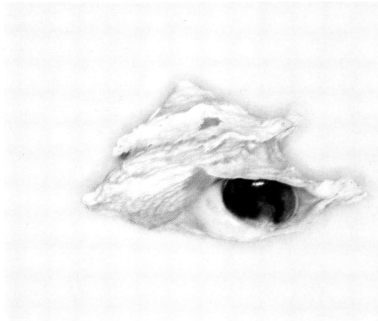

00

301
TURBINIDAE
Round Turban Shell
Astralium rotularia
Lamarck, 1822

The exquisite rosette shape and its availability make this species very popular. Easily found on intertidal reefs where it lives on algae and is quite common. Range: northern W.A. to N.T. Size: 45 mm. Common.

298
TURBINIDAE
Jourdan's Turbo
Turbo jourdani
Kiener, 1839

T. jourdani is by far the largest turbo in southern Australia. Living below tide level amongst algae covered reef to 40 metres, they are collected mainly by divers. The animal is black in colour and sensitive to light and movement during the day. Not often seen on the move, they prefer the nocturnal hours for feeding on algae. Range: S.A. to southern W.A. Size: grows to over 220 mm in height. Uncommon.

301

302

302
TURBINIDAE
Blue Mouthed Turban
Astralium stellaris
Gmelin, 1791

The blue columella and operculum make it readily identifiable. Some collectors believe that by cutting off the mollusc's operculum (which is used for jewellery) without actually killing the mollusc, their actions are consequential in preserving the species. Without an operculum for protection the mollusc will soon succumb to natural predators, if it survives the surgery! Range: Qld. to northern W.A. Size: 30 mm. Common.

303

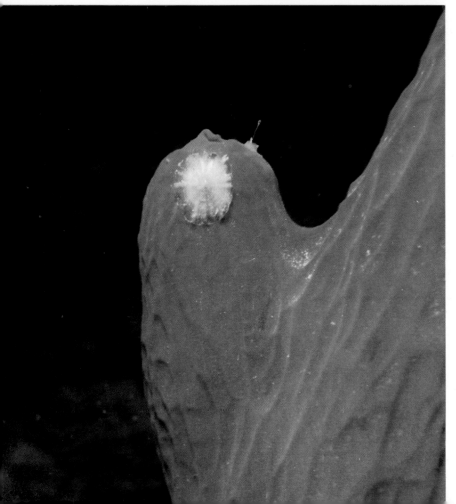

305

304

303
TURBINIDAE
Sydney Turbo Shell
Turbo torquatus
Gmelin, 1788

Very common on intertidal reef platforms along the entire south coast, they are prone to variable shell characteristics. Quite edible, this species and many others are the subject of wholesale exploitation as food by some communities. Already a number of the low tide populations have been noticeably reduced in easily accessible reefs around heavily populated areas. Range: southern Aust. Size: 100 mm. Common.

304
TURRIDAE
Botany Bay Turrid
Daphnella botanica
Hedley, 1918

A beautiful little shell sometimes mistaken for a volute, *D. botanica* has a creamy animal with black eyes. Specimens are usually found beneath rocks in sand or rubble from low tide level down to 15 metres. Range: Qld., N.S.W. to W.A. Size: 19 mm. Moderately common.

305
TYLODINIDAE
Small Umbrella Shell
Tylodina corticalis
Tate, 1889

One of the smallest umbrella shells it is also one of the rarest. The animal is bright yellow with the flat clear limpet like shell attached to its back. It feeds exclusively on sponges and can be found from low tide level down to 60 metres. Range: N.S.W., Vic., S.A. Size: 30 mm. Rare.

306, 307
UMBRACULIDAE
Umbrella Shell
Umbraculum sinicum
Gmelin, 1783

This animal is a large, lumpy, grey, yellowish mass. The mollusc's thin shell sits in the centre of the dorsal surface mostly covered in algae. Found in intertidal rock pools all around Australia's eastern, northern and western coasts down to 20

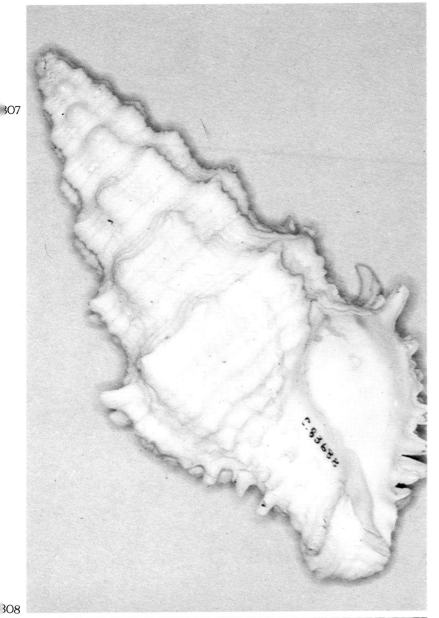

307

metres subtidally. Recorded specimens in N.S.W. lay a typical opistobranch egg ribbon, usually between December and March, and feed mostly on sponges. Not always an easy shell to find, they tend to appear in cycles. Range: coastal Aust. Size: diameter of 152 mm.

308
TURBINELLIDAE
Flinder's Vase Shell
Vasum flindersi
Verco, 1914

For many years these shells were known only from dead specimens inhabited by hermit crabs taken in craypots. With the increase of abalone divers and scuba sport divers along the south and south-west coasts, these shells are now being taken alive on rocky reef. Shells are subtidal dwellers living in depths of between 20 and 250 metres. Several colour forms have been recorded but the majority are brilliant orange. Range: S.A. to W.A. Size: 180 mm. Uncommon.

309
VERMETIDAE
Common Worm Shell
Serpulorbis sipho
Lamarck, 1818

Very common below tide level, these shells attach themselves to rocks, reef and to other shells. The colours and patterns of the animal of this species seems to be fairly consistent. Range: N.S.W., Vic., Tas., S.A., southern W.A. Size: 130 mm. Common.

308

309

103

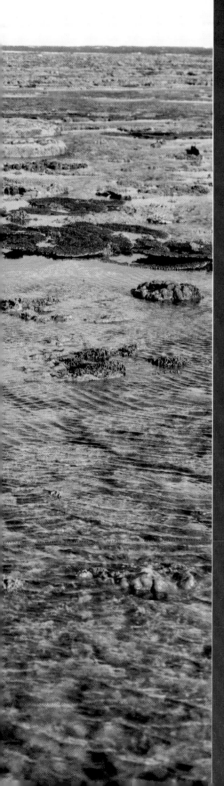

Part 3
Coral reefs

Coral reefs

311

Coral reefs — the very words conjure up visions of rare and beautiful species amid palm fringed islands and azure blue waters of the tropics. Indeed it is very true of some places, for the shells inhabiting coral reefs are amongst the most beautiful to be found in any habitat.

Australia has the most extensive coral reefs in the world; over 3,000 kilometres of reef formations exist off the eastern, northern and western coasts. The coral reefs of the west are not as extensive as those of the east and are mainly fringing reefs. Nevertheless they possess large communities of superb animals and produce some very rare shells. The species found on the eastern, northern and western coral reefs are often coalescent and many are widely distributed over thousands of kilometres.

Although corals grow from mid-tide level down to many hundreds of metres, the reef building forms are usually restricted to the vicinity of 50 metres. Between these two extremes live the majority of shells available to the collector.

A large part of intertidal coral reef flats are not living coral but cemented causeways of beach rock covered by thousands of pieces of dead and living coral clumps. Beneath these clumps and their associated slabs of coral or beach rock the main body of accessible shells is to be found. A diver may turn up a rare species now and then but he cannot cover the area or see as much as a fossicker on the low tide.

Intertidal coral reefs are susceptible to damage by the unthinking and the ignorant, large tracts can be laid waste in a short time by people smashing coral and leaving rocks overturned. It is every person's responsibility not to take more shells than needed, to leave behind those with healed breaks, growth marks, juveniles or females on eggs. At all times every effort must be made to leave the habitat as it was found.

Shells, like most living things, are subject to differences within the species. Early conchologists believed that the geographical variations shown in some species to be worthy of specific or subspecific rank. Because nothing much was known then regarding distribution, habitat, natural history or in some cases locality, many shells of the same species received different names. As the misconceptions of the past are corrected so new names must be learnt. This has led to much confusion throughout the years and is one of the reasons why the world of the shell collector is forever changing.

312

313

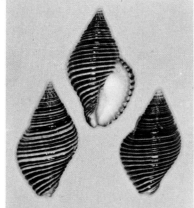

314

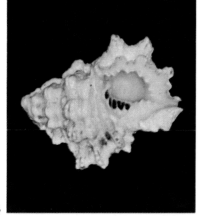

315

316

312
AGLAJIDAE
Pleasant Long Tailed Slug
Chelidonura amoena
Bergh, 1905

Not a common species, this mollusc usually inhabits short algae covered sand pockets on submerged reefs. Range: northern W.A. Size: 35 mm. Uncommon.

313
BUCCINIDAE
Little Banded Whelk
Pisania fasciculata
Reeve, 1846

A small elongated shell quite commonly found under coral slabs on the Great Barrier Reef where it has two distinct colour forms. Animals are dark red and sexual dimorphism does not seem to be evident. Range: Qld. Size: 25 mm. Common.

314
BUCCINIDAE
Waved Buccinid
Cantharus undosus
Linnaeus, 1758

With a heavy periostracum to protect them these shells are usually found in good condition. Very common on the Great Barrier Reef, they live under dead coral on the reef flats and causeways. Range: Qld. Size: 35 mm. Common.

315
BURSIDAE
Blood Stained Frog Shell
Bursa cruentata
Sowerby, 1835

Normally living below tide level, these little bursids shelter under coral slabs and in dead coral on the Great Barrier Reef. Specimens are nearly always heavily encrusted with marine growths. The dark splashes of colour above the columella plaits make them easy to identify. Range: Qld. Size: 40 mm. Moderately common.

316
BURSIDAE
Granulated Bursa
Bursa granularis
Roeding, 1798

Probably the most commonly encountered species of *Bursa,* this species inhabits mainland and offshore reefs. Shells from different areas can be very variable, some being almost smooth while others are heavily granulated. The best specimens are located beneath rocks and dead coral slabs. Range: N.S.W. to W.A. Size: 38 mm. Common.

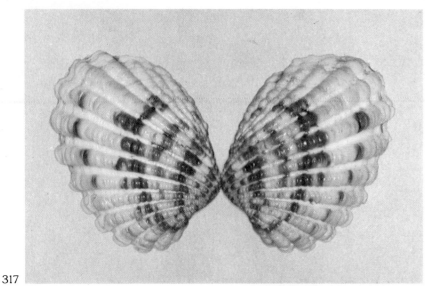

317

317
CARDITIDAE
Thickened Cardita
Cardita incrassata
Sowerby, 1825

This species is usually found beneath rocks or coral either intertidally or in shallow water. It is a filter feeder. Range: Qld., N.T., W.A., S.A. Size: specimens often grow as large as 50 mm. Moderately common.

318
CERITHIIDAE
Wandering Cerith
Pseudovertagus aluco
Linnaeus, 1758

Living intertidally on coral reef, sand and rubble, this shell is subject to erosion on the dorsum. Range: Qld. to northern W.A. Size: 58 mm. Fairly common.

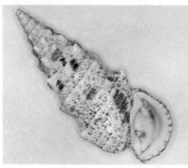

318

319, 320
CERITHIIDAE
Pillar Creeper
Cerithium columna
Sowerby, 1834

Figured specimens were found in 5 metres of water on fans of dead *Acropora* coral on the Great Barrier Reef. These shells are unusually coloured for ceriths but are always heavily covered in encrusting coraline growths. Range: N.S.W. to northern W.A. Size: 60 mm. Common.

319

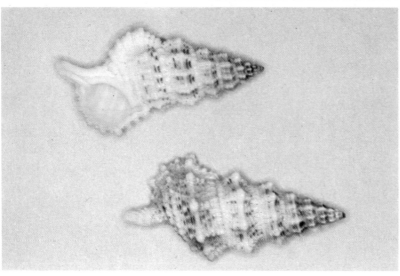

320

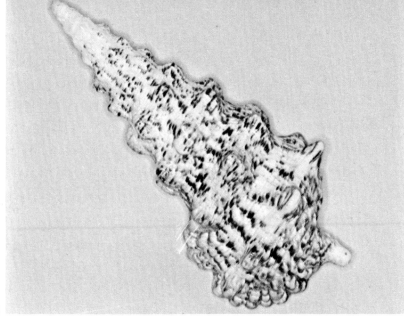

321

322

323

321
CERITHIIDAE
Nodulose Coral Creeper
Cerithium nodulosum
Bruguiere, 1792

Quite a large cerith, this shell is found on coral reefs along the Qld. coast. Often heavily encrusted with coraline algae large adult specimens have eroded spires. Range: Qld. Size: 100 mm. Common.

322
CHAMIDAE
Reflected Chama
Chama reflexa
Reeve, 1846

This shell is often found attached to dead coral and rocks above or below low water; also lives beneath rocks which have water flowing under them. Quite an attractive shell, skill is needed to remove the shell from the substrate in one piece. Range: Qld. to N.T. Size: 50 mm. Common.

323
CHITONIDAE
Giant Gem Chiton
Acanthozostra gemmata
Iredale and Hull, 1926

A large, very common species which lives on coral rock just below high tide level. These chitons have their own particular hole or hollow to which they return after foraging. They feed mainly during the night on algae scraped from surrounding rock surfaces. Range: Qld. to northern W.A. Size: 100 mm. Common.

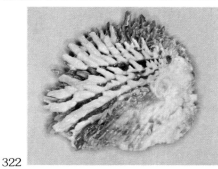

324

324
CONIDAE
Cat Cone
Conus cattus
Hwass in Bruguiere, 1792

Fairly common in sand pockets on reef, it is found in many colours and patterns. Reported to be a fish eater. The species should be handled with care, as should all cones. Range: Qld. Size: 50 mm. Common.

325
CONIDAE
Astrologer's Cone
Conus chaldaeus
Roeding, 1798

This cone lives in the same habitat as *C. ebraeus* and also has the same range. Often the two may be confused although *C. chaldaeus* always displays finer wavy white lines separating its darker colour. Range: N.S.W. to northern W.A. Size: 40 mm. Not as common as *C. ebraeus*.

325

326
CONIDAE
Scarlet Cone
Conus coccineus
Gmelin, 1791

This shell is taken by divers working in 10 to 20 metres of water off the reef edges. This little cone hides away in small sand pockets in caves and under ledges in coral heads and bommies. Range: Qld. to N.T. Size: 30 mm. Rare.

326

327

328

327
CONIDAE
Coronated Cone
Conus coronatus
Gmelin, 1791

Very common in small sand pockets on reef ramparts. They are often covered in encrusting coraline algae and have many colour forms. Range: N.S.W. to northern W.A. Size: 35 mm. Common.

328
CONIDAE
Hebrew Cone
Conus ebraeus
Linnaeus, 1758

In the main, this intertidal species is found on rocky reef platforms and coral reef rims. It prefers small pockets and indents in the reef and is often disfigured with hard coraline growths and erosion. Range: N.S.W. to northern W.A. Size: 40 mm. Very common.

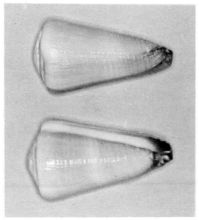

329

329
CONIDAE
Emaciated Cone
Conus emaciatus
Reeve, 1849

C. emaciatus has a thick heavy periostracum and occurs on reef platforms intertidally. Although this species is somewhat similar in shape to *C. virgo*, it can be distinguished by its slightly concave sides and spiral ribbing. Range: N.S.W. to Qld. Size: 50 mm. Moderately common.

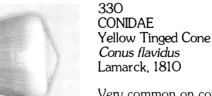

330

330
CONIDAE
Yellow Tinged Cone
Conus flavidus
Lamarck, 1810

Very common on coral reef flats and causeways, this species is usually covered in a thick coating of coraliñe algae. The spires of larger adult specimens are mostly eroded and marred by boring from marine animals. Range: N.S.W. to Qld. Size: 50 mm. Common.

332   331

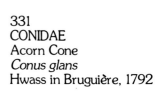

331
CONIDAE
Acorn Cone
Conus glans
Hwass in Bruguière, 1792

A small uncommon species occasionally found in broken coral beds and under coral slabs on intertidal reefs. Also found by diving in similar habitat down to 10 metres. The animal is red, which contrasts with the vivid blue of the shell. Pure white specimens have been found but these are very rare. Shell feeds on worms. Range: Qld. to northern W.A. Size: 30 mm. Uncommon.

332
CONIDAE
Imperial Cone
Conus imperialis
Linnaeus, 1758

Not often found in good condition these shells are very susceptible to erosion, marring coraline algae growth and healed breaks. They live intertidally on dead rubble reef usually fairly close to shore. Food consists mainly of worms. Range: Qld. Size: 76 mm. Uncommon.

111

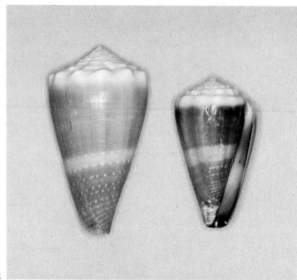

333

333
CONIDAE
Livid Cone
Conus lividus
Hwass in Bruguiere, 1792

Lives in similar circumstances to *C. flavidus*. Although it is quite common, collectors have a hard time finding perfect specimens. Range: N.S.W. to W.A. Size: 50 mm. Common.

334
CONIDAE
Mile Cone
Conus miles
Linnaeus, 1758

Perfect specimens of *C. miles* are not easy to find although it is a very common species. It lives on intertidal reef flats and causeways usually in the open in rocks and holes. Invariably this cone has thick coatings of coraline growths and is very susceptible to healed breaks and growth marks. Range: N.S.W. to northern W.A. Size: 80 mm. Common.

334

335
CONIDAE
Music Cone
Conus musicus
Bruguière, 1792

Found on intertidal reef ramparts. These little shells live in small pockets and crevices in the reef and sometimes occur in sandy holes. They are usually covered in encrusting coraline algae and are subject to erosion which may be severe in large adults. Range: Qld. to N.T. Size: 20 mm. Moderately common.

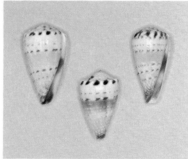

335

336
CONIDAE
Weasel Cone
Conus mustellinus
Bruguière, 1792

Superficially similar to *C. capitaneus*, this species can be distinguished by its slimmer shape and more elevated spire. Mostly found on intertidal reef, either exposed or under rock edges. Range: Qld. to N.T. Size: 55 mm. Moderately common.

336

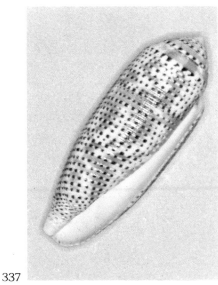
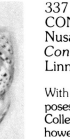

337

337
CONIDAE
Nusatella Cone
Conus nusatella
Linnaeus, 1758

With such a distinct form *C. nusatella* poses no problems in identification. Collecting it alive is not as easy, however, for it is a fairly uncommon species and lives amongst live coral reef usually under several layers of broken coral. Range: Qld. Size: 65 mm. Uncommon.

338

338
CONIDAE
Young Cone
Conus parvulus
Link, 1807

C. parvulus lives on reef flats. It is not easy to find, and even when found, its identity is not clear until the specimen is cleaned. Coraline algae usually covers its dorsal surface. Range: Qld., N.T. Size: 40 mm. Moderately common.

339

339
CONIDAE
Ringed Cone
Conus planorbis
Born, 1778

Living exposed intertidally on coral reefs, this shell is also found on rocky reefs. Under these conditions it has a fairly thick brown periostracum. Shells taken subtidally in depths of 20 metres are more brightly coloured and have a thinner periostracum. Range: Qld. to W.A. Size: 65 mm. Common.

340
CONIDAE
Rat Cone
Conus rattus
Hwass in Bruguière, 1792

C. rattus lives on reef flats and causeways, where it can be found in sand pockets, under stones or amongst coral. It feeds mostly on worms. Range: Qld. to northern W.A. Size: 45 mm. Common.

340

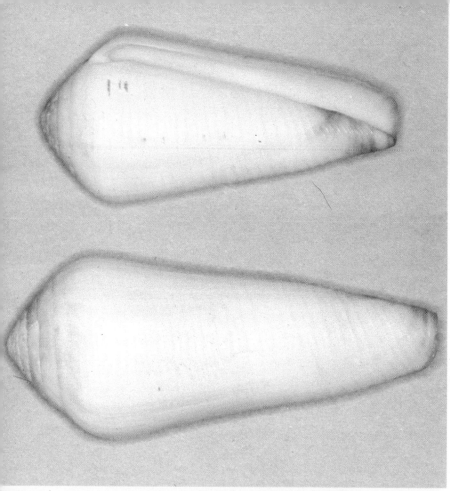

341
CONIDAE
Auger Cone
Conus terebellum
Linnaeus, 1758

Usually a white base colour, *C. terebellum* also has a thick brown periostracum. Occasionally found on intertidal coral reef they seem to prefer a below tide level habitat, living on coral outcrops under dead coral. Range: Qld. to northern W.A. Size: 100 mm. Uncommon.

342
CONIDAE
Flag Cone
Conus vexillum
Gmelin, 1791

This cone seems to prefer a fairly rough water habitat and can be often found under large coral slabs on the seaward side of some Great Barrier Reef islands, just below tide level. Quite a large species, it has a black animal and a well developed operculum. Range: Qld. to northern W.A. Size: 150 mm. Uncommon.

341

342

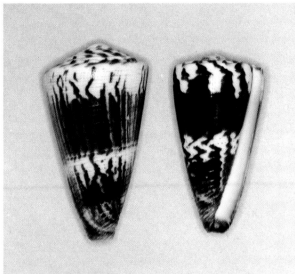

44 343

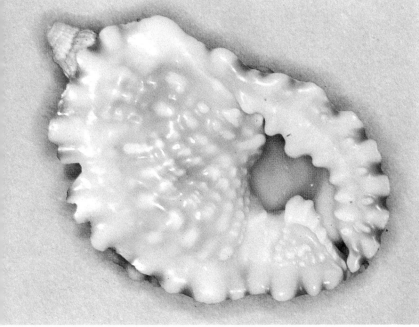

345

346

343
CONIDAE
Calf Cone
Conus vitulinus
Hwass in Bruguière, 1792

Found on reef flats amongst rubble and under small ledges, this cone is a pleasure to find as most specimens are in good condition. Also found over the edge of the reef to depths of 10 metres on dead coral. Range: Qld. Size: 60 mm. Uncommon.

344
CYMATIIDAE
Distorted Triton
Distorsio anus
Linnaeus, 1758

Not always an easy shell to find, specimens live below tide level under large coral slabs on the Great Barrier Reef. In life they have a thin sparsely haired periostracum. Care must be taken when handling this shell to adequately protect the thin flattened ventral shield as it is quite fragile. Range: Qld. to N.T. Size: 90 mm. Not common.

345
CYMATIIDAE
Jewel Triton
Septa gemmata
Reeve, 1844

These shells live beneath coral slabs on islands and bays of the Great Barrier Reef, and are found intertidally and subtidally. They have a yellow periostracum, and large adults may often be badly eroded. Not as plentiful in Australia as in other Indo Pacific areas. Range: Qld. Size: 35 mm. Not common.

346
CYMATIIDAE
Tadpole Triton
Gyrineum gyrinum
Linnaeus, 1758

Mostly found beneath coral slabs in shallow water along the Great Barrier Reef. This species is not commonly taken alive. The animal itself is yellowish with brown markings on the tentacles. Range: Qld. to N.T. Size: 25 mm. Uncommon.

348   347

347 See 352

348
CYMATIIDAE
Sea Shore Triton
Ranularia lotoria
Linnaeus, 1758

A moderately large species, *R. lotoria* lives amongst coral reef from low tide level down to 10 metres. It has a very thick periostracum. Old adult shells are subject to erosion and disfiguring coraline growths. Range: Qld. Size: 150 mm. Uncommon.

349
CYMATIIDAE
Bent Triton
Septa nicobarica
Roeding, 1798

These shells live on hard substrate beneath coral slabs on shallow water reefs. Shells grow to 70 mm and at this size are often eroded. Range: N.S.W. to W.A. Size: 70 mm. Moderately common.

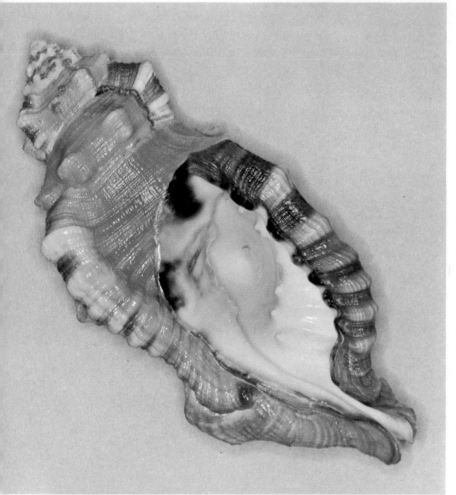

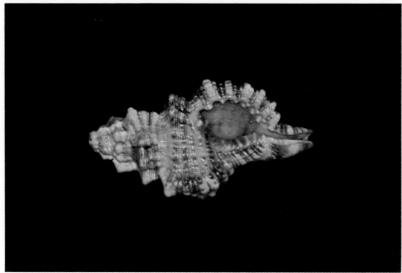

349

350
CYMATIIDAE
Northern Hairy Triton
Septa pileare
Linnaeus, 1758

Rather a common species over its entire distribution. These shells usually have a thin hairy periostracum, but in several areas on the Great Barrier Reef adult shells have their periostracum worn away thus allowing marine growths and erosion to mar the shells. Found on intertidal reef under coral slabs *S. pileare* also lives in deeper waters. Range: Qld. to W.A. Size: 90 mm. Common.

351
CYMATIIDAE
Rose Coloured Tadpole Triton
Gyrineum roseum
Reeve, 1844

These shells are difficult to find as they are always heavily encrusted with coraline algae. On the Great Barrier Reef they live below tide level under dead coral. Range: Qld. to W.A. Size: 40 mm. Uncommon.

352
CYMATIIDAE
Robin Redbreast Triton
Septa rubecula
Linnaeus, 1758

More commonly found dead than alive, *S. rubecula* is found on intertidal reef under coral slabs and rocks and subtidally to 20 metres. Its colour is variable but the majority of shells are orange, red or brown. Range: Qld. to W.A. Size: 40 mm. Uncommon.

350

351

352

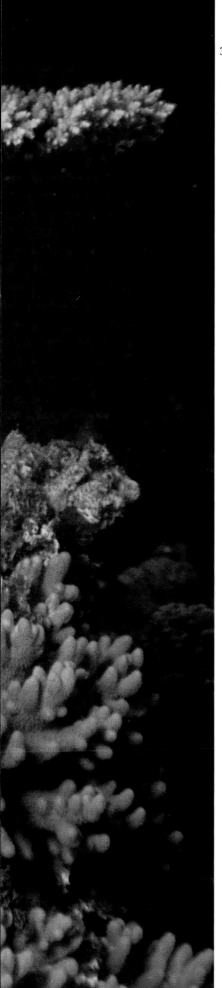

353

353
CYMATIIDAE
Giant Triton Shell
Charonia tritonis
Linnaeus, 1758

This largest of Australian tritons has become almost a household word over the past few years. As a predator on echinoderms its diet includes the crown of thorns sea star. For this reason the government has fully protected this species, banning all collecting. From the time the young tritons hatch it takes up to 3 years before they reach their maximum size of 457 mm. Range: Qld. to W.A. Size: 457 mm. Uncommon.

354

354
CYMATIIDAE
Wasp Triton
Septa vespaceum
Lamarck, 1822

Fairly common on intertidal coral reef where it lives under dead coral slabs. Also found by snorkelling to depths of around 5 metres. Very variable in colour. Food includes encrusting compound ascidians. Range: Qld. Size: 30 mm. Common.

355
CYPRAEIDAE
Ringed Money Cowry
Cypraea annulus
Linnaeus, 1758

One of the commonest species of cowry in Australia, these shells inhabit coral reefs and rocky reefs. They are restricted to intertidal areas and usually occur towards the mid tide or high tide level. Shells can be found under stones or coral in crevices, holes or pools. Range: N.S.W. to W.A. Size: 25 mm. Common.

355

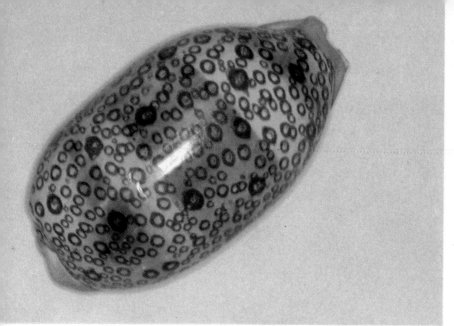

356

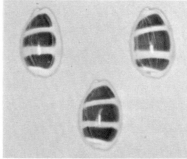

357

358

359

356
CYPRAEIDAE
Eyed Cowry
Cypraea argus
Linnaeus, 1758

A very easily recognised species but not commonly found alive *C. argus* lives in caves and holes under reef edges from 5 to 30 metres. They seem to prefer areas of maximum water movement similar to *C. mappa*. Range: northern N.S.W. to northern W.A. Size: 100 mm. Uncommon.

357
CYPRAEIDAE
Little Ass Cowry
Cypraea asellus
Linnaeus, 1758

Mainly restricted to low tide reef this species lives under rocks and dead coral. Quite often shells are marred by growth lines. Range: N.S.W. to northern W.A. Size: 18 mm. Moderately common.

358
CYPRAEIDAE
Serpent's Head Cowry
Cypraea caputserpentis
Linnaeus, 1758

Another common cowry found along the coasts and islands of its range. They live under rocks, coral and in holes and crevices in the tops of rocks and reefs, etc., usually on the outer edge of the reef where the surf breaks. Range: N.S.W., Qld., N.T., W.A. Size: 25 mm. Common.

359
CYPRAEIDAE
Purple Mouthed Cowry
Cypraea carneola
Linnaeus, 1758

Living mostly beneath coral and rocks on intertidal reef flats, these shells are difficult to find in good condition. They are almost all marred by growth scars and healed breaks. Easily recognisable by their deep purple aperture, they are also taken subtidally to 10 metres. Range: N.S.W. to W.A. Size: 50 mm. Moderately common.

360
CYPRAEIDAE
Thick Edged Cowry
Cypraea caurica
Linnaeus, 1758

Quite common along the Great
Barrier Reef, they cling to the
underside of rocks and coral on tidal
reefs down to 16 metres. On many
occasions several shells may be·
found under the same rock. Range:
N.S.W. to W.A. Size: approx.
50 mm. Common.

361
CYPRAEIDAE
Chinese Cowry
Cypraea chinensis
Gmelin, 1791

Not commonly found in Australia,
these shells live intertidally beneath
rocks and corals as well as subtidally
down to 40 metres. Quite an easily
distinguished species, they are held in
high regard by collectors. Range:
N.S.W. to W.A. Size: 50 mm.
Uncommon.

362
CYPRAEIDAE
Clandestine Cowry
Cypraea clandestina
Linnaeus, 1767

A very common shell over its entire
range, this species lives an intertidal
existence beneath rocks and dead
coral. *C. clandestina* has a jet black
animal with an occasional small white
pappilae. The females lay a white egg
mass and partake of no food during
the brooding. Range: N.S.W. to W.A.
Size: 20 mm. Common.

360

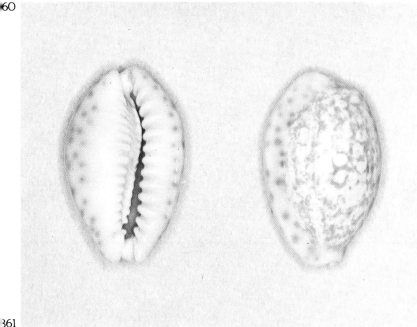

361

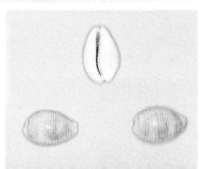

362

363

363
CYPRAEIDAE
Tan & White Cowry
Cypraea cribaria
Linnaeus, 1758

Not a rare cowry, but still regarded as quite a prize whenever found alive. They can be found under stones and coral slabs at low water and down to 8 metres. Range: N.S.W. to W.A. Size: 25 mm. Uncommon.

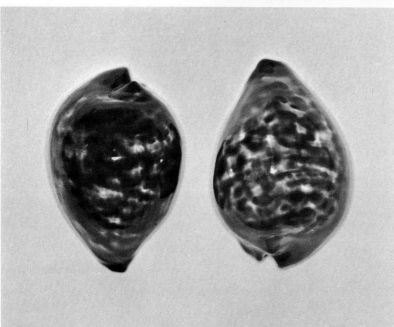

364

364
CYPRAEIDAE
Hump-Backed Cowry
Cypraea decipiens
Smith, 1880

Commonly collected by pearl divers in northern W.A. during the height of pearling activities early in the 20th century, *C. decipiens* is not as available today. Living from below tide level down to 80 metres, this species lives on sponges and is the only shell in the *Zolia* sub-genus of which the egg capsules are unknown. Range: northern W.A. Size: 60 mm. Common.

365

365
CYPRAEIDAE
Elongate Cowry
Cypraea eglantina
Duclos, 1833

Common intertidally under dead coral slabs and rocks, *C. eglantina* has a black animal and is usually found in pairs. Pink egg masses are laid in early summer on the underside of rocks. Shell is similar to *C. arabica* but is lighter and more cylindrical with a dark spire. Range: Qld. to W.A. Size: 75 mm. Common.

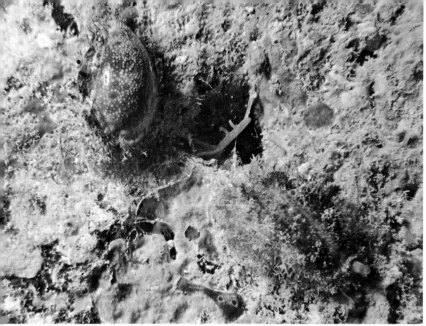

366

366
CYPRAEIDAE
Eroded Cowry
Cypraea erosa
Linnaeus, 1758

These shells live under rocks and coral mostly around the low tide level; have also been taken by diving down to 6 metres. The females deposit their egg capsules in the winter months and sit on them till they hatch. Range: N.S.W., Qld., N.T., W.A. Size: 37 mm. Common.

367
CYPRAEIDAE
Cat Cowry
Cypraea felina
Gmelin, 1791

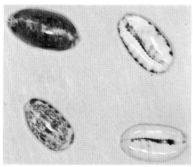

367

Lives on coral reef ramparts under large dead coral heads mostly on the seaward sides. Usually found in pairs, this species is subject to melanism. Although not completely understood, this process causes the shell to take on a rostrate shape and become black. These melanistic shells are very popular amongst collectors. Range: N.S.W. to Qld. Size: 25 mm. Uncommon.

368
CYPRAEIDAE
Fringed Cowry
Cypraea fimbriata
Gmelin, 1791

368

A small delicately coloured shell, *C. fimbriata* lives beneath small stones and coral mostly in the intertidal zone. Also found below tide level to 5 metres. Range: N.S.W. to W.A. Size: 12 mm. Moderately common.

369

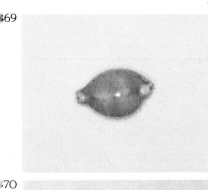

369
CYPRAEIDAE
Globular Cowry
Cypraea globulus
Linnaeus, 1758

Although quite commonly washed up on beaches along the Great Barrier Reef, live specimens of this shell are uncommon. They live inside corals and coral heads and come out of their nooks and crannies only at night. Range: Qld. to W.A. Size: 20 mm. Uncommon.

370
CYPRAEIDAE
Hammond's Cowry
Cypraea hammondae
Iredale, 1939

A rather smallish shell, specimens inhabit reef ramparts under dead coral rock. Also collected under stones on rocky reefs and by diving. Animal is bright orange and is fairly uncommon. Range: N.S.W. to W.A. Size: 20 mm. Uncommon.

70

371

371
CYPRAEIDAE
Honey Cowry
Cypraea helvolva
Linnaeus, 1758

A beautiful little shell, this species is mainly a snorkeller's shell. Even though numbers are found at low tide under rocks and coral slabs they are more prevalent below tide level. Range: N.S.W. to W.A. Size: 25 mm. Common.

372
CYPRAEIDAE
Swallow Cowry
Cypraea hirundo
Linnaeus, 1758

Because of its small size *C. hirundo* is not the easiest of shells to find. It lives under dead coral and rock. Shells seem more prolific below tide level, although the species inhabit intertidal reefs. Range: N.S.W. to northern W.A. Size: 15 mm. Uncommon.

372

373
CYPRAEIDAE
Humphrey's Cowry
Cypraea humphreysii
Gray, 1825

Not commonly found in many areas, this delightful little shell lives intertidally down to at least 20 metres. Sometimes taken on sponge or in bryozoans the deep water forms are of a much lighter colour. Range: N.S.W. to Qld. Size: 16 mm. Uncommon.

373

374
CYPRAEIDAE
Isabell Cowry
Cypraea isabella
Linnaeus, 1758

A beautiful species, *C. isabella* is collected beneath rocks and dead coral on intertidal reef. It has a black mantle. Range: N.S.W. to W.A. Size: 35 mm. Uncommon.

375
CYPRAEIDAE
Kiener's Cowry
Cypraea kieneri
Hidalgo, 1906

Found under similar conditions to *C. hirundo,* this little shell is sometimes mistaken for that species. Mantle is a transparent cream colour and specimens are sometimes marred by healed breaks. Range: N.S.W. to northern W.A. Size: 18 mm. Uncommon.

374

375

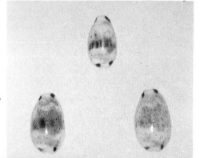

376, 377
CYPRAEIDAE
The File Cowry
Cypraea limacina
Lamarck, 1810

This species has one of the most beautiful and well developed mantles of all the Cypraeidae family. When found underwater this pink coloured mantle with long filaments makes the shell difficult to distinguish from its surroundings. It lives beneath rocks, under coral and sponge. Range: N.S.W. to W.A. Size: 35 mm. Uncommon.

377

378
CYPRAEIDAE
Lynx Cowry
Cypraea lynx
Linnaeus, 1758

This shell seems to grow larger in W.A. It lives under rock and coral slabs in the intertidal zone and lays a white egg mass in the late winter. Range: N.S.W. to northern W.A. Size: 5 mm. Fairly common.

378

379
CYPRAEIDAE
Map Cowry
Cypraea mappa
Linnaeus, 1758

One of the most beautiful of the larger cowries, there is an almost artificial look about them. Collected from low tide level down to 30 metres, they seem to prefer the caves and holes in coral over the edge of the reef. Range: N.S.W. to Qld. Size: 76 mm. Uncommon.

380

381

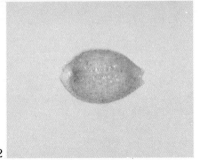

382

383

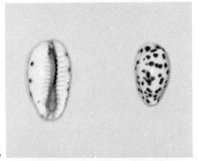

384

385

380 See 363

This shell is an albanistic colour variation of *C. cribaria*.

381
CYPRAEIDAE
Money Cowry
Cypraea moneta
Linnaeus, 1758

A common species, *C. moneta* lives under stones and coral as well as under ledges and in holes. Found on intertidal rocks and coral reefs. They seem to prefer areas of mid tide level. Occasionally beautiful golden forms of this shell are discovered. Range: N.S.W. to W.A. Size: 30 mm. Very common.

382
CYPRAEIDAE
Nut Cowry
Cypraea nucleus
Linnaeus, 1758

Rare in Australia this unique little shell lives under and in coral heads usually in exposed areas of reef. The mantle palps are remarkably long and of a similar colour to the shell. Range: northern Qld. to northern W.A. Size: 25 mm. Rare.

383
CYPRAEIDAE
Purple Based Cowry
Cypraea poraria
Linnaeus, 1758

Australian forms of this shell are found on coral reef ramparts in holes and crevices and occasionally under rocks. Range: N.S.W. to northern W.A. Size: 16 mm. Uncommon.

384
CYPRAEIDAE
Punctate Cowry
Cypraea punctata
Linnaeus, 1771

With a brilliant red mantle and a yearning for dark places *C. punctata* is an extremely elusive shell. Specimens have been taken on intertidal reef under and in dead coral or rock along the Qld. coast and Great Barrier Reef. Range: Qld. Size: 25 mm. Uncommon.

385
CYPRAEIDAE
Mouse Cowry
Cypraea scurra
Gmelin, 1791

Another member of the *Arabica* group, this species is the smallest and the least common. Found intertidally beneath dead coral on reef ramparts their finding always brings a victory shout from even the most experienced collector. Range: N.S.W. to Qld. Size: 40 mm. Uncommon.

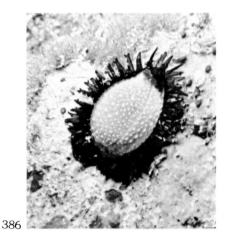

386

386
CYPRAEIDAE
Pustulose Cowry
Cypraea staphylea
Linnaeus, 1758

Found under dead coral and rocks. This interesting species has a dark plum coloured mantle and is often located amongst a similar coloured encrusting sponge upon which it feeds. Range: N.S.W. to W.A. Size: 33 mm. Uncommon.

88   387

387
CYPRAEIDAE
Fool's Cowry
Cypraea stolida
Linnaeus, 1758

Because of their beauty and relative elusiveness this species is considered by many to be quite a prize. They inhabit reefy areas under rocks, coral slabs and soft coral from low tide down to 10 metres. Range: N.S.W. to W.A. Size: 25 mm. Moderately common.

388
CYPRAEIDAE
Mole Cowry
Cypraea talpa
Linnaeus, 1758

Living under coral slabs just below the intertidal zone, *C. talpa* is right in the snorkeller's zone. It has a black-blue mantle peppered with white flecks. The large palps are a curious aspect of this mantle. Range: N.S.W. to northern W.A. Size: 90 mm. Uncommon.

389
CYPRAEIDAE
Tortoise Shell Cowry
Cypraea testudinaria
Linnaeus, 1758

It is doubtful whether this species has been found alive in Australia. A number of dead specimens have been recorded but their localities are obscure. There is every possibility that in the near future their habitat will be discovered on the northern reefs. Range: Qld. to northern W.A. Size: 120 mm. Rare.

390
CYPRAEIDAE
Tiger Cowry
Cypraea tigris
Linnaeus, 1758

Very common in shallow lagoons on the Great Barrier Reef, this species can be found at low tide level on the tops of micro atolls in the open. Below water they live in caves and ledges under reef ramparts or bommies down to 30 metres. Range: N.S.W. to W.A. Size: 120 mm. Common.

391
CYPRAEIDAE
Milk Spot Cowry
Cypraea vitellus
Linnaeus, 1758

Probably one of the best known cowries in Australia, they can be found on reefs under rocks, coral and in caves, from low water to 12 metres. Collected by reefing at low tide and diving. Range: N.S.W., Qld., W.A. Size: 70 mm. Common.

392
CYPRAEIDAE
Ziczac Cowry
Cypraea ziczac
Linnaeus, 1758

Rarely collected at low tide level, the species has been found by divers in several localities in W.A. A sub-specific form is also known from the east coast. Range: W.A. Size: 25 mm. Uncommon.

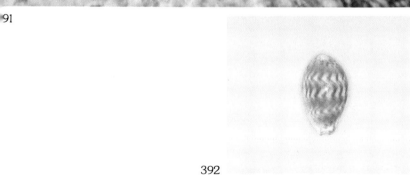

392

393
DORIDIDAE
Gold-Spotted Nudibranch
Halgerda aurantiomaculata
Allan, 1932

Fairly common below tide level down to 30 metres, this species is mostly found between 5 and 15 metres. It inhabits caves and ledges and has rather large gill plumes and rhinophores. It is firm to touch and varies little in colour over its Australian range. Range: Qld. Size: 76 mm. Common.

394
DORIDIDAE
Cespit Nudibranch
Asteronotus cespitosus
van Hasselt, 1824

A much nicer looking animal than its name suggests, *A. cespitosus* is recognisable by its large warty protrudences and wavy edged mantle. It lives beneath coral slabs in shallow waters along the northern W.A. coast. Range: W.A. to Qld. Size: grows to over 200 mm. Fairly common.

394

395

396

395
DORIDIDAE
Co's Nudibranch
Chromodoris coi
Risbec, 1956

Unmistakably patterned, *C. coi* is fairly common over the entire Great Barrier Reef. Mostly found subtidally in depths of 5 to 20 metres, it lives on exposed coral bommies and reef outcrops. Egg ribbons are laid in mid winter months with the small nudibranchs hatching in early summer. Range: Qld. Size: 50 mm. Common.

396
DORIDIDAE
Red Coral Nudibranch
Ceratosoma corallinum
Odhner, 1917

Seldom encountered, this exquisitely coloured mollusc inhabits intertidal areas of northern Australia where it lives in the open on rocky and coral reefs. Range: W.A. to N.T. Size: 55 mm. Moderately uncommon.

397
DORIDIDAE
Horned Nudibranch
Ceratosoma cornigerum
A. Adams & Reeve, 1850

A large species of *Ceratosoma*, these nudibranches grow to over 120 mm. They inhabit coral reef areas along the Great Barrier Reef and live in the open to depths of 20 metres. Mating takes place in mid-winter. Range: Qld. to W.A. Size: 120 mm. Common.

397

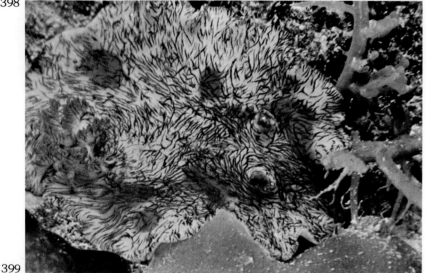

398

399

398
DORIDIDAE
Red Splashed Platydorid
Platydoris cruenta
Quoy & Gaimard, 1833

Found beneath coral rock on the Great Barrier Reef from low tide to 2 metres, this species is easily recognisable. Range: Qld. to W.A. Size: 100 mm. Common.

399
DORIDIDAE
Marginate Nudibranch
Chromodoris sp.

A large white and very soft species with an orange mantle edge. It inhabits subtidal coral along the Great Barrier Reef to depths of 10 metres. Range: N.S.W., Qld., W.A. Size: grows to around 80 mm. Uncommon.

400
DORIDIDAE
Scabby Nudibranch
Platydoris scabra
Cuvier, 1804

Common under coral slabs from low tide level to 10 metres. A firm flat nudibranch, it tends to adhere to flat surfaces very tightly making it difficult to remove. The gills and rhinophores can be retracted very quickly when the animal is disturbed. Range: Qld. to northern W.A. Size: 76 mm. Common.

401

401
DORIDIDAE
Slimy Nudibranch
Trippa spongiosa
Kelaard, 1858

Although fairly large in size, *T. spongiosa* is not of common occurrence. It lives below tide level beneath slabs of dead coral to depths of 10 metres and is soft and slimy to handle. Range: Qld. Size: 100 mm. Uncommon.

402
DORIDIDAE
Mauve-Spotted Nudibranch
Chromodoris inornata
Pease, 1871

Usually located beneath rocks or coral slabs on the low tide. *C. inornata* is soft and flabby to touch. Range: W.A. to Qld. Size: 76 mm. Common.

403
ELYSIIDAE
Ornate Nudibranch
Elysia ornata
Swainson, 1840

This species is almost always found on or in the vicinity of green algae. Often the juveniles found on algae are a little different in colour to the adults. It lives from low tide level to 15 metres and can be mistaken for a small sea hare. Range: N.S.W. to W.A. Size: 50 mm. Moderately common.

402

403

404

404
FASCIOLARIIDAE
Filamented Spindle Shell
Pleuroploca filamentosa
Roeding, 1798

Common tropical species, this shell lives on intertidal coral reefs down to 10 metres. It is carnivorous and feeds on other molluscs, especially trochids, attacking the victims through their aperture. Range: Qld. Size: 100 mm. Common.

405
FASCIOLARIIDAE
Australian Peristernia
Peristernia australiensis
Reeve, 1847

Very common on the Great Barrier Reef where it lives under dead coral and amongst reef on the intertidal zone. Often covered with marine growths it is still an easily identifiable species. Range: Qld. Size: 28 mm. Common.

405

406
FASCIOLARIIDAE
Sloping Peristernia
Peristernia fastigium
Reeve, 1847

Found on dead coral in shallow water on the Great Barrier Reef, these shells are always heavily coated in coraline growths. Well camouflaged they are often overlooked by collectors and do not seem to be in many collections. They are easily recognised by their purple aperture and prominent tooth on the outer lip. Range: Qld. Size: 30 mm. Moderately common.

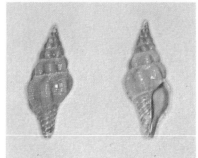

406

407
FASCIOLARIIDAE
Gibbose Latirus
Latirus gibbulus
Gmelin, 1791

A fairly heavy species, often marred by healed breaks, shells are usually heavily encrusted with marine growths. Fairly common on the Great Barrier Reef. They live on reef flats at low tide down to 5 metres below tide level and feed on other molluscs. Range: Qld. Size: 65 mm. Common.

407

408

409

410

408
FASCIOLARIIDAE
Flesh Coloured Peristernia
Peristernia "incarnata"
Kiener, 1840

Fairly common beneath rocks and coral intertidally. An attractive little shell, it can be separated from other small representatives of its family by its bright orange colour which varies little over its entire range. Range: Qld. to W.A. Size: 25 mm. Common.

409
FASCIOLARIIDAE
Fine Net Peristernia
Peristernia nassatula
Lamarck, 1822

Common beneath dead coral on reef flats in the Great Barrier Reef, *P. nassatula* is easily separated from others of its family by the deep purple aperture. Range: Qld. to N.T. Size: 35 mm. Common.

410
FASCIOLARIIDAE
Many Angled Latirus
Latirus polygonus
Gmelin, 1791

Certainly one of the most spectacular species of latirids, *L. polygonus* is fairly common beneath coral slabs in the intertidal zone of the Great Barrier Reef islands. Subject to flaws, healed breaks and marine encrustations, a good specimen is nevertheless worth the effort to clean. It is a major predator on molluscs and other small invertebrates. Range: Qld. Size: 65 mm. Common.

411

412

411
FASCIOLARIIDAE
Precious Stone Shell
Latirolagena smaragdula
Linnaeus, 1758

Another species which is very prevalent on the Great Barrier Reef, *L. smaragdula* lives on reef flats intertidally and is found beneath dead coral and amongst rocks. It has an entirely different shape from most other fasciolarids. Like the others of its family it is carnivorous, feeding mostly on other small molluscs. Range: Qld. Size: 30 mm. Common.

412
FASCIOLARIIDAE
Turreted Latirus
Latirus turritus
Gmelin, 1791

It is not always easy to find good specimens of *L. turritus* which lives from low tide level down to 8 metres, beneath dead coral or rocks and is often encrusted with a thick coating of coraline algae. Range: Qld. Size: 38 mm. Moderately common in some areas.

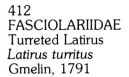

414

413
HALIOTIDAE
Asses's Ear
Haliotis asinina
Linnaeus, 1758

This species belongs to the same family as abalone or mutton fish. They belong to class Gastropoda, and are herbivorous and quite agile. In certain localities a small commensal crab lives in close association with this species — one of the few recorded instances of crustacean commensalism in Australian gastropods. Collected on reefs at low tide and by diving. Range: Qld., N.T., northern W.A. Size: length up to 150 mm. Common.

414
HALIOTIDAE
Sheep's Ear Shell
Haliotis ovina
Gmelin, 1791

This shell is mostly found below tide level on islands and cays of the Great Barrier Reef. It lives beneath large coral slabs during daylight hours and is a nocturnal herbivore feeding on algae. Often coated with a liberal amount of encrustations. Range: Qld. Size: 80 mm. Moderately common.

413

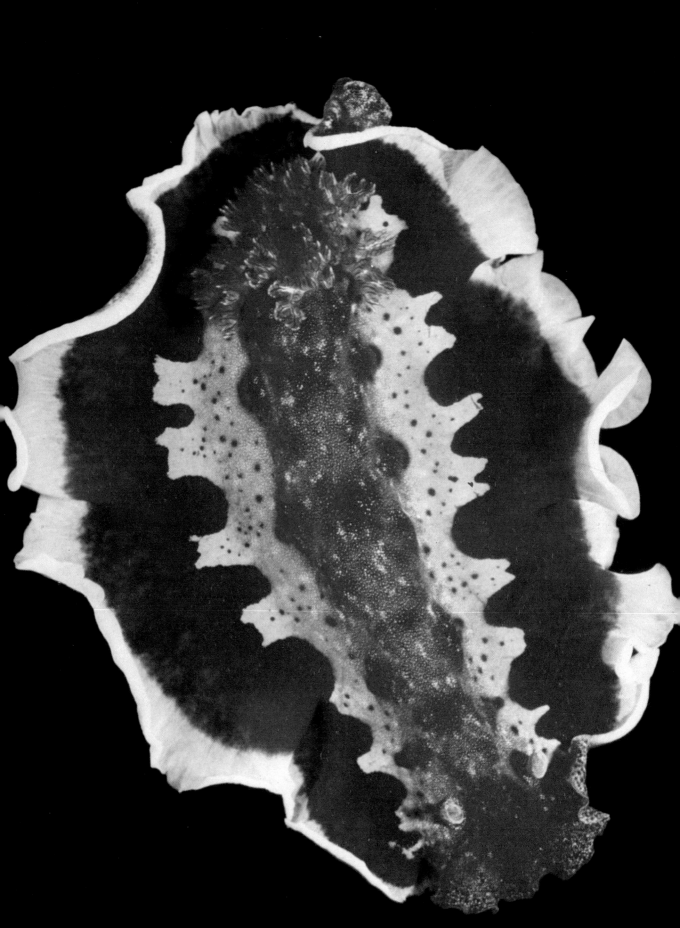

416

415, 416
HEXABRANCHIDAE
Bloody Spanish Dancer
Hexabranchus sanguinea
Rueppell & Leuckart, 1828

Found on both the east and west
coasts, *H. sanguinea* is the most
common large nudibranch in
Indo-Pacific waters. It lays bright
red egg ribbons. Occasionally this
species has a small commensal
shrimp living on its body or in its
gills. The adult shrimps are almost
identical in colour to their host.
Range: N.S.W. to W.A. Size:
300 mm. Common.

415

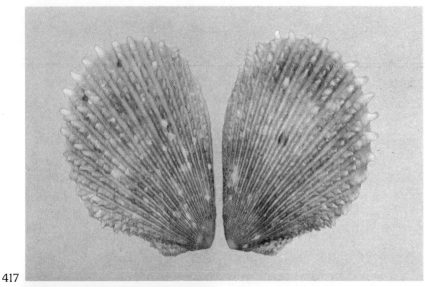

417

LIMIDAE
Giant File Shell
Lima lima vulgaris
Link, 1807

The giant file shell inhabits the underside of dead coral slabs and is attached by a byssus. It sometimes has a greenish tinge to its shell and often has small white worm shells attached. Shells can be found at low tide but diving produces better specimens. Range: Qld. to northern W.A. Size: 60 mm. Common.

418

418
LIMIDAE
Fragile File Shell
Limea fragilis
Gmelin, 1791

This shell is probably known as the swimming file shell. It lives beneath rocks and coral from low tide level to 5 metres. The animal itself is very colourful: bright red with red and white striped filamentous mantle extensions. These extensions are extremely fragile and of an adhesive nature. When separated from the animal they twist and turn like dozens of small worms. Range: N.S.W. to northern W.A. Size: 35 mm. Common.

420

419
MAGILIDAE
Ornamented Coral Shell
Coralliophila costularis
Lamarck, 1816

C. costularis lives mostly subtidally. The species can be found singularly, in pairs or groups on certain types of hard corals. Yellow eggs are laid in clear capsules that are brooded within the female shell. A certain amount of sexual dimorphism seems evident with adult females being larger than the males. Range: Qld. to W.A. Size: 64 mm. Fairly common.

420
MAGILIDAE
Staghorn Coral Shell
Quoyula madreporarum
Sowerby, 1832

Living amongst the stems of several species of branching corals, this shell is very firmly attached. Usually found towards the base of the corals, their apertures are often moulded to the shape of the coral stem. Range: N.S.W. to W.A. Size: 30 mm. Fairly common.

421
MAGILIDAE
Soft Coral Shell
Rapa rapa
Linnaeus, 1758

It is a keen collector indeed who finds this shell alive for it lives embedded in the base of large tropical soft corals and feeds on their juices. Only a small breathing hole discloses its whereabouts. Range: Qld. to W.A. Size: 60 mm. Uncommon.

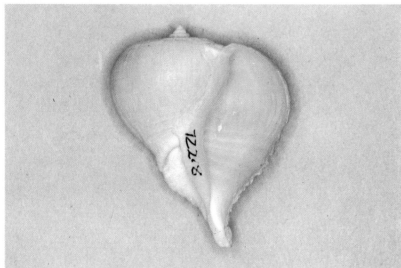

421

419

422

422
MAGILIDAE
Violet Mouthed Coral Shell
Coralliophila violacea
Kiener, 1836

This species is found on large live coral heads. Shells tend to congregate in crevices or hollows in the coral and are usually heavily encrusted with coraline algae. Females are the largest and lay large flat, oval transparent capsules half filled with pink eggs. These capsules are kept with the shell and brooded, the young being released only after hatching. Range: Qld. to northern W.A. Size: 25 mm. Common.

423

423
VANIKORIDAE
Cherished Velvet Shell
Vanikoro foveolata
Souverbie & Montrouzier, 1866

V. foveolata resembles a moon snail but differs by having external shell cancellations beneath a soft yellowish periostracum. Picture shows both male and female shell, the female being on the bottom. Green eggs in transparent capsules are laid in early summer and the female broods these till hatching takes place. Range: N.S.W., Qld. Size: 15 mm. Uncommon.

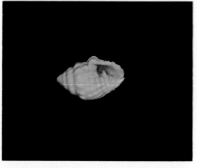

424

424
COSTELLARIIDAE
Nodulose Mitre
Vexillum cancellarioides
Anton, 1839

A rather rare little mitre in Australia, this species occurs mostly on exposed reef ramparts in small crevices or holes in the reef. Range: restricted to Qld. and the Great Barrier Reef. Size: 18 mm. Uncommon.

425

425
MITRIDAE
Strawberry Mitre
Mitra cucumerina
Lamarck, 1811

Found under stones and dead coral slabs all along the Great Barrier Reef this little mitre can be very easily overlooked. Its round shape and bright red colour blends in with the many similar surrounding coloured sponges and ascidians. Range: Qld. to N.T. Size: 12 mm. Common.

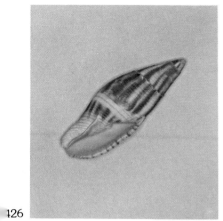

426
MITRIDAE
Brown Mottled Mitre
Mitra eremitarum
Roeding, 1798

Found on intertidal and subtidal coral reef, this shell is usually encrusted with marine growths. It lives exposed or under coral on rubble or reef. Range: Qld. to W.A. Size: 40 mm. Moderately common.

428
MITRIDAE
Banded Black Mitre
Mitra scutulata
Gmelin, 1791

Fairly common under dead coral on the Great Barrier Reef, this shell also lives beneath rocks in other areas. Often covered in marine growths. Range: N.S.W. to W.A. Size: 30 mm. Common.

426

427
MITRIDAE
Mournful Mitre
Mitra lugubris
Swainson, 1821

Mostly found on reef under dead coral, this little shell may be coated with coraline growths. Range: N.S.W. to Qld. Size: 25 mm. Fairly common.

429
MITRIDAE
Little Tavern Mitre
Mitra tabanula
Lamarck, 1811

Not commonly encountered, this little shell lives intertidally and subtidally on coral reef and is found beneath coral slabs on the Great Barrier Reef. It is sometimes covered by marine growths. Range: Qld. Size: 10 mm. Uncommon.

427

430
MITRIDAE
Telescope Mitre
Mitra telescopium
Reeve, 1844

Quite often found dead in rubble banks on islands and cays of the Great Barrier Reef, *M. telescopium* is rarely taken live. It lives subtidally and is usually found beneath coral and coral slabs. Almost always completely covered in coraline algae, perfect shells are extremely difficult to find. Range: Qld. Size: 20 mm. Rare.

428

429

430

143

431

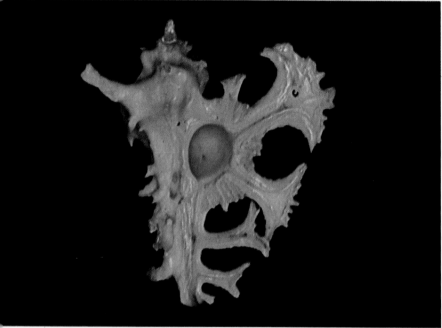

432

431
MITRIDAE
Brown Mouthed Coral Mitre
Mitra ticaonica
Reeve, 1844

Fairly common on coral and under coral slabs, these shells are always heavily covered with coraline growths and subject to marring healed breaks. Range: Qld. to W.A. Size: 30 mm. Common.

432
MURICIDAE
Skeleton Murex
Homolocantha anatomica
Perry, 1811

One of the most difficult muricids to find. Usually the shells are completely covered in thick coatings of coraline algae and marine growths. They can be found on the surface of larger coraline covered reef subtidally to 25 metres where they blend perfectly with their surroundings. Occasionally discovered at the low tide level where they may be in the open amongst dead rubble or beneath dead coral plates. Tube worms make up the greater part of their diets. Range: Northern N.S.W. to W.A. Size: 63 mm. Rare.

433
MURICIDAE
Armed Thaid
Thais armigera
Link, 1807

Living at the extreme intertidal edge of coral reef ramparts, *T. armigera* seems to prefer areas exposed to excessive water movement. It is quite a large shell and is almost always heavily encrusted with marine organisms. Range: Qld. Size: 80 mm. Common.

434
MURICIDAE
Girdled Murex
Murexiella balteata
Beck in Sowerby, 1841

This shell has been recorded on reefs north of Australia and there is reason to believe that it occurs in Australian waters. Range: Known range is so far restricted to New Guinea. Size: 20 mm. Rare.

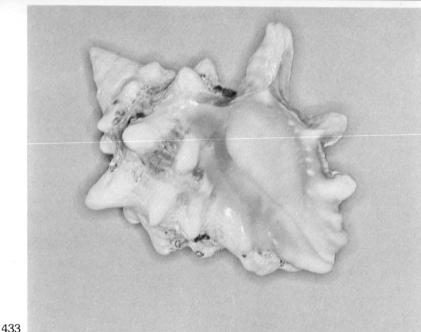

433

434

435
MURICIDAE
Two-Winged Murex
Pterynotus bipinnatus
Reeve, 1845

Smaller than similar shells, this
species can almost always be
distinguished by its purple aperture. It
lives at low tide level and down to 10
metres in areas of dead coral rubble
on the Great Barrier Reef. Range:
Qld. Size: 35 mm. Rare.

436
MURICIDAE
Quadrangular Murex
Favartia brevicula
Sowerby, 1834

Found in dead coral areas on the
Great Barrier Reef, it lives exposed or
beneath dead coral. Fairly common
in some localities it nevertheless
remains elusive to most collectors as
it is very well camouflaged. Range:
Qld. to W.A. Size: 25 mm.
Uncommon.

437
MURICIDAE
Coleman's Typhis
Pterotyphis colemani
Ponder, 1972

A small white shell found from low
tide level to 20 metres usually in
areas of dead coral and rubble.
Located beneath coral slabs they
are usually covered in a chalk like
coating and are difficult to
distinguish from their
surroundings. Range: Qld. to W.A.
Size: 20 mm. Rare.

438, 439
MURICIDAE
Dogwood Drupe
Drupella cornus
Roeding, 1798

A fairly variable shell over its
distribution, specimens are usually
white with orange or white
apertures. It lives in shallow waters
subtidally on coral reef and feeds
on coral polyps and tissues.
Gregarious by nature, this species
is extremely common although
because of marine encrustations
only small numbers are noticeable.
Several species of corals are
preyed upon and in badly infested
areas large white patches of dead
coral can be seen. Range: N.S.W.
to W.A. Size: 50 mm. Common.

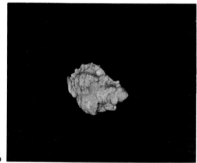

35

36

37

438

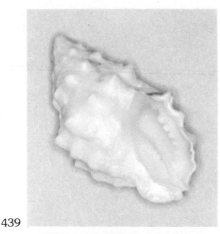

439

440
MURICIDAE
Spiked Coral Shell
Murexiella cuspidatus
Sowerby, 1879

Living exposed on algae covered dead coral slabs, rubble or bommies these shells are mostly subtidal dwellers. Always covered in marine growths they are difficult to locate and live on reefs and islands off the Great Barrier Reef. Animal is a translucent white with opaque white markings and black eyes. Range: Qld. Size: 36 mm. Uncommon.

440

441
MURICIDAE
Yellow Mouthed Drupe
Drupa grossularia
Roeding, 1798

Easily recognised by its bright yellow mouth, *D. grossularia* lives exposed on reef ramparts. Specimens are usually very heavily encrusted with marine growths and often marred by small holes. Range: Qld. to W.A. Size: 40 mm. Fairly common.

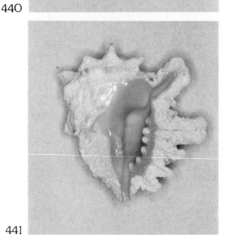

441

442
MURICIDAE
Confused Murex
Chicoreus akritos
Radwin & D'Attilio, 1976

Moderately common in several areas of Qld., this shell is found from low tide level under dead coral down to and beyond 30 metres. They feed on small chama, other bivalves and tube worms and are usually covered with an orange sponge. Shell colours usually waver between pink, white and brown. Animal is cream with brown and black flecks. Range: Qld. Size: 35 mm. Common.

442

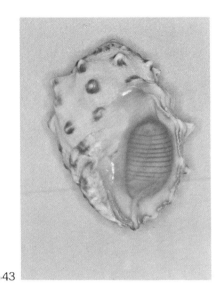

443

443
MURICIDAE
Pimpled Thaid
Mancinella mancinella
Linnaeus, 1758

A heavy, thick shell found intertidally, it lives exposed on reef ramparts, and is usually covered in thick encrustations of coraline algae. It feeds on worms and bivalves. Range: N.S.W. to W.A. Size: 50 mm. Common.

444
MURICIDAE
Windowed Murex
Pterynotus martinetanus
Roeding, 1798

Only a few specimens of this species are recorded from Australia. It lives amongst dead and live coral to depths below 20 metres. Heavily encrusted in marine growths it takes a lot of patience to find one or to clean it. Three of the four specimens found have been in staghorn coral brought up on fishing lines. Range: Qld. to W.A. Size: 30 mm. Rare.

444

445
MURICIDAE
Short Fronded Murex
Chicoreus microphyllus
Lamarck, 1816

Not as large as *C. torrefactus,* this shell's main distinguishing characteristics are its stripes and the presence of small denticles on the columellar. It seems to be restricted to the northern areas of the east coast where it is considered uncommon. The shell is found beneath coral slabs at low tide and subtidally to 30 metres. It feeds mostly on bivalves and is often heavily encrusted with coraline algae. Range: Qld. Size: 76 mm. Uncommon.

446
MURICIDAE
Grained Vitularia
Vitularia miliaris
Gmelin, 1791

An attractive shell found in association with corals and beneath rocks and coral slabs in the intertidal zone. A number of different colour variations have been recorded together with noticeable sexual dimorphism. Range: Qld. Size: 35 mm. Uncommon.

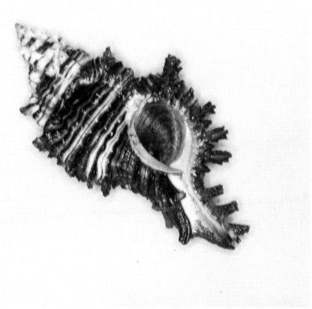

445

446

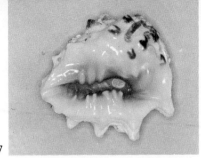

447

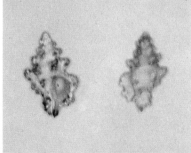

449 448

447
MURICIDAE
Purple Mouthed Drupe
Drupa morum
Roeding, 1798

Lives on reef ramparts and boulders at low tide level. Usually very heavily infested and overgrown with marine organisms. Although difficult to find on occasions it is nonetheless common. Range: Qld. to N.T. Size: 35 mm. Common.

448
MURICIDAE
Noduled Spiny Drupa
Muricopsis noduliferus
Sowerby, 1841

This species lives subtidally to depths of 20 metres and is found living in the open amongst dead coral or on coral bommies covered with coraline algae. Always heavily encrusted with marine growths the shells have to be literally carved from their encasement. To date only a few specimens have been found in Australian waters and little is known of their natural history. Range: restricted to the Great Barrier Reef off northern Qld. Size: 20 mm. Rare.

449
MURICIDAE
Rose Fronded Murex
Chicoreus foliatus
Perry, 1810

First Australian record of this species was from a specimen found by pioneer skindiver Allan Power. The shell was photographed by Allan in 5 metres of water off Heron Island, Qld. in 1965. Since then several others have been found, one being caught on a fishing line at 30 metres. Range: Qld. Size: 150 mm. Rare.

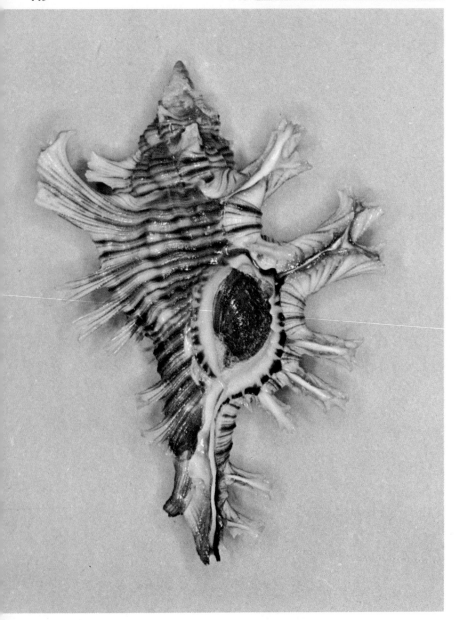

450

450
MURICIDAE
White-Toothed Drupe
Drupa ricinus
Linnaeus, 1758

Fairly common on exposed reef ramparts and under the edges of boulders, specimens seem to be more prevalent below tide level. Encrusted with coraline algae they blend in with their habitat extremely well. They are omnivorous, and feed on worms as well as coraline algae and other organisms. Range: Qld. to northern W.A. Size: 25 mm. Common.

451
MURICIDAE
Wheel Murex
Homolocantha zamboi
Burch & Burch, 1960

Rather a rare shell in Australia, *H. rota* lives beneath coral slabs on the Great Barrier Reef from low water to 20 metres. Figured specimen is from off Townsville. Range: Qld. Size: 50 mm. Rare.

452
MURICIDAE
Red Mouthed Drupe
Drupa rubusidaeus
Roeding, 1798

One of the larger drupes, it lives behind exposed intertidal reef ramparts, under boulders and in pools and depressions in the reef. Specimens can also be found subtidally. Range: Qld. Size: 55 mm. Common.

451

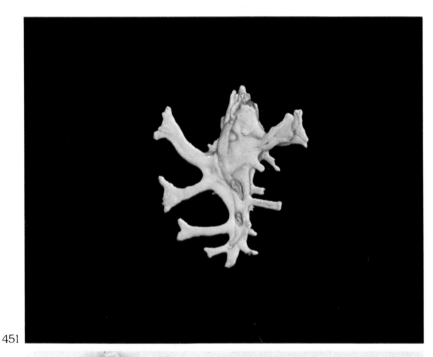

452

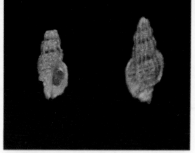

453

454

453
MURICIDAE
Sculptured Murex
Phrygiomurex sculptilis
Reeve, 1844

Living under dead coral on the reef flats of the Great Barrier Reef, *P. sculptilis* is not a shell often encountered by the collector. In its live state it is almost completely covered with encrusting lime and it takes many patient hours to clean. Range: N.S.W., Qld. Size: 20 mm. Rare.

454
MURICIDAE
Garland Thaid
Nassa serta
Bruguière, 1789

Common under stones and coral on intertidal reef flats this shell is sometimes also found on the open reef. Egg capsules are laid in winter months beneath coral slabs. Various numbers are laid, usually between 60 to 90, the capsules are white and contain yellow eggs. Range: N.S.W. to northern W.A. Size: 40 mm. Common.

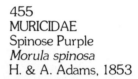

455

455
MURICIDAE
Spinose Purple
Morula spinosa
H. & A. Adams, 1853

Although this little shell is normally very heavily encrusted with coraline algae, young adults can be quite attractive. They live under boulders and dead coral at low tide level on coral reefs. Below tide level shells can be found exposed on dead coral. Range: N.S.W. to W.A. Size: 30 mm. Common.

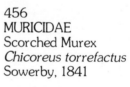

456
MURICIDAE
Scorched Murex
Chicoreus torrefactus
Sowerby, 1841

An interesting, wide ranging species, *C. torrefactus* can be found at low tide under coral slabs and also subtidally to 30 metres on the Great Barrier Reef. External shell features differ in some areas as does colour. The form pictured is from northern W.A. where specimens are taken by diving in caves and ledges of submerged reefs or surge gutters. Egg capsules are laid in early summer beneath ledges and rocks and are white in colour. Superficially similar in some cases to *C. brunneus*, *C. torrefactus* can usually be distinguished by the orange aperture colouring and shorter spines. Range: Qld. to W.A. Size: 120 mm. Uncommon.

456

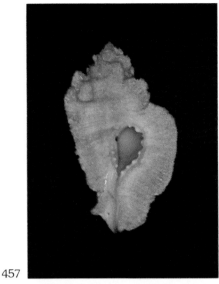

457

457
MURICIDAE
Lace Murex
Pterynotus tripterus
Born, 1778

Taken in very small numbers beneath coral slabs on the Great Barrier Reef, *P. tripterus* lives from low tide level to 30 metres. Some specimens are very badly encrusted with coraline algae and are impossible to clean without damaging the delicate sculpture of the shell. This species is easily recognised by the tooth-like nodules on its columella. Range: Qld. Size: 60 mm. Uncommon.

458
MURICIDAE
Three Cornered Murex
Naquetia triqueter
Born, 1778

Rarely found alive in Australia, *P. triqueter* lives amongst coral reef and rubble on the Great Barrier Reef below low tide level. Cyclones are often responsible for depositing fairly large numbers of these shells on shingle beaches which indicates that they are there in reasonable quantities. Range: Qld. Size: 70 mm. Uncommon.

58

459
MURICIDAE
Cluster Purple
Morula uva
Roeding, 1798

Very common on intertidal and subtidal reefs, *M. uva* is usually found in small groups or pairs. It lives in the open and is a distinctive little species. Range: N.S.W. to W.A. Size: 25 mm. Common.

459

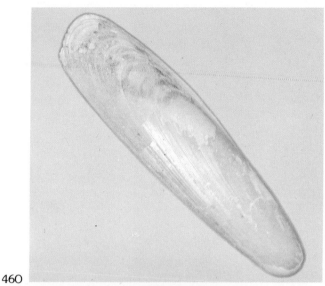

460

460
MYTILIDAE
Golden Date Mussel
Lithophaga obesa
Philippi, 1847

Usually found in large solid coral heads these shells tend to occur in groups. Very difficult to remove in many circumstances, they live mostly from the intertidal zone down to 10 metres. The animal has a dark coloured siphon. Range: Qld. to W.A. Size: 80 mm. Common.

461
MYTILIDAE
Chocolate Date Mussel
Lithophaga teres
Philippi, 1846

This shell is found burrowed into corals on northern reefs, and it occurs both intertidally and subtidally. It is a filter feeder and plays a large part in the erosion of coral reefs. Range: Qld. to W.A. Size: 70 mm. Common.

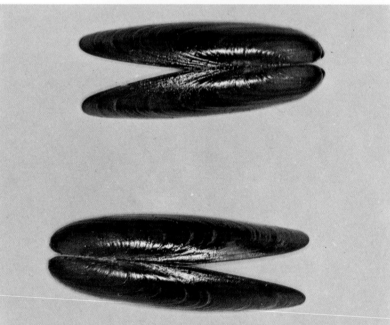

461

462
OSTREIDAE
Leaf Oyster
Lopha folium
Linnaeus, 1758

Fairly common on tropical reefs attached to black coral, hydroids and gorgonians. They live from low tide level down to and beyond 30 metres. Many specimens have a beautiful golden internal hue. Range: N.S.W. to northern W.A. Size: Grow to just over 50 mm. Common.

462

463
GRYPHAEIDAE
Giant Coxcomb Oyster
Hyotissa hyotis
Linnaeus, 1756

The largest of the edible oysters, *H. hyotis* lives attached to reef or coral from low tide level to 20 metres. The shell is extremely thick and at times almost defies destruction. Although stronger in taste than the smaller commercial oyster, *H. hyotis* is still relished by sea food gourmets. Range: Qld. to northern W.A. Size: 200 mm. Common.

463

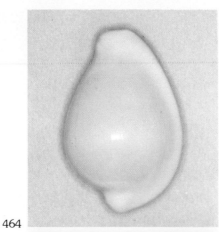

464
OVULIDAE
Costellate Egg Cowry
Ovula costellata
Larmarck, 1810

Although *O. costellata* is similar in shape to *O. ovum* it only grows to half its size and is nowhere near as common. Whereas *O. ovum* has a black mantle with white specks, *O. costellata* has a bright orange mantle. This shell lives on soft corals to depths of 30 metres. Range: N.S.W. to Qld. Size: 50 mm. Uncommon.

464

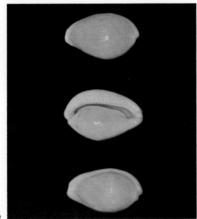

465
OVULIDAE
Milky Ovulid
Calpurnus lacteus
Lamarck, 1810

Found on similar soft corals to *C. verrucosus*, *C. lacteus* has a green patterned mantle and is not commonly collected. It lives intertidally down to 2 metres. Range: Qld. to northern W.A. Size: 20 mm. Uncommon.

466   465

466, 467
OVULIDAE
Egg Cowry
Ovula ovum
Linnaeus, 1758

Very common from N.S.W. to W.A., *O. ovum,* like others of its family, is associated with soft corals upon which it feeds. In Qld. the most common host is *Sarcophyton trocheliophorum,* a large, usually green, very prolific soft coral found on reef flats and down to and beyond 20 metres. In N.S.W. and northern and southern W.A. several other hosts have been recorded. Eggs are laid in summer mostly under the flaps of the soft coral. Occasionally subject to various diseases which mar and discolour the shells; these imperfect specimens should be left for breeding purposes. Range: N.S.W. to W.A. Size: 120 mm. Common.

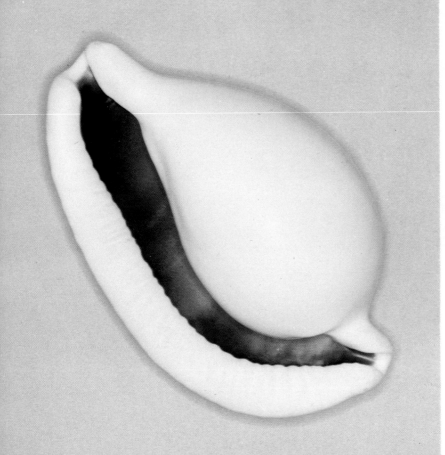

467

468

468
OVULIDAE
Toe Nail Cowry
Calpurnus verrucosus
Linnaeus, 1758

These exquisite little allied cowries are unique in having at each end of the shell a small callus from which their common name is taken. They are restricted to living around the low tide level and can be found on soft corals. Circular translucent egg capsules are laid on the host soft corals in early summer. Range: Qld. to N.T. Length: 25 mm. Common.

469

469
PECTINIDAE
Painted Scallop
Chlamys pallium
Linnaeus, 1758

One of the most beautiful northern scallops. Although the valves are quite commonly found washed up on beaches, live shells are not easy to locate. They live subtidally beneath slabs of dead coral or in live coral where they are attached by a byssus. While the external features of the shell are most attractive they cannot compare with the internal colour of a live taken shell. Range: Qld. to northern W.A. Size: 50 mm. Uncommon.

470
PECTINIDAE
Flat Ribbed Scallop
Semipallium radula
Linnaeus, 1758

Not commonly found alive. This scallop usually inhabits areas of dead coral and may be attached beneath larger slabs or even in the depths of living coral reef from low tide to 10 metres. Range: Qld. to W.A. Size: 60 mm. Uncommon.

470

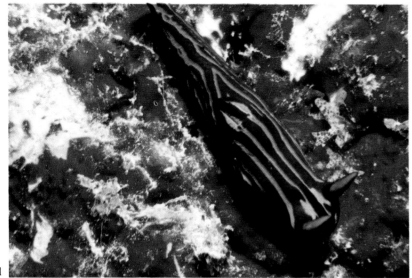

471

471
POLYCERIDAE
Bordered Nudibranch
Tambja affinis
Eliot, 1903

A distinctly coloured species, *T. affinis* prefers a subtidal habitat and is usually encountered by divers at depths of 15 to 20 metres. Found on bommies or the sides of caves, it is a carnivorous species and will occasionally feed on other nudibranchs. Range: Qld. to W.A. Size: 65 mm. Moderately rare.

472

472
PHYLLIDIIDAE
Celestial Nudibranch
Phyllidia coelestis
Bergh, 1905

Although belonging to the prolific *Phyllidia* genus, this species is not often seen. It lives in caves and beneath ledges subtidally to 20 metres. Range: Qld. to W.A. Size: 30 mm. Uncommon.

473
PHYLLIDIIDAE
Ocellate Nudibranch
Phyllidia ocellata
Cuvier, 1804

An outstanding species, this mollusc feeds on sponges and can be found to depths of 20 metres. Though variable in colour, its constant pattern makes it an easily recognised species. Range: Qld. to W.A. Size: 50 mm. Common.

473

474, 475
PHYLLIDIIDAE
Ruppell's Nudibranch
Fryeria ruppelli
Bergh, 1869

F. ruppelli lives under caves and ledges off northern W.A. This species extrudes a mucus from pores in its back which is toxic to other small marine creatures. It has been recorded at depths of 20 metres. Range: Qld. to northern W.A. Size: 100 mm. Common.

474

475 See 474

476
PINNIDAE
Flag Razor Shell
Atrina vexillum
Born, 1778

Although located from N.S.W. to
W.A., *A. vexillum* is prominent on
various sections of the Great Barrier
Reef. They are usually embedded
deep into the reef growths and
anchored by a strong byssus. Those
found by diving usually have their
shells gaping and mantle edges
exposed. Occasionally they are
mistaken for pearl shells which
behave in a similar manner. The
adductor muscles are edible, either
cooked or marinated in vinegar.
Range: N.S.W. to W.A. Size:
300 mm. common.

477

477
PLANAXIDAE
Furrowed Clusterwink
Planaxis sulcatus
Born, 1780

Very common on intertidal beach
rock on many islands of the Great
Barrier Reef, these shells are usually
found in clusters or groups in
exposed positions. Range: Qld. to
W.A. Size: 22 mm. Common.

478
POLYCERIDAE
Kubary Nembrotha
Nembrotha kubaryana
Bergh, 1877

One of the many strikingly coloured
nudibranchs, this mollusc is found
below tide level on the sides of reef
gutters and in caves off northern
W.A. Specimens have been recorded
to depths of 8 metres. Range: W.A.
Size: 50·mm. Uncommon.

479
PTERIIDAE
Penguin Pearl Shell
Pteria penguin
Roeding, 1798

Growing to almost 300 mm this
magnificent species is generally taken
below tide level to depths of 30 or
more metres. It lives attached by a
byssus to other marine growths
including hydroids and black corals.
Specimens have also been found
attached to pilings, nets, ropes and
the bottoms of moored boats. Range:
Qld. to W.A. Size: 300 mm. Fairly
common.

478

479

480

480
PTERIIDAE
Black Lipped Pearl Shell
Pinctada margaritifera
Linnaeus, 1758

Many years ago these bivalve shells
were one of two species on which
the pearling industry depended. Even
today they are gathered in their
juvenile forms and used as hosts for
cultivating cultured pearls. Like most
bivalves, they are filter feeders sifting
the plankton from the surrounding
water. They live from low tide level
down to and beyond 40 metres.
Range: Qld., N.T., northern W.A.
Size: 230 mm in diameter. Common.

481

481
PTERIIDAE
Red Winged Pearl Shell
Pteria saltata
Iredale, 1931

Found attached to sea whips and
gorgonian coral fans growing on
and around reefs in 8 to 40
metres. Collected by trawling,
dredging and skindiving. Range:
N.S.W. to northern W.A. Size:
150 mm. Common.

482

482
COLUMBELLIDAE
Punctate Pyrene
Pyrene punctata
Bruguière, 1789

One of the largest pyrenes, this shell lives under rocks and coral between the tides and down to 5 metres. Usually gregarious, several specimens may be found beneath the same slab. Range: Qld. to northern W.A. Size: 22 mm. Common.

483
SPONDYLIDAE
Northern Thorny Oyster
Spondylus ducalis
Roeding, 1798

Fairly common on the Great Barrier Reef, usually attached to dead coral or reef from low tide to 10 metres. They are mostly covered in coraline algae and are extremely difficult to clean. Not a very exciting shell but certainly a challenge for the collector who does not have a specimen. Range: Qld. to N.T. Size: 80 mm. Common.

483

484

484
SPONDYLIDAE
Ocellate Thorny Oyster
Spondylus zonalis
Lamarck, 1819

Deeply inbedded in coral heads and rocky reef, this species is able to burrow so far into its substrate that only partial destruction of that substrate will allow its removal. Found from low tide level to around 8 metres. It sometimes plays host to a small commensal crab. Range: N.S.W. to W.A. Size: 140 mm. Common.

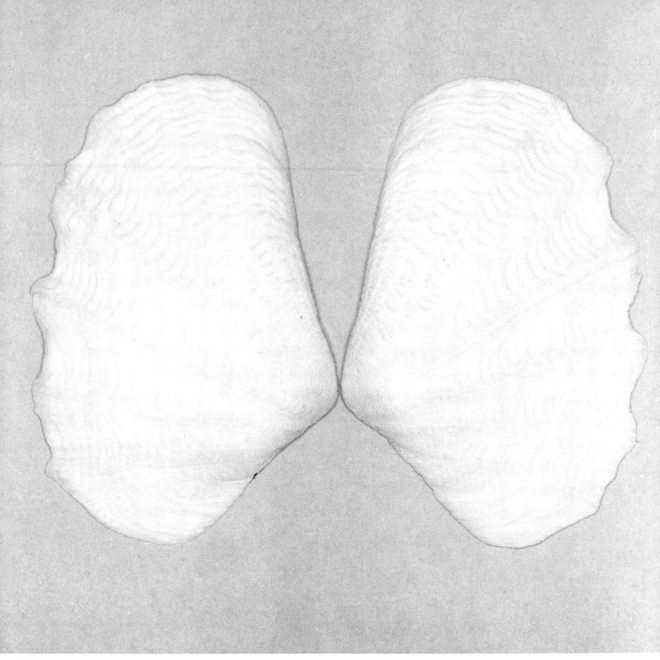

485

485, 486
TRIDACNIDAE
Burrowing Clam
Tridacna crocea
Lamarck, 1819

Deeply imbedded in coral heads
and rocky reef, this species is able
to burrow so far into its substrate
that only partial desruction of that
substrate will allow its removal.
Found from low tide level to
around 8 metres. It sometimes
plays host to a small commensal
crab. Range: N.S.W. to W.A. Size:
140 mm. Common.

487

487
TRIDACNIDAE
Horse's Hoof Clam
Hippopus hippopus
Linnaeus, 1758

One of the few free living species of clams found on the Great Barrier Reef. It lives on the reef flats and at low tide it can be seen lying with its valves a few inches apart. Should it be disturbed the valves can shut with amazing swiftness shooting a jet of water high into the air. Some ignorant people poke sticks into these molluscs to make them squirt. No thought is given to the injuries sustained by the mollusc which may well be fatal. They are extremely susceptible to wholesale human predation and so should not be wantonly destroyed. Range: Qld. to northern W.A. Size: 300 mm. Common.

486

488

488
TRIDACNIDAE
Burrowing Clam
Tridacna maxima
Roeding, 1798

This shell lives partially embedded in coral attached to the substrate by its byssus which protrudes through a hole at the base of the valves. Primarily a filter feeder, its mantle tissues house millions of minute algae, zooxanthellae. These organisms are apparently responsible for the mantle's brilliant patterning. Range: N.S.W. to W.A. Size: 200 mm. Common.

489
TRIDACNIDAE
Fluted Giant Clam
Tridacna squamosa
Lamarck, 1819

Easily recognised in the field by its size and the characteristic sculpture of leaf-like flutes, *T. squamosa* displays very beautiful mantle lobes. It is a filter feeder and lives below tide level in the shallow waters of coral reefs. Specimens can be found on sand or in coral to depths of 10 metres. Range: Qld. to W.A. Size: 400 mm. Fairly common in some areas.

489

490

490
TRITONIIDAE
White Tritoniopsid
Tritoniopsis alba
Baba, 1949

This nudibranch feeds on soft corals and breathes through the multitude of fine membraneous branchiae covering its dorsal surface. Range: Qld. to W.A. Size: 30 mm. Fairly common.

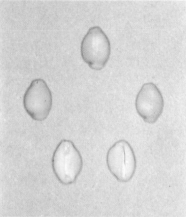

491

491
TRIVIIDAE
Little Rice Cowry
Trivirostra oryza
Lamarck, 1810

Very common on intertidal reef beneath stones and dead coral. On the reef rims of Great Barrier Reef islands this species is almost always found beneath dead coral where it is associated with a soft brown encrusting ascidian upon which it feeds. The shell's mantle blends perfectly with the ascidian. Range: N.S.W. to northern W.A. Size: 8 mm. Very common.

492

492
TROCHIDAE
Lacinate Dolphin Shell
Angaria delphinus
Linnaeus, 1758

Often mistaken for a turbo shell because of its shape, *A. delphinus* lives exposed on coral and rocky reefs. It feeds on algae and its spines are often covered with marine growths, making it difficult to separate it from its surroundings. Range: Qld. to northern W.A. Size: 76 mm. Fairly common.

493
TROCHIDAE
Elongate Trochid
Thalotia elongatus
Wood, 1828

Not an easy shell to find alive, this species inhabits intertidal areas of coral rubble and broken reef. The external colour of the shell is often badly eroded exposing the nacerous underlayers, particularly in the vicinity of the spire. Range: Qld. Size: 25 mm. Moderately common.

494
TROCHIDAE
Button Trochus
Trochus niloticus
Linnaeus, 1767

493

494

By far the largest trochid in Australia this shell grows to over 150 mm and lives intertidally and subtidally on the Great Barrier Reef. In pre-war years this shell supported a thriving fishery in northern Australia. Shells were collected mainly by diving in shallow water to depths of 10 metres. The molluscs were boiled, extracted and the flesh smoke dried, the shells being sold for the manufacture of buttons. Although quite prolific on reefs off the Qld. coast this species seems to be less abundant in N.T. and northern W.A. Shells breed in the early winter months and are mostly found on the exposed sides of reefs where they feed on algae. Range: Qld., N.T., northern W.A. Size: 150 mm. Common.

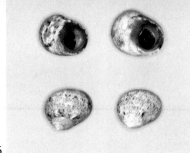

495

496

497

495
TROCHIDAE
Paradox Trochus
Chrysostoma paradoxum
Born, 1780

Not at all shaped like a normal trochus shell this species is quite commonly found washed up on the beaches of Great Barrier Reef islands. It lives amongst dead coral rubble intertidally and, owing to its secretive ways it is not easily found alive. Range: Qld. to northern W.A. Size: 15 mm. Moderately common.

496
TROCHIDAE
Pyramid Trochid
Trochus pyramis
Born, 1778

T. pyramis is a herbivore and feeds on short fine algae growing on coral and rocky reefs intertidally. Fairly easily identified by its shape, colour and angled axial striae. Range: Qld. to W.A. Size: 75 mm. Common.

497
TURBINIDAE
Scaley Turban
Turbo argyrostomus
Linnaeus, 1758

Fairly common shell on offshore islands. They live under, around and on coral rocks from low tide down to 6 metres. Range: Qld., northern W.A. Size: 50 mm. Common.

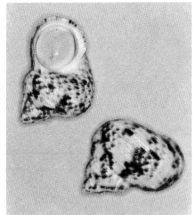

498

498
TURBINIDAE
Little Burnt Turbo
Turbo bruneus
Roeding, 1798

Very common beneath rocks and coral slabs on intertidal reef flats of the Great Barrier Reef. *T. bruneus* is, fairly variable in external shell features and colour patterns. Range: Qld. Size: 25 mm. Common.

499

499
TURBINIDAE
Spurred Turban Shell
Astralium calcar
Linnaeus, 1758

Not commonly collected, they live on algae covered reef flats and are invariably covered in a thick coating of coraline growth, topped by a mat of brown algae. So well do they blend with their habitat that it is mostly by accident that they are located at all. Specimens are moderately common subtidally on algae covered dead coral although always heavily encrusted with marine growths. Range: Qld. Size: 35 mm. Uncommon.

500
TURBINIDAE
Onion Turban
Turbo cepoides
Smith, 1880

Restricted to Lord Howe Island off the N.S.W. coast, this shell can be found by diving from just below tide level to 20 metres. It lives hidden away beneath ledges and amongst corals. Good specimens are difficult to locate as the shells live in exposed areas and suffer from healed breaks. They are preyed upon heavily by the double headed wrasse. Range: L.H.I. and several adjacent reefs. Size: 100 mm. Uncommon.

503

501

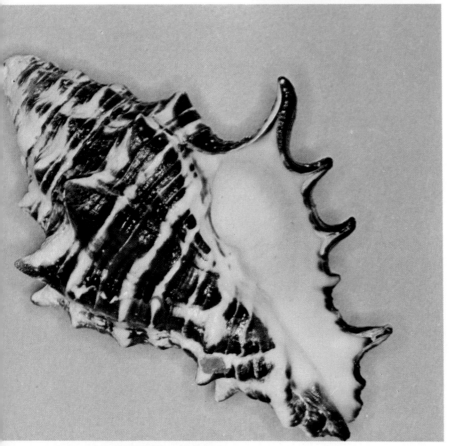

501
TURBINIDAE
Gold Mouthed Turban
Turbo chrysostomus
Linnaeus, 1758

Fairly common intertidally and subtidally to 10 metres, these shells are found around or under coral slabs. They are herbivores and can be easily recognised by their golden aperture. Range: Qld. Size: 55 mm. Common.

502
TURBINIDAE
Cat's Eye Turban
Turbo petholatus
Linnaeus, 1758

The most beautiful of all the turbos, their trapdoors or operculums are used for jewelry and decorative purposes. The shell itself displays a natural high polish. It inhabits coral reefs. Range: Qld. to W.A. Size: 76 mm. Common.

503
TURBINELLIDAE
Ceramic Vase Shell
Vasum ceramicum
Linnaeus, 1758

Fairly common on tropical reefs, they live intertidally and also below tide level to 10 metres. This species is usually very overgrown with encrusting marine organisms, and is often found with an eroded spire. Range: Qld. to N.T. Size: 130 mm. Common.

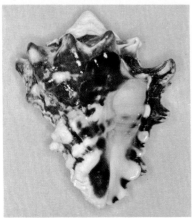

504
TURBINELLIDAE
Knobby Vase Shell
Vasum tubinellus
Linnaeus, 1758

Common intertidally on reef ramparts and dead coral heads; in Western Australia it tends to prefer deeper water. The author has recently found specimens living on limestone reef in 15 metres off N.W. Cape. Range: Qld. to northern W.A. Size: 50 mm. Common.

505
VERMETIDAE
Great Coral Worm Shell
Dendropoma maxima
Sowerby, 1825

A sessile shell which lives attached to coral reef ramparts on the Great Barrier Reef, usually in areas of permanent water movement with only minimum exposure to air. The tube grows to about 150 mm with a diameter of 25 mm. The animal is reported to be a plankton feeder. Range: Qld. Uncommon.

504

505

Part 4
Sand and rubble

Sand and rubble

These two habitats have been combined because of the numbers of similar species of molluscs which live in either, or both.

Sand may range from the white intertidal beaches on the east coast to the stark red of the west. It can be flour fine or comprised solely of shell grit. Rubble may be any of these on which larger pieces of broken coral or rock, shells and other bottom detritus has accumulated. In time this rubble will eventually become grit and then sand. On, in and amongst these combined habitats live some of the most exciting and coverted species of molluscs known to man.

The sand and rubble dwellers are diverse in colour, shape and form and because of their hidden ways some have remained on the rare lists for hundreds of years. It is here that the majority of the bivalve shells live. The species are many and varied and often have their own special grade of sand or rubble to live in. Bivalves are filter or detritus feeders and almost always have two siphons, an intake and an outlet. Water pumped into the intake siphon has two functions, it provides the oxygen necessary for survival and the planktonic animals used for food. The wastes and water are then pumped out of the exhalent siphon.

Reproduction occurs by the shedding of sperm and eggs into the surrounding waters. The fertilized eggs become larvae and drift with the plankton until settling to the bottom. Bivalves have many predators including man as they are almost all edible.

Confined solely to a sand and rubble habitat are the tusk shells. These uncommon molluscs are easily identified, for as their common name suggests, they are always shaped like a tusk. Although there are many species within Australia, they are not often encountered by the average collector. These eyeless, heartless and gilless molluscs spend most of their lives head down in the sand or mud, feeding on minute, single celled creatures called forams.

Almost all the sand dwelling univalves are carnivores, either boring holes in other shells and rasping the flesh out with their radula or smothering their prey in the folds of their voluminous foot. Some species live on worms, and swallow these succulent invertebrates whole.

Collecting shells from these habitats can be accomplished at low tide, by diving, dredging or trawling. Intertidal sand banks are very susceptible to over collecting and in some areas mollusc populations have been decimated by over enthusiastic collectors and tourists. It may well be necessary for future interests that some areas be closed for a certain time allowing species to build up in numbers once again.

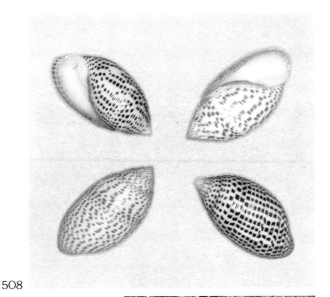

508

508
ACTAEONIDAE
Solid Pupa Shell
Pupa solidula
Linnaeus, 1758

These shells are found on intertidal
sand banks. They are the largest of
the pupa shells and have two main
colour variations, the pink forms
being the most common. These shells
are carnivorous. Range: Qld. to N.T.
Size: 30 mm. Common.

509
AEOLIDIIDAE
Plume-Ringed Nudibranch
Cerberilla affinis
Bergh, 1889

Found intertidally burrowing in sand
or fine rubble, this species has
dozens of cerata lining its back.
These cerata act as gills and can
absorb oxygen from the water as it
passes over them. Range: Qld. Size:
50 mm. Uncommon.

510
AEOLIDIIDAE
Twin-Plumed Nudibranch
Cerberilla ambonensis
Bergh, 1905

C. ambonensis lives deep in intertidal
sand banks and feeds on other small
molluscs. A very rare animal the
figured specimen is the first to be
recorded in Australia and only the
second since the initial discovery of
the species. Range: N.T. Size:
20 mm. Rare.

509

510

512
AGLAJIDAE
Troubridge Philinopsis
Philinopsis troubridgensis
Verco, 1909

A sand burrowing form, this species
is mostly nocturnal. It feeds on other
molluscs which it swallows whole.
Range: S.A. Size: 200 mm.
Uncommon.

511

512

513

514

511
AGLAJIDAE
Striped Philinopsis
Philinopsis lineolata
H. & A. Adams, 1854

P. lineolata lives under the sand in
the intertidal zone, and surfaces on
the rising tide in search of small
molluscs and other invertebrates
upon which it feeds. The prey is
swallowed whole and the
undigestible parts are regurgitated.
This species is quite rare, the
specimen figured being the only
one recorded from Australia for
120 years. Range: Qld. Size:
33 mm. Rare.

513
ALOIDIDAE
Little Basket Shell
Corbula vicaria
Iredale, 1930

Very common in sand and sandy
mud in Sydney Harbour, this easily
recognised little bivalve lives beneath
the sub-surface to a depth of
100 mm. Usually found in the same
vicinity as small heart urchins, they
can be collected by dredging or
diving to depths of 20 metres. Range:
N.S.W. Size: 25 mm. Common.

514
ARCIDAE
Navicula Ark
Arca subnavicularis
Iredale, 1939

Common in the rubble bottomed
channels of Qld. estuaries, this
species is one of the most attractive
of the ark family. In its live state it
has a medium thick periostracum
and is usually attached to rubble or
other shells by its byssus. Figured
specimens were taken in 20 metres
of water and their size averages
55 mm. Range: Qld., N.T. Size:
55 mm. Common.

515
ARMINIDAE
Variable Armina
Armina variolosa
Bergh, 1904

Living under the sandy mud this
species was recorded in Cockburn
Sound, W.A. It is found down to 20
metres and is mostly nocturnal.
Range: Qld. to W.A. Size: 150 mm.
Uncommon.

516

516
HAMINOEIDAE
Cylindrical Bubble Shell
Aliculastrum cylindricus
Helbling, 1779

Very commonly washed up on
beaches in Qld., *A. cylindricus* lives
on intertidal sand banks and is
preyed upon by other carnivorous
molluscs, including nudibranchs.
Range: Qld. Size: 25 mm. Common.

517
BUCCINIDAE
Ribbed Cominella
Cominella eburnea
Reeve, 1846

Found on intertidal sand flats down
to 10 metres. Included in its diet are
decaying marine organisms. This
mollusc is extremely variable in
colour and pattern. Range: Vic., Tas.,
S.A. Size: 35 mm. Common.

517

518
BULLIDAE
Vernicose Bubble Shell
Bulla vernicosa
Gould, 1859

Found under sand and algae on
the Great Barrier Reef where it
lives and feeds on other small
molluscs. Range: N.S.W. to Qld.
Size: 35 mm. Common.

518

519
CANCELLARIIDAE
Antique Cancellaria
Trigonostoma antiquata
Hinds, 1843

Inhabiting subtidal areas of sand and
rubble, this species has been found to
depths of 20 metres. The animal
itself is cream in colour with orange
banded tentacles and black eyes.
Most cancellaria's do not have
operculums but are able to retreat
deep into their shells when danger is
near. This shell has only been found
on a few occasions in Australia and is
very rare. Range: Qld. to W.A. Size:
25 mm. Rare.

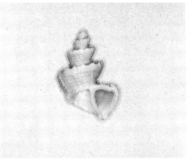

519

520
CARDIIDAE
White Half Cockle
Fragum fragum
Linnaeus, 1758

A smaller shell than *F. unedo*, *F.
fragum* is usually found in sandy
areas along the Great Barrier Reef.
It lacks the pronounced deep red
tubercules of the former shell and
is often distinguished by a yellow
or orange streak on the interior
wall of the valves. Range: Qld.
Size: 30 mm. Common.

520

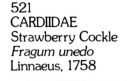

521

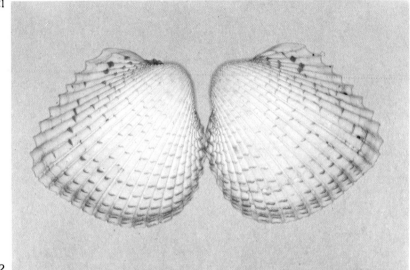

522

521
CARDIIDAE
Strawberry Cockle
Fragum unedo
Linnaeus, 1758

One of the most common northern species of cockles, *F. unedo* frequents sandy flats both intertidally and subtidally It has an easily recognisable shell. Range: N.S.W. to northern W.A. Size: 50 mm. Common.

522
CASSIDAE
Checker Board Helmet
Phalium areola
Linnaeus, 1758

Because of their unique colour pattern this species is much in demand for tourist novelties. As they live on both coastal and offshore island sand banks, their habitat offers easy access to collectors. They come up out of the sand on the turn of the tide and crawl on the surface seeking food. Range: N.S.W. to W.A. Size: 65 mm. Common.

523
CASSIDAE
Banded Helmet
Phalium bandatum
Perry, 1811

Common on shallow water sand banks down to 40 metres. Eggs are laid in Sept. usually attached to some solid object. One egg case has been observed attached to a mangrove leaf. Their food consists mainly of sand dwelling echinoderms, particularly sand dollars. This species is very popular with shell ornament manufacturers, who turn them into salt and pepper shakers. Range: N.S.W. to W.A. Size: 88 mm. Common.

523

524
CASSIDAE
Giant Helmet Shell
Cassis cornuta
Linnaeus, 1758

Because of their size this shell has been very popular with collectors and tourists for many years. Easily accessible habitats on the sea floor and lagoons of the Great Barrier Reef have made them susceptible to over collecting. Their diet consists mainly of echinoderms including an occasional crown of thorns sea star. The government has fully protected these shells and under no circumstances should they be collected. Range: Qld. to N.T. Size: 355 mm.

525
CASSIDAE
Fimbriate Helmet
Cassis fimbriata
Quoy & Gaimard, 1833

An easily identified common species, *C. fimbriata* is by far the largest southern helmet found in Australia. Variable in colour pattern it lives in sand from low tide level down to 200 metres. Adult shells are occasionally eroded on the back due to a habit some shells have of not burying completely into the sand. Range: Vic. to W.A. Size: 120 mm. Common.

526
CASSIDAE
Ponderose Helmet
Casmaria ponderosa
Gmelin, 1791

A small solid shell, *C. ponderosa* lives on intertidal sand banks and also below tide level. Like all cassids it is carnivorous, feeding mostly on other molluscs and echinoderms. Range: N.S.W. to W.A. Size: 45 mm. Common.

525

526

527
CASSIDAE
Pear Helmet
Phalium pyrum
Lamarck, 1822

Although a fairly common and variable species this shell is not found alive by collectors in any numbers. Living from low tide level to beyond 60 metres it feeds on sand dwelling echinoderms. Pictured shell is from Jervis Bay, N.S.W., at a depth of 30 metres. Range: N.S.W., Vic., Tas., S.A. Size: 70 mm. Moderately common.

528
CASSIDAE
Labiate Helmet
Phalium labiata
Perry, 1811

P. labiata is usually found in sand around reef intertidally and down to 20 metres. They feed mostly on sea urchins and other echinoderms which are attacked mostly through their anal orifice. Mating takes place in summer with eggs being laid a short time after, often in communal circumstances as pictured. Range: Qld. to Vic. Siz 80 mm. Common.

528

529
CASSIDAE
Red Helmet Shell
Cypraecassis rufa
Linnaeus, 1758

Although it is the second largest
species of helmet shell in Australia,
C. rufa is rarely collected. Its habitat
seems to be in subtidal sand patches
and flats near beds of eel grass.
There have been several
unconfirmed findings throughout the
years resulting in conjecture as to
whether the species really existed in
Australian waters. Skin divers in Qld.
and W.A. have since confirmed its
presence. Range: Qld. to W.A. Size:
203 mm. Rare.

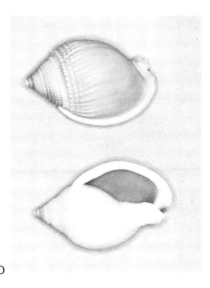

530

530
CASSIDAE
Half-Grained Helmet
Phalium semigranosum
Lamarck, 1822

This easily recognised species is
reasonably common on low tide sand
banks. They are also taken by divers
in shallow water and to 400 metres
by trawling. Range: Vic., Tas., S.A.,
W.A. Size: 35 mm. Common.

531
CERITHIIDAE
Banded Creeper
Rhinoclavis fasciata
Bruguière, 1792

Living beneath sand from low tide
level to 20 metres along the northern
reefs these shells are very common
at depths of around 5 to 10 metres.
The shells live in communities and
criss-cross the sand with their trails.
Many a snorkeller has cursed their
existence after repeated dives have
resulted in finding only dozens of
these ceriths. Range: Qld. to northern
W.A. Size: 76 mm. Common.

532
CERITHIIDAE
Acquitted Creeper
Rhinoclavis sinensis
Gmelin, 1791

Occurring in sand from low tide level
to 10 metres, *R. sinensis* is an
attractive solid species. It lives in
colonies and is preyed upon by other
carnivorous molluscs and fish. Range:
Qld. to W.A. Size: 50 mm. Common.

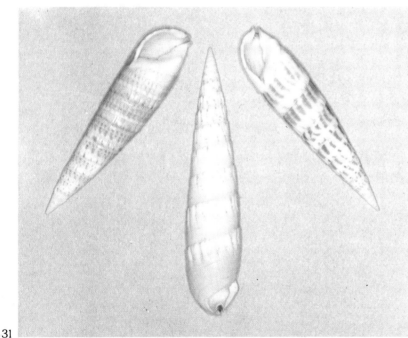

31

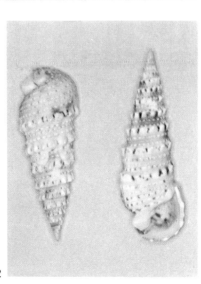

29

532

533
CERITHIIDAE
Symbol Creeper
Campanile symbolicum
Iredale, 1917

The largest of this family in Australia, *C. symbolicum* grows to well over 180 mm. It lives on sand patches amongst reef and rubble in shallow water. Endemic to southern W.A., the species is extremely common, although adults with good lips are hard to come by. Range: W.A. Size: 180 mm. Common.

534

534
CERITHIIDAE
Ribbed Cerith
Rhinoclavis vertagus
Linnaeus, 1758

Shorter and stouter than *R. fasciata* it can be easily distinguished from that shell by the folds or nodules along the sutures. Very common, it lives under the sand in shallow water and varies considerably in colour. Range: Qld. to northern W.A. Size: 60 mm. Common.

535

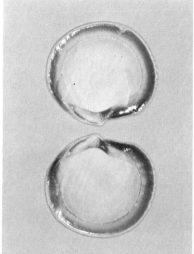

535
LUCINIDAE
Punctate Codakia
Codakia punctata
Linnaeus, 1758

Usually found in sand or sand patches from low tide level to 20 metres. Although white in colour the interior of a live taken shell is bright yellow bordered by a red margin. Range: N.S.W. to northern W.A. Size: 80 mm. Common.

536
FASCIOLARIIDAE
Flame Spindle Shell
Fusinus pyrulatus
Reeve, 1847

This species lives amongst sand and rubble to depths of 80 metres. Divers find live specimens near underwater reefs between 20 and 40 metres. This carnivorous species feeds mostly on other molluscs. Range: N.S.W., Vic., S.A. Size: 76 mm. Uncommon.

537
COLUBRARIIDAE
Twisted Colubraria
Colubraria tortuosa
Reeve, 1844

Hardly ever taken alive this species inhabits areas of sandy rubble. It is easily identified by its fine beaded sculpture and twisted spire. Range: Qld. to W.A. Size: 50 mm. Uncommon.

536

533

537

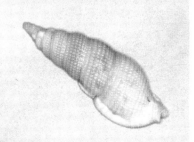

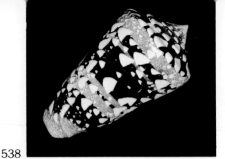

538

539

538
CONIDAE
Admiral's Cone
Conus ammiralis
Linnaeus, 1758

These cones are amongst the most beautifully patterned in Qld. waters. Primarily an offshore species, they can be found in sand and coral rubble on the islands and cays of the Great Barrier Reef at low tide, and by diving and dredging to 10 metres. Range: Qld. Size: grows to over 50 mm in length. Uncommon.

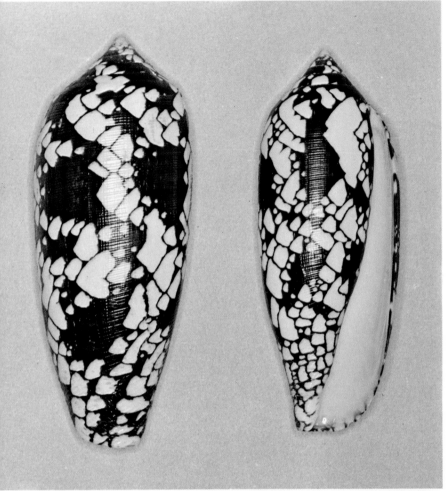

539
CONIDAE
Court Cone
Conus aulicus
Linnaeus, 1758

The largest of the tent cones in Australia this species is not considered common. Specimens have been found in N. Qld. in sand under large coral heads and rocks. Shell has been recorded as a stinger; injuries inflicted by a large specimen could well prove fatal. Range: Qld. to N.T. Size: 140 mm. Uncommon.

540
CONIDAE
Betuline Cone
Conus betulinus
Linnaeus, 1758

A large heavy shell with a fairly thick periostracum. This species lives on sand or sandy mud intertidally and subtidally in shallow water. Not often collected in Australia. Range: Qld. to N.T. Size: 100 mm. Uncommon.

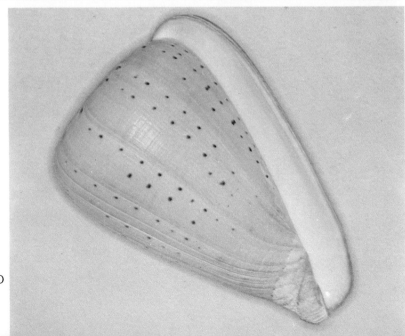

540

541
CONIDAE
Captain's Cone
Conus capitaneus
Linnaeus, 1758

This species lives under boulders and coral, and can be found at low tide under rocks and coral slabs, or by diving. When taken alive it is covered with a skin or periostracum. Range: N.S.W. to northern W.A. Size: 76 mm. Moderately common.

541

542

542
CONIDAE
Fig Cone
Conus figulinus
Linnaeus, 1758

These shells live on intertidal sand banks and have a brown periostracum. Large pink egg capsules are laid in summer, and usually anchored deep in the sand. As there is no cone in Australia similar to this species, it is easy to identify. Range: Qld. Size: 80 mm. Moderately common.

543
CONIDAE
Geographic Cone
Conus geographus
Linnaeus, 1758

This large cone is usually found in sandy pockets near the reef edge, under dead coral or amongst reef. It feeds on small fishes, harpooning them with a poisonous barbed dart which is an extension of its radula. A very dangerous species recorded to have caused several human deaths. Range: Qld. to northern W.A. Size: 120 mm. Uncommon.

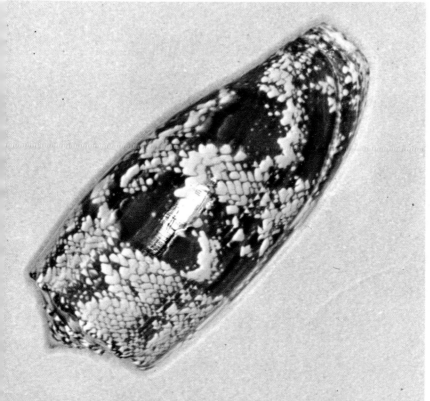

543

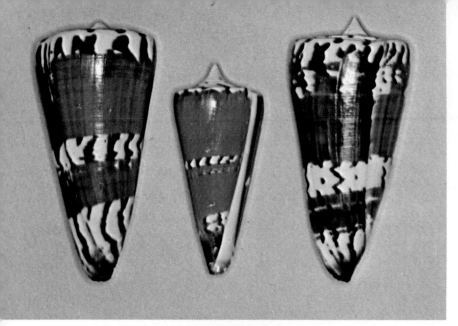

544
CONIDAE
General Cone
Conus generalis
Linnaeus, 1767

A well known and fairly common species, this shell is quite variable in colour and has a thick brown periostracum. It lives on sand under coral slabs but is also found exposed on sandy rubble areas. It occurs from low tide level down to 10 metres on the Great Barrier Reef and is trawled in deep water off the Qld. coast. Range: Qld. to W.A. Size: 80 mm. Common.

545
CONIDAE
Leopard Cone
Conus leopardus
Roeding, 1798

Quite common on sandy rubble and muddy rubble flats, this species is usually found on the surface in the open. It has a thick yellow brown periostracum to which, in silty areas, the mud clings, making its detection difficult. Range: Qld. to N.T. Size: 115 mm. Common.

546
CONIDAE
Marbled Cone
Conus marmoreus
Linnaeus, 1758

C. marmoreus inhabits sandy areas where it lives under dead coral or in sand around coral heads or soft corals. It has a very striking colour pattern which doesn't assist it in remaining hidden from its enemies. Although it feeds on other molluscs it has been recorded as dangerous to man. Range: Qld. Size: 76 mm. Common.

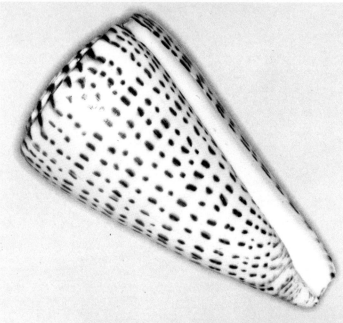

545

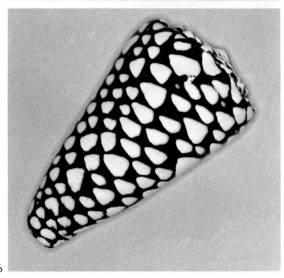

546

194

547

547
CONIDAE
Military Cone
Conus miliaris
Bruguière, 1792

A very solid, brightly coloured shell, this species is very common on reef ramparts where it lives intertidally in sand pockets under coral. Sometimes covered in coraline algae, specimens are subject to erosion and healed breaks. They feed on worms. Range: N.S.W. to Qld. Size: 25 mm. Common.

548

548
CONIDAE
Omaria Cone
Conus omaria
Hwas in Bruguière, 1792

One of the exquisite textile group of cones. They seem to prefer sandy patches in reefs and hide during the day under stones and coral heads. Their habitat is not restricted, however, for although living at low tide level divers locate specimens down to 10 metres. This species has been recorded as dangerous to man. Range: Qld. to W.A. Size: 76 mm. Uncommon.

549
CONIDAE
Yellow Cone
Conus quercinus
Solander, 1786

This very common species lives on sand along the Great Barrier Reef. Although found intertidally, more specimens can be located below low tide level. Egg capsules are pink and the shells join in communal egg laying in summer months. Colour varies between gold and white. Range: Qld. Size: 100 mm. Common.

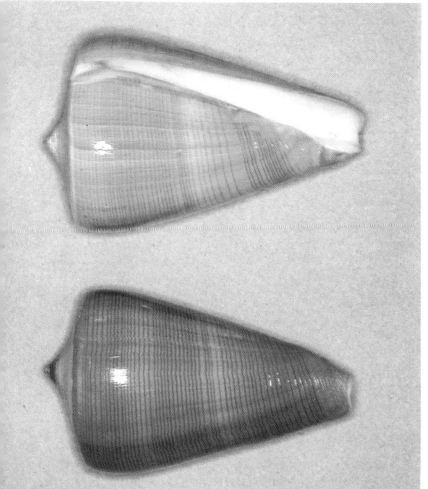

549

550

550
CONIDAE
Segrave's Cone
Conus segravei
Gatliff, 1891

A delicate, pastel coloured shell, it has been considered fairly rare in the past. Howerver, in recent years divers have discovered shells living in sandy bottoms down to 40 metres. The first of the southern Australian shells to be recorded as a fish eater. It should be regarded as potentially dangerous to man. Range: Vic., S.A., southern W.A. Size: 30 mm. Uncommon.

551
CONIDAE
Striated Cone
Conus striatus
Linnaeus, 1758

Very popular amongst collectors, this species has many colour forms and patterns. Found in sand pockets and on reef under stones or dead coral. It has a bad reputation for incurring injuries to humans. Range: Qld. to northern W.A. Size: 100 mm. Common.

553
CONIDAE
Textile Cone
Conus textile
Linnaeus, 1758

C. textile lives in sand beneath coral and rocks. Very variable in pattern and colour, larger specimens may have eroded backs and are useless as collector's items. These cones should be handled with care as they are attributed to have caused several fatalities. A good rule in the collection of cones is to pick them up by the thick (posterior) end and keep the thin (anterior) end away from contact with the body. Range: N.S.W. to northern W.A. Size: 120 mm. Common.

551

552

552 CONIDAE
Tessellated Cone
Conus tessulatus
Born, 1778

This very beautiful little cone is found intertidally on sand banks. It lives under the sand coming up on an incoming tide, particularly during night time lows. Range: Qld. Size: 40 mm. Common in some areas.

553

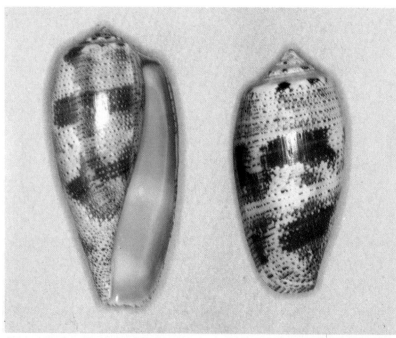

554

554
CONIDAE
Tulip Cone
Conus tulipa
Linnaeus, 1758

Although smaller than *C. geographus*, *C. tulipa* is nevertheless a potential danger to man. It feeds on fish and its poison is extremely strong. Lives in sand under coral heads and dead coral on the Great Barrier Reef. Range: Qld. Size: 70 mm. Uncommon.

555
CONIDAE
Virgin Cone
Conus virgo
Linnaeus, 1758

A large heavy shell, *C. virgo* has a thick brown periostracum when found alive. It lives on sand flats and also on rubble bottom from low tide to 15 metres along the Great Barrier Reef. Easily distinguished from other similar species by its dark purple anterior. Range: Qld. Size: 150 mm. Common.

555

556

556
CORBIDAE
Fimbriated Basket Shell
Fimbria fimbriata
Linnaeus, 1758

A very eash shell to identify, *F. fimbriata* lives subtidally in coral reef sand patches. It is quite a large species and often has a yellow tinged interior. Range: Qld. to N.T. Size: 76 mm. Common.

557
CYMATIIDAE
Two Humps Triton
Gyrineum bituberculare
Lamarck, 1822

Still very rare in Australian waters, this shell has been taken on a rubble bottom beneath small coral nodules at a depth of 20 metres. Range: So far is restricted to the Great Barrier Reef off Prosperpine, Qld. Size: 25 mm. Rare.

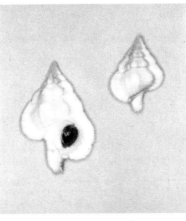

557

558
DONACIDAE
Pipi
Donax deltoides
Lamarck, 1818.

One of the main commercial fish bait species, *D. deltoides* inhabits areas of coarse sandy surf beaches where it lives at low tide to several fathoms in large gregarious colonies. On many of the beaches frequently mined and those in heavily populated areas used for swimming the shells have become almost non-existent. It is against the law to collect this species by mechanical means. Range: Qld., N.S.W., Vic., S.A. Size: 60 mm. Common.

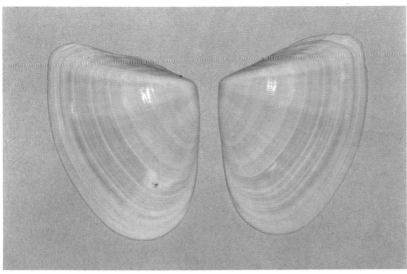

558

559

559
DORIDIDAE
Freckled Dorid
Chromodoris tinctoria
Rueppell & Leuckart, 1828

Inhabiting a shell and rubble bottom amongst weed beds, *C. tinctoria* is found mostly below tide level in shallow water. This attractive species is able to retract its gills and rhinophores very quickly. Range: N.S.W., Qld., W.A., S.A. Size: 70 mm. Common.

560

560
EPITONIIDAE
Precious Wentletrap
Epitonium scalare
Linnaeus, 1758

Extremely popular amongst collectors, these exquisitely shaped shells live below tide level in areas of sandy mud. Often washed up on Qld. beaches in numbers after storms, they have still to be located in natural habitat. Their food host is unknown but is thought to be a sea anemone. Range: Qld. Size: 50 mm. Moderately common.

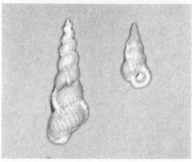

561

561
EPITONIIDAE
Rough Wentletrap
Cirsotrema varicosa
Lamarck, 1822

One of the larger wentletraps, this species in its live state has for many years been considered quite rare. Recently live specimens have been discovered in association with large sand anemones on islands and reefs off the Qld. coast. They feed by inserting their proboscis into the anemone, and deriving nourishment from its body juices. Range: Qld. to N.T. Size: 38 mm. Uncommon.

562

562
GLAUCIDAE
Serrate Nudibranch
Phyllodesmium serrata
Baba, 1949

This species inhabits sandy tide pools in northern W.A., but is occasionally seen in the vicinity of soft corals. Range: Qld. to W.A. size: 35 mm. Uncommon.

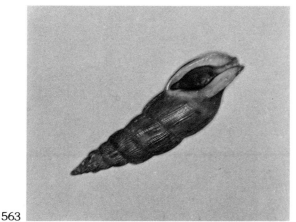

563

563
COLUBRARIIDAE
Brazier's Colubraria
Colubraria brazieri
Angas, 1869

Living in sand subtidally to 50 metres, this shell is not often encountered alive. Specimens have been taken by dredging and diving off the coast. Range: N.S.W. Size: 65 mm. Uncommon.

564

564
FLABELLINIDAE
Western Nossis
Nossis westralis
Burn, 1964

N. westralis is found at low tide on sandy mud flats where it lives in association with small hydroid colonies, upon which it feeds. Range: northern W.A. Size: 30 mm. Locally common.

565

565
GARIIDAE
Faded Sunset Shell
Asaphis deflorata
Linnaeus, 1758

Found in sand or sandy mud intertidally and in shallow water. They have a horny periostracum which cracks and flakes if the shells are left in the sun. Internal colours are quite attractive. Range: Qld. to W.A. Size: Large specimens reach 55 mm. Common.

566
HARPIDAE
Lesser Harp Shell
Harpa amouretta
Roeding, 1798

One of the smallest tropical harp shells found in Australia, *H. amouretta* lives in sand beneath coral slabs in shallow water on the Great Barrier Reef. It is a carnivore and feeds on small invertebrates. Range: Qld. Size: 65 mm. Not common.

566

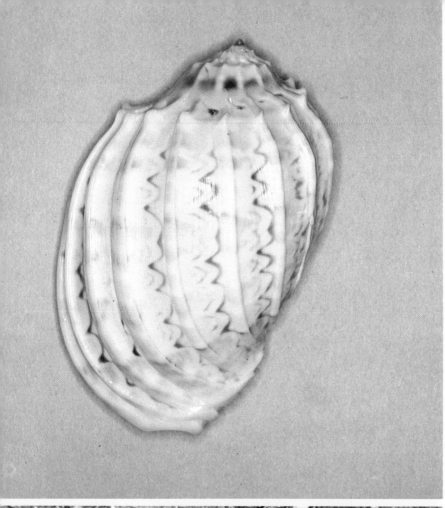

567
HARPIDAE
Greater Harp Shell
Harpa major
Roeding, 1798

The figured specimen was taken at low tide in sand 32 kilometres off Cairns, Qld. by Mrs Jean Robertson. This species is one of the largest of the harps and is rare in Australia. Range: Qld. Size: 100 mm. Rare.

568
HYDATINIDAE
Rose Petal Bubble Shell
Hydatina physis
Linnaeus, 1758

A large spectacular bubble, this shell is cyclic, appearing in shallow waters to spawn usually in summer. It can be found in a variety of habitats from sandy mud to rocky reef and from low tide level down to 10 metres. They are very delicate in structure and care must be exercised in collecting and cleaning specimens. Range: N.S.W. to W.A. Size: 50 mm. Common.

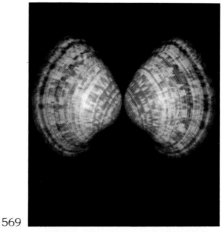

569

569
VENERIDAE
King's Cockle
Notocallista kingii
Gray, 1853

One of the most colourful southern bivalves, *N. kingii* can be taken by trawling and dredging along the coasts. In the past this species was thought only to inhabit deep water, recently the author discovered a bed of shells living in 3 metres of water in Sydney Harbour. Range: N.S.W., Qld. Vic. Size: 38 mm. Common.

570

570
MARGINELLIDAE
Creeping Margin Shell
Plicaginella formicula
Lamarck, 1822

Very common subtidally in southern Tas., these little shells come out of the sand at the turn of the tide and at dusk in search of food. Range: Vic., Tas. Size: 12 mm. Common.

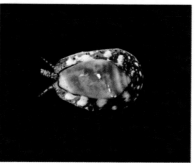

571

571
MARGINELLIDAE
Translucent Margin Shell
Mesoginella translucida
Sowerby, 1846

Very common from low tide level to 10 metres in estuaries along the N.S.W. coast. Range: N.S.W., Vic., Tas., S.A., W.A. Size: 6 mm. Common.

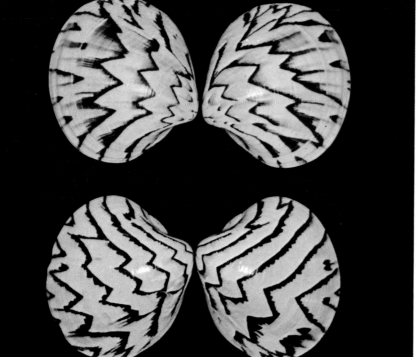

572

572
VENERIDAE
Tent Venus Shell
Lioconcha castrensis
Linnaeus, 1758

A fairly common shell taken subtidally in sand along the Great Barrier Reef; they are collected by dredging or diving. *L. castrensis* has one of the most attractive patterns in the bivalve class and live shells have a thin yellowish periostracum. Range: Qld. to W.A. Size: 50 mm. Common.

573

573
MITRIDAE
Cardinal Mitre
Mitra cardinalis
Gmelin, 1791

Another of the larger mitrids, *M. cardinalis* inhabits sand and sandy patches and is usually found beneath stones or coral. Range: Qld. Size: 76 mm. Fairly common.

574
MITRIDAE
Chestnut Mitre
Scabricola casta
Gmelin, 1791

Not of common occurrence in Australia, *S. casta* frequents sandy areas amongst reef subtidally. The brown bands around the shell are not true shell colouring, only the outer skin or periostracum. It can be collected by dredging or trawling off the Great Barrier Reef. Range: Qld. Size: 30 mm. Uncommon.

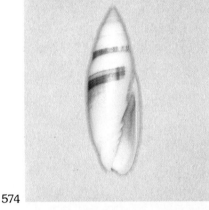

574

575
MITRIDAE
Cone Mitre
Imbricaria conularis
Lamarck, 1811

At first glance *I. conularis* can be mistaken for a small cone shell. Certainly when viewed from the dorsal surface the resemblance to a cone shell is unmistakable. It is not until the aperture of the shell is examined that its main distinguishing feature is seen. Like all mitrids, *I. conularis* possesses columellar plaits, a simple easily recognised characteristic for their family. The shell is reasonably uncommon, and lives under the sand on intertidal and subtidal sand banks where it feeds on worms. Range: Qld. to N.T. Size: 25 mm. Uncommon.

575

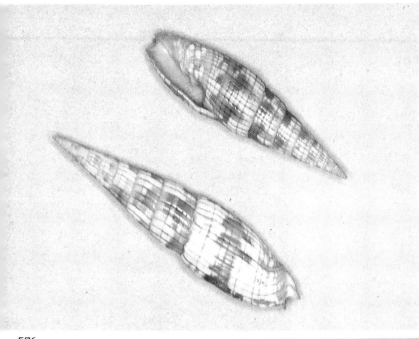

576

576
COSTELLARIIDAE
Star Mitre
Vexillum costatum
Gmelin, 1791

This shell seems to be taken mostly in northern areas of the Great Barrier Reef and lives subtidally in sand to 5 metres. Range: Qld. Size: grows to just óver 51 mm. Uncommon.

577
COSTELLARIIDAE
Vexate Mitre
Vexillum exasperatum
Gmelin, 1791

Fairly common on intertidal sand flats of the Great Barrier Reef, shells are also prevalent subtidally to 10 metres. They show remarkable differences in shell characteristics in various areas. Range: Qld. Size: 25 mm. Common.

578
MITRIDAE
Thread Mitre
Cancilla filaris
Linnaeus, 1771

Usually in sand pockets below low tide level, *C. filaris* is also often found beneath coral slabs in sand. Fairly variable in shape they occur mostly on the Great Barrier Reef. Range: Qld. Size: 30 mm. Moderately common.

577

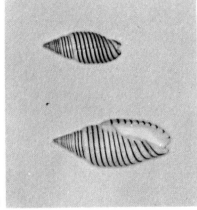

578

579

579
MITRIDAE
Giant Mitre
Mitra mitra
Linnaeus, 1758

The largest and best known of the Australian mitres, they live all along the Great Barrier Reef. Restricted to a single environment they are found in sand tracks from low tide down to 10 metres on offshore islands, cays and reefs. Range: Qld. to W.A. Size: 150 mm. Common.

580

581

582

580
MITRIDAE
Papal Mitre
Mitra papalis
Linnaeus, 1758

Although specimens are found on the Great Barrier Reef, this species is not common. It lives in sand amongst sea grass or algae at, or just below, low tide level. Range: Qld. Size: 100 mm. Uncommon.

581
MITRIDAE
Butterfly Mitre
Neocancilla papilio
Link, 1807

A fairly distinct species, this shell is found in sand patches or coral pools on the Great Barrier Reef. Range: Qld. Size: 60 mm. Common.

582
MITRIDAE
Circula Mitre
Neocancilla circula
Kiener, 1838

A delicate, finely striated mitre, this species lives from low tide level to 5 metres on the Great Barrier Reef. Mostly located by fanning in sand patches below tide level. Range: Qld. Size: 25 mm. Not common in Australia.

583

583
COSTELLARIIDAE
Plaited Mitre
Vexillum plicarium
Linnaeus, 1758

Similar to *V. rugosum,* this shell can be distinguished by its smoother surface and shallower spiral grooves. Found in sand patches on reef or in sand, their dorsal surface is often eroded. Range: Qld. to W.A. Size: 50 mm. Uncommon.

584
COSTELLARIIDAE
Juke's Mitre
Vexillum vulpercula jukesii
A. Adams, 1853

Found intertidally in sandy patches or amongst algae on rubble reef these shells are subject to disfiguring erosion. These chalky specimens are useless for any purpose and should be left where found. Range: Qld. to W.A. Size: 50 mm. Moderately common.

585
MITRIDAE
Pontifical Mitre
Mitra stictica
Link, 1807

Living in sand usually beneath coral slabs or rocks, *M. stictica* can be located fairly regularly on islands and cays of the Great Barrier Reef, and is found both intertidally and subtidally. The animal is translucent white in colour with heavier white spots. Range: Qld. Size: 50 mm. Moderately common.

584

585

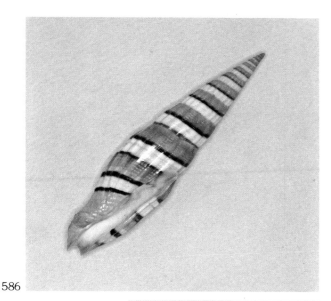

586

586
COSTELLARIIDAE
Ribbon Mitre
Vexillum taeniatum
Lamarck, 1811

One of the most beautiful species of mitres, these shells live from low tide level down to 40 metres. They frequent sandy or sandy mud areas. Very popular with collectors. Range: Qld. Size: 76 mm. Uncommon.

587
MITRIDAE
Variable Mitre
Mitra variabilis
Reeve, 1844

Usually found intertidally on sand, sandy mud rubble or under coral. This shell feeds mostly on worms. Range: Qld. to W.A. Size: 35 mm. Common in some areas.

587

588
MURICIDAE
Spinous Murex
Murex acanthostephes
Watson, 1883

Abundant on intertidal sandy and sandy mud beaches in northern W.A., this delicately spined *Murex* has been trawled down to 72 metres on mud bottom in northern Australia Specimens from different geographical localities differ in spine length with deep water forms generally having exceptionally long spines. As in a number of species within the *Murex* genus the tips of the spines are sometimes dark purple to black in colour. They feed mostly on bivalves. In summer they lay a white column of egg capsules which is fixed to a suitable base anchored in the sand. Range: northern Aust. Size: 110 mm. Common.

588

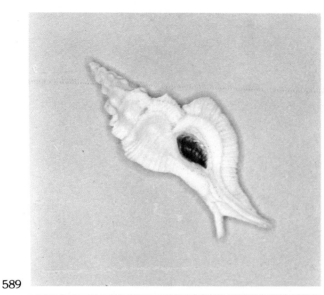

589

589
MURICIDAE
Winged Murex
Pterynotus alatus
Roeding, 1798

Dredged off the coast of Qld. on rubble bottom in depths of 60 metres, this shell is also taken by divers working on reefs to the north of Darwin, N.T. Although not a rare shell, specimens in perfect condition are difficult to find. Range: Qld. to N.T. Size: 60 mm. Moderately uncommon.

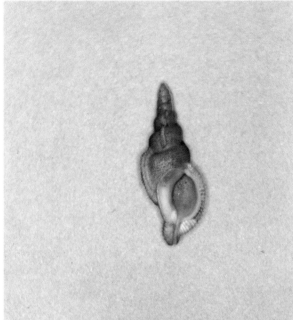

590

590
MURICIDAE
Convolute Muricid
Phyllocoma convoluta
Broderip, 1833

Hardly ever taken alive, this rare species lives from low tide level to at least 10 metres in sandy rubble beneath coral slabs. Range: Qld. Size: 25 mm. Rare.

591
MURICIDAE
Elongate Murex
Pterynotus elongatus
Lightfoot, 1786

Very rarely found alive, this species lives in dead coral rubble areas of the Great Barrier Reef. Most specimens are known only from dead shells washed up on the beaches or blown ashore by cyclones. Range: Qld. to N.T. Size: 76.2 mm. Very rare.

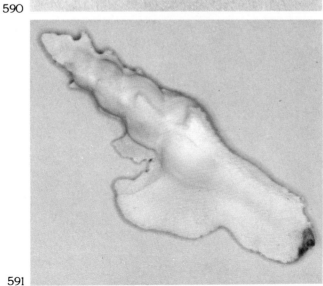

591

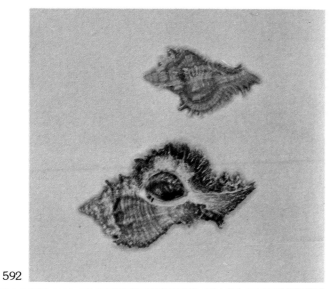

592

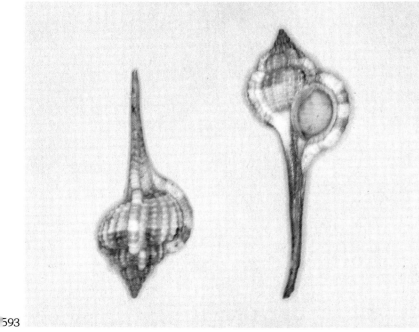

593

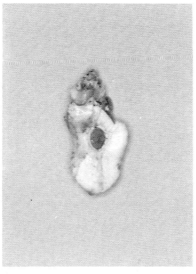

594

592
MURICIDAE
Lacinate Murex
Chicoreus lacinatus
Sowerby, 1841

Living subtidally from 20 to 50 metres off Qld. and the Great Barrier Reef, *C. lacinatus* is found on a rubble weed covered bottom. Difficult to locate in natural habitat. The animal is an ochre colour, peppered with small brown and black flecks. Range: Qld. Size: 50 mm. Uncommon.

593
MURICIDAE
Plicated Murex
Haustellum multiplicatum
Sowerby, 1895

Fairly uncommon over its entire geographical distribution, *H. multiplicatum* lives intertidally in sand banks. A number have been taken by divers working in shallow waters off northern W.A. Eggs are laid in white capsules interlaced amongst the branches of sea whips and are deposited between November and February. On occasions the shell will climb over 400 mm up into the higher branches of the sea whips before the eggs are laid. Range: N.T. to W.A. Size: 65 mm. Uncommon.

594
MURICIDAE
Occluse Typhis
Typhisopsis occulosum
Garrard, 1963

This shell was first recorded alive in the early 1960s when Mr Tom Nielson dredged two specimens off the Great Barrier Reef in 34 metres and presented them to the Australian Museum. Several years later two other live specimens were taken in 10 metres by the author. They live on a coral mud rubble bottom amongst broken shells and assorted marine life. Shells tend to be fairly eroded and contain a white animal. Range: Qld. Size: 25 mm. Rare.

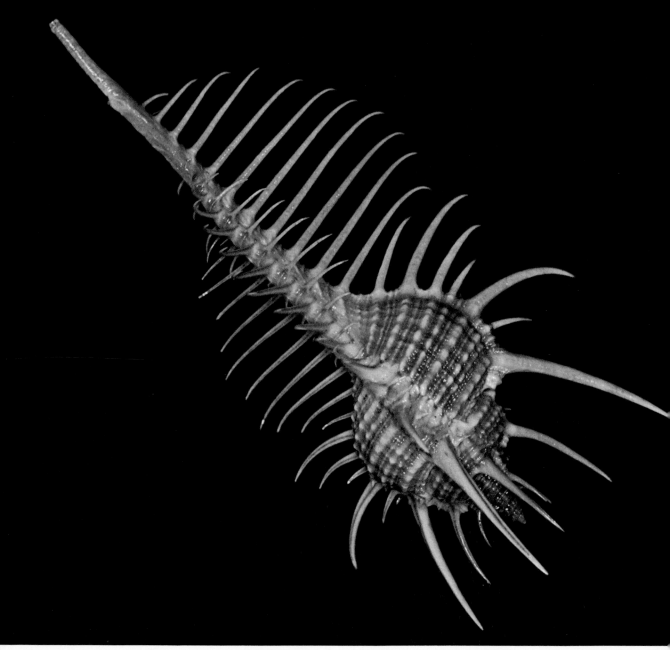

595
MURICIDAE
Venus Comb Murex
Murex pecten
Solander, 1786

This species is one of the many
wonders of the molluscian kingdom.
Its fine delicate spines and graceful
architecture make it a must for every
collector. Not common in Australia, it
lives in sand off Qld. and the Great
Barrier Reef and is collected mainly
by dredging. Range: Qld. Size:
120 mm. Uncommon.

596
MURICIDAE
Giant Murex
Chicoreus ramosus
Linnaeus, 1758

By far the largest of all murex shells
in Australia, *C. ramosus* can be found
intertidally on sandy rubble reef on
some islands off the Great Barrier
Reef. A little commoner below tide
level, they live under similar
circumstances and on muddy, broken
reef in northern areas. Bivalves
make up the greater part of their
diets although univalves are
sometimes eaten. Range: Qld. to
northern W.A. Size: 300 mm.
Reasonably uncommon.

596

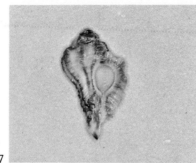

597

597
MURICIDAE
Tate's Murex
Subterynotus tatei
Verco, 1895

Only recently rediscovered by S.A. cray fisherman Mr Dennis Pearson this species is still a very rare shell. It lives on a sandy rubble bottom in depths of 20 to 40 metres in S.A. Well known W.A. shell diver Mr Bob Hancy of Bunbury has also found specimens in southern W.A. Range: S.A. to W.A. Size: 28 mm. Rare.

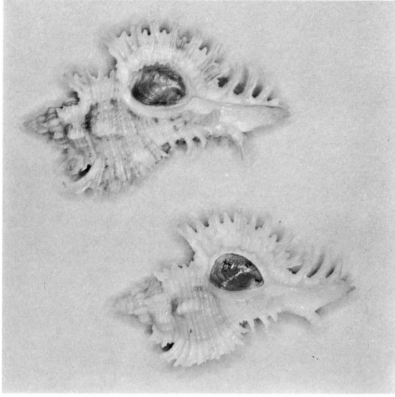

598

598
MURICIDAE
Territory Murex
Chicoreus territus
Reeve, 1845

These shells are found intertidally to around 20 metres living on either muddy or sandy rubble bottom. Shells can feature long, well developed varice extensions or some may completely denuded. They feed mostly on bivalves including oysters and charmas. Eggs are deposited in early summer and are laid on testes of ascidians, bivalve shells or substrate. Shell colours include brown, purple, white and orange. Range: Qld. Size: 70 mm. Moderately common.

599

599
MURICIDAE
Three-Winged Murex
Pterochelus triformis
Reeve, 1845

These shells enjoy several habitats – rocky reef, sandy rubble and mud flats, from low tide to 40 metres. The best specimens are found amongst broken reef and rubble in sea grass beds. Eggs are laid in summer on reef or in bivalve shells. A number of shell colours are recorded including brown, black, purple, yellow and orange, with brown to black being the most prevalent. Range: Vic. to W.A. Size: 76 mm. Common only in S.A.

214

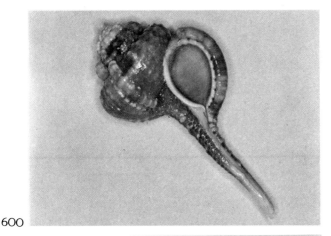

600

600
MURICIDAE
Wilson's Murex
Haustellum wilsoni
D'Attilio and Old, 1971

A living animal of this species is still to be located although dead specimens are found fairly regularly in craypots and by divers working along the southern W.A. coast. *H. wilsoni* was named in honour of Dr Barry Wilson of the Perth Museum who figured in the discovery of the original specimens. Range: W.A. Size: 70 mm. Uncommon.

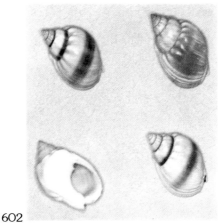

601

601
NASSARIIDAE
Box Dog Whelk
Nassarius arcularius
Linnaeus, 1758

A thick, heavy shell. This species is located on sand flats at midtide level usually in the same vicinity as *N. coronatus,* although it is not as common as that shell. Range: Qld. Size: 30 mm. Common.

602

602
NASSARIIDAE
Coronated Dog Whelk
Nassarius coronatus
Bruguière, 1789

Very common on sandy flats, these little shells emerge from the sand on the receding and flooding tide to search for food. Found in several colours and combinations of colours. Range: Qld. to northern W.A. Size: 25 mm. Common.

603
NASSARIIDAE
Acorn Dog Whelk
Nassarius glans
Linnaeus, 1758

Largest of the dog whelks, *N. glans* inhabits intertidal and subtidal areas of sand, rubble and reef. Its animal is extremely active and feeds on smaller molluscs and by scavenging. Range: Qld. to W.A. Size: 50 mm. Common.

603

604

604
NASSARIIDAE
Papillose Dog Whelk
Nassarius papillosus
Linnaeus, 1758

One of the easiest dog whelks to recognise, it is fairly common on cays and islands along the Great Barrier Reef and is usually found below tide level in shallow water. Range: N.S.W. to N.T. Size: 50 mm. Common.

605
NASSARIIDAE
Banded Nassarius
Nassarius pyrrhus
Menke, 1843

Very common on low tide sand banks in Vic., these rather pretty little shells can also be found in sand to depths in excess of 40 metres. Range: S.A. and southern W.A. Size: 20 mm. Common.

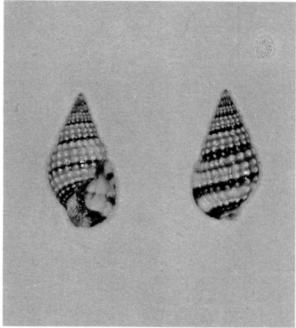

605

606
NATICIDAE
Conical Sand Snail
Conuber conicum
Lamarck, 1822

An extremely common and widely distributed species, *C. conicum* occurs on sand and muddy sand flats intertidally, and preys on small bivalves. This snail lays thousands of tiny eggs which are housed in a clear sausage shaped mass of firm jelly. The eggs are laid in summer and are conspicuous on many southern estuary beaches. Range: Qld., N.S.W., Vic., Tas., S.A., W.A. Size: 30 mm. Common.

606

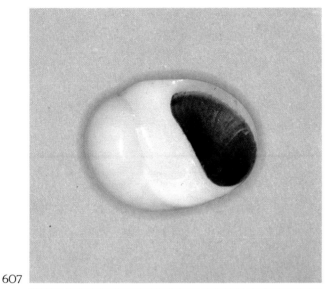

607

607
NATICIDAE
Yellow Sand Snail
Polinices auranticus
Roeding, 1798

Conspicuous by its bright yellow colouring, *P. auranticus* lives in sand patches amongst reef. Coming to the surface in search of prey it is often found on flooding tides on the Great Barrier Reef. However, it is more prevalent subtidally in shallow water where it feeds mostly on small bivalves. When drilling holes through the shell of its prey it seems to prefer a location near the umbo. Once selected, the site is softened by an acid secretion and drilled with a radula. The proboscis is then poked through into the living tissues of the bivalve where the helpless victim is rasped into small pieces and devoured. Range: N.S.W. to N.T. Size: 40 mm. Common.

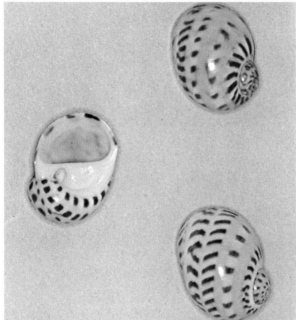

608

608
NATICIDAE
Chestnut Sand Snail
Natica onca
Roeding, 1798

With its outstanding colour pattern, this species is readily identifiable. It lives intertidally on sandy mud flats and predates on small bivalves. An attractive shell, it does not seem to be as prolific as others of its family. Range: Qld. to N.T. Size: 25 mm. Moderately common.

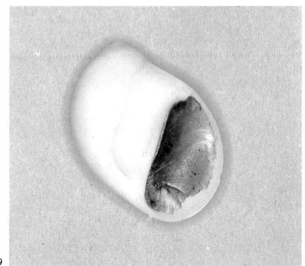

609

609
NATICIDAE
Tumid Sand Snail
Polinices tumidus
Swainson, 1840

Similar in shape to *P. auranticus*, *P. tumidus* is white in colour and more elongated. It is a carnivorous species which lives in intertidal and subtidal sand patches. Like all sand snails this species can pump water into its body to assist in the expansion of its large foot. This often gives the impression that the animal is too big for the shell. This water is squirted out of pores in the foot upon retraction. Range: Qld. to W.A. Size: 50 mm. Common.

610

610
NATICIDAE
Seychell Moon Snail
Natica seychellium
Watson, 1886

Although fairly common in areas of Qld., *N. seychellium* is extremely variable in the amount of patterning on its dorsal surface. It lives on sand or sandy mud flats and can be found at low tide. The species grows to 25 mm but the majority of shells found are smaller. Range: Qld., N.T. Size: 25 mm. Moderately common.

611
OLIVIDAE
Ringed Olive
Oliva annulata
Gmelin, 1791

Living on sand banks intertidally and subtidally to 10 metres, *O. annulata* is mainly confined to islands and cays of the Great Barrier Reef. Occasionally pale colour forms are encountered. Range: Qld. Size: 60 mm. Fairly common in some areas.

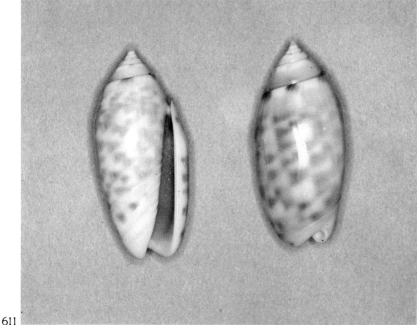

611

612
OLIVIDAE
Australian Olive
Oliva australis
Duclos, 1835

O. australis is fairly common in S.A. and W.A. where it lives from low tide level down to 20 metres or more. Found in sand, they live on other small molluscs and also scavenge. Quite variable in colour, the N.W. Australian form seems to be narrower and lighter in shell structure than its southern counterparts. Range: Vic. to W.A. Size: 25 mm. Fairly common in some areas.

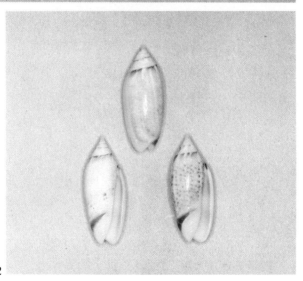

612

613

614

613
OLIVIDAE
Purple Mouthed Olive
Oliva caerulea
Roeding, 1798

A very solid shell with a deep purple mouth; features that tend to make it easily recognisable. It is found on exposed sand banks and subtidally to 10 metres. Range: Qld. to W.A. Size: 50 mm. Common.

614
OLIVIDAE
Carnelion Olive
Oliva carneola
Gmelin, 1791

This species seems to be more prevalent towards the northern extremeties of the Great Barrier Reef. It is fairly constant in pattern although colour and size of stripes vary. Range: Qld. Size: 20 mm. Uncommon.

615
OLIVIDAE
Elongate Ancilla
Amalda elongata
Gray, 1847

This beautiful species of mollusc is found on intertidal sand and sandy mud flats. Abundant in some areas. The animal is much larger than the shell and cannot be withdrawn. In times of stress it has been known to swim by frequent backward and forward motions of its large foot. Range: Northern W.A. to N.T. Size: 45 mm. Common.

615

616

616
OLIVIDAE
Wood Olive
Oliva lignaria
Marrat, 1868

Common on sand flats in W.A., these shells are also recorded from N.T. and Qld. Like so many olives their colours are extremely variable; *O. lignaria* may range from white with brown speckles through to deep chocolate. Range: W.A., N.T., Qld. Size: 50 mm. Common.

617

617
OLIVIDAE
Marginate Ancilla
Amalda marginata
Lamarck, 1811

Mostly found in shallow water sand flats, specimens of this carnivorous species are obtained by dredging or diving. Range: N.S.W., Vic., Tas., S.A. Size: 35 mm. Common.

618
OLIVIDAE
Red Mouthed Olive
Oliva miniacea
Roeding, 1798

O. miniacea are the largest species of this family in Australia, and inhabit sandy areas on both the mainland and offshore islands. Easy method of collecting these shells is at night on the low tide, for on the turn of the tide they emerge out of the sand. Range: Northern N.S.W., around north coast to W.A. Size: 63 mm. Common.

618

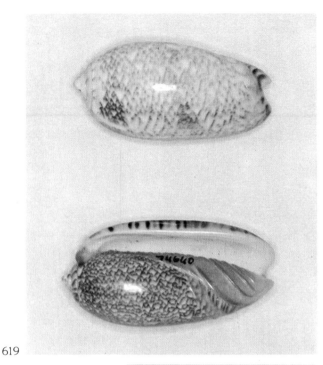

619

619
OLIVIDAE
Bloody Olive
Oliva reticulata
Roeding, 1798

Restricted in areas in Qld. where it lives on intertidal sand flats. This species usually has an orange or red callus and columella. Range: Qld. Size: 50 mm. Moderately common.

620
OVULIDAE
Tokio Ovulid
Phenacovolva tokioi
Cate, 1973

Never an easy shell for the inexperienced collector to locate, they are found by either using a look-box or diving. They live on gorgonians from low tide level down to 30 metres. It is important when collecting the dependant host shells that they are not indiscriminately torn up as this will delete the food in the area, along with the shells. Range: Qld. Size: 35 mm. Uncommon.

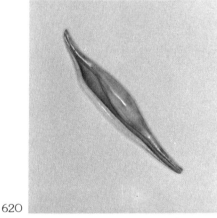

620

621
OVULIDAE
Depressed Ovulid
Hiata depressa
Sowerby, 1875

Living from low tide level down to 3 metres along the north-west coast, this shell is associated with gorgornians upon which it feeds. Mating takes place in mid summer and eggs are laid on the host soon after. Common in some areas, there doesn't seem to be a marked difference in size between males and females. Range: Qld. to W.A. Size: 30 mm. Moderately common.

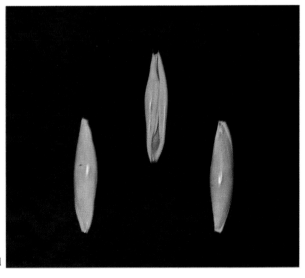

621

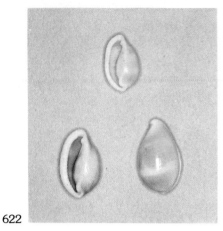

622

622
OVULIDAE
Short Ovulid
Prionovolva brevis
Sowerby, 1828

This species lives from just below tide level to 10 metres on alcyonarian corals, and is sometimes found at extreme low tides. Their eggs are laid amongst the inner branches of the soft coral and are white in colour. Range: N.S.W., Qld. Size: 15 mm. Uncommon.

623
OVULIDAE
Hayne's Ovulid
Aclyvolva haynesi
Sowerby, 1889

Sometimes this species, which lives from low tide level down to 20 metres, is found on several species of gorgonoids. It has an extremely brightly coloured and distinctively patterned mantle. Range: Qld. to W.A. Size: 35 mm. Uncommon.

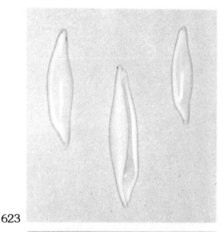

623

624
OVULIDAE
Traill's Ovulid
Crenavolva striatula traillii
A. Adams, 1855

A rather small but interesting subspecies, *C. s. traillii* lives on gorgonians from low tide level down to and beyond 40 metres. Their mantles tend to be a deep red colour similar to the shell with small white or light coloured markings. This is almost identical to the red of their host gorgonian polyps. Not always easily collected on the Qld. mainland at low tide, their abundance coincides with the drought years Range: Qld.. Size: 12 mm. Uncommon.

624

625
OVULIDAE
Elongated Egg Cowry
Volva volva
Linnaeus, 1758

A very distinct species, *V. volva* is a fairly common shell usually collected by trawlers in depths below 20 metres off the Qld. coast. These shells are associated with soft corals and have been taken by divers down to 25 metres in N.S.W and Qld. They have a rapid growth to adulthood and, should a colony consume all of their host alcyonarian corals in the area, mass migration to other areas sometimes occur. Range: N.S.W. to northern W.A. Size: 100 mm. Moderately common.

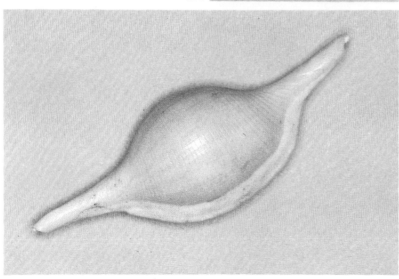

625

26

27

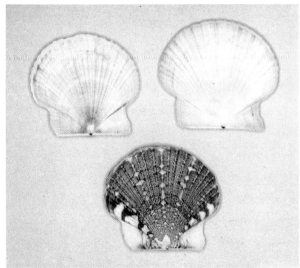

628

626
PECTINIDAE
Queen Scallop
Chlamys bifrons
Lamarck, 1819

Commercially fished by scallop boats in Tas. this species is one of the largest southern scallops. It is very big in Tas. where shells have been recorded to 150 mm. In mainland waters its average size is between 76 and 100 mm. Although usually purple in colour, albinistic specimens frequently occur. Many shells have a green look about them but this is mostly algae or erosion. Divers find the shells very plentiful in some localities, especially in S.A. where they are found in *Posidonia* sea grass beds and amongst rubble reef. Range: N.S.W. to S.A. Size: see above. Common.

627
PECTINIDAE
Cuming's Scallop
Chlamys cumingi
Reeve, 1853

Confined to areas along the Qld. coast, *C. cumingi* lives on a sandy rubble bottom and is often taken by trawlers and scallop boats. Not large enough for commercial use they are usually shovelled back into the water. Quite common in some of the larger bays and estuaries of southern Qld. Range: Qld. Size: 40 mm. Common.

628
PECTINIDAE
Complete Scallop
Pecten isomeres
Iredale, 1939

An intertidal species which inhabits areas of sandy mud flats on the Qld. coast. *P. isomeres* is very variable in colour and can be found lying in shallow depressions with their flat side up. Range: Qld. Size: 25 mm. Uncommon.

629
PECTINIDAE
King Scallop
Pecten meridonalis
Tate, 1887

This shell is similar in shape to the well-known sign on service stations. It is the basis of the Tas. scallop fishery. Invariably, it lives on sandy mud bottom, lying in small pockets, flat surface up. These shells, like all scallops, have amazing agility. By continuous flapping movements of the valves water is forced out from the mantle cavity enabling the scallops to jet backwards in spasmodic jerks. Range: Tas. Size: grows to over 150 mm. Common.

630
PLEUROBRANCHIDAE
Hill's Side-Gilled Slug
Pleurobranchus hilli
Hedley, 1896

The largest Australian side gilled slug, *P. hilli* lives on sand and mud below tide level to 10 metres. It is not a common species and there have only been a few isolated records of its presence in any numbers. Range: N.S.W. to S.A. Size: 400 mm. Uncommon.

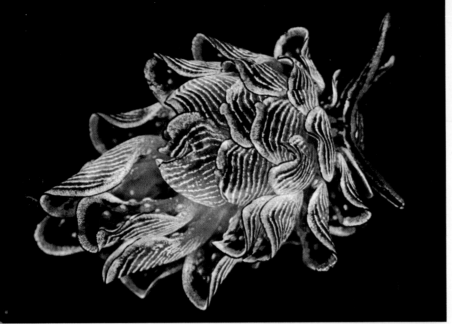

631

631
POLYBRANCHIDAE
Black Cyerce
Cyerce nigricans
Pease, 1860

This opisthobranch inhabits sandy tide pools on the north-west coast of Australia. It is very delicate and often when any of its cerata are dislodged they will pulsate for quite some time after. Range: Qld. to W.A. Size: 50 mm. Common.

632
POLYCERIDAE
Ceylonese Nudibranch
Gymnodoris ceylonica
Kelaart, 1859

Occasionally observed intertidally, *G. ceylonica* lives beneath the coarse shell sand on islands and cays of the Great Barrier Reef. It feeds on other small invertebrates. Range: Qld. to W.A. Size: 50 mm. Uncommon.

632

633
POLYCERIDAE
Striated Sand Nudibranch
Gymnodoris sp.

Found in sand and occasionally on sand under rocks, this little nudibranch dwells beneath the sand surface. Its gills are especially adapted to a burrowing existence and specimens have been recorded from low tide level to 2 metres. Range: Qld. to W.A. Size: 18 mm. Uncommon.

633

634
PYRAMIDELLIDAE
Iredale's Pyramid Shell
Mormulastra iredalei
Laseron, 1959

Fairly uncommon even in beach drift, this species is one of the many pyramid shells of which almost nothing is known in regard to the living animal or its food host. It lives in sand intertidally on the islands and cays of the Great Barrier Reef. Range: Qld. Size: 40 mm. Uncommon.

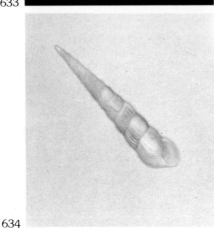

634

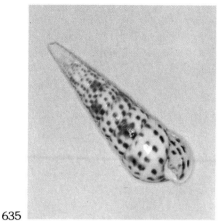

635
PYRAMIDELLIDAE
Spotted Pyramid Shell
Pyramidella acus
Gmelin, 1791

One of the largest of the
Australian Pyramids, *P. acus* can
be found on sand or mud
intertidally. Like most of their
family they prey on other
invertebrates and have specially
adapted mouth parts for sucking
the juices from their hosts. Range:
Qld. to N.T. Size: 45 mm.
Moderately common.

636
SOLENIDAE
Large Chinese Fingernail Shell
Solen grandis
Dunker, 1861

S. grandis lives in sandy mud below
tide level. They seem to congregate in
groups and are not always easy to dig
up. One of the largest members of
this family in Australia, the shells are
easily identified by their red
markings. Range: Qld. to N.T. Size:
often reaches a length of 110 mm.
Moderately common.

637
CUTTELLIDAE
Knife Finger Oyster
Phaxas hilaris
Iredale, 1936

Quite common on sandy mud flats in
Qld., the shells are usually buried to a
depth of around 200 mm. The
molluscs are quite agile and can
move very quickly back into
substrate that is covered by water.
Range: Qld. to northern W.A. Size:
70 mm. Common.

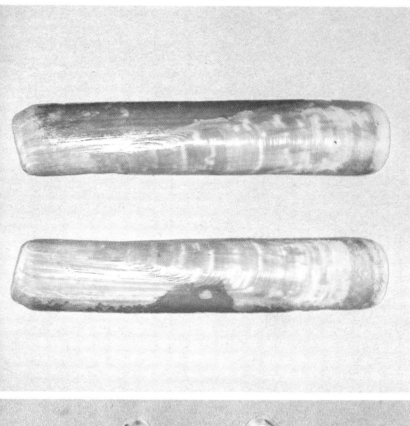

637

638
STROMBIDAE
Diana's Stromb
Strombus aurisdianae
Linnaeus, 1758

Found on offshore islands on the Great Barrier Reef, this species lives intertidally on sand banks and occasionally in rubble patches. It is also found below tide level on sheltered algae covered sand to 5 metres. Not considered a common species by Australian collectors. Range: Qld. Size: 60 mm has been recorded.

639
STROMBIDAE
Bull Stromb
Strombus bulla
Roeding, 1798

S. bulla is found on intertidal and subtidal algae covered sand flats on coral cays in northern Qld. It is a burrowing species and spends a lot of time under the sand. Range: northern Qld. Size: 60 mm. Rare.

638

639

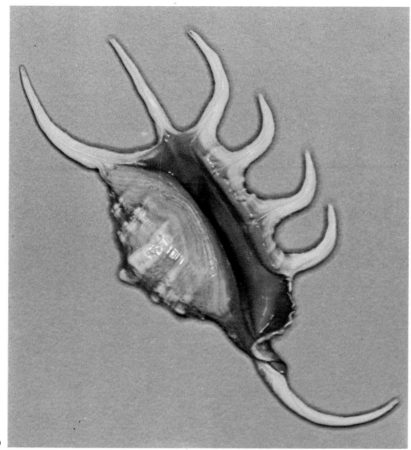

40

640
STROMBIDAE
Crocate Spider Shell
Lambis crocata
Link, 1807

The crocate spider shell is not commonly collected in Australia. It lives on sandy rubble in the northern Barrier Reef areas and prefers a subtidal existence. Range: Qld. to N.T. Size: 120 mm. Uncommon.

641
STROMBIDAE
Dilate Stromb
Strombus dilatus
Swainson, 1821

Not often collected in Australia, it lives in muddy sand rubble channels inbetween mainland islands on the Great Barrier Reef down to 20 metres. Range: Qld. Size: 45 mm. Uncommon.

642
STROMBIDAE
Fish Stromb
Strombus erythrinus
Dillwyn, 1817

S. erythrinus inhabits areas below tide level in silty sand and algae covered rubble down to 20 metres. Range: restricted to Qld. and the Great Barrier Reef. Size: 30 mm. Uncommon.

641

642

229

643

643
STROMBIDAE
Labiate Stromb
Strombus labiatus
Roeding, 1798

Found in large colonies along the Qld. offshore islands, *S. labiatus* can be distinguished from similar species by the dark brown aperture and orange columella. Seems to prefer a silty sand habitat amongst algae covered rubble. Range: Qld. Size: 30 mm. Common.

644
STROMBIDAE
Scorpion Shell
Lambis scorpius
Linnaeus, 1758

Although not generally collected in Australia this shell nevertheless inhabits areas of northern Australia where it lives on a sandy rubble bottom below tide level. Range: Qld. to N.T. Size: 150 mm. Uncommon.

645
STROMBIDAE
Common Spider Shell
Lambis lambis
Linnaeus, 1758

Very common on reef flats and rubble patches at low tide. Specimens have been taken by divers down to 10 metres. Female shells are generally larger than the males and eggs are laid during summer. They feed exclusively on short fine algae growing on dead coral and rocks. In some areas beautiful dwarf specimens are collected on mud with abnormally long apertural projections. This very popular shell is used in many tourist orientated advertisements for the Great Barrier Reef. Range: Qld. to northern W.A. Size: 228 mm. Common.

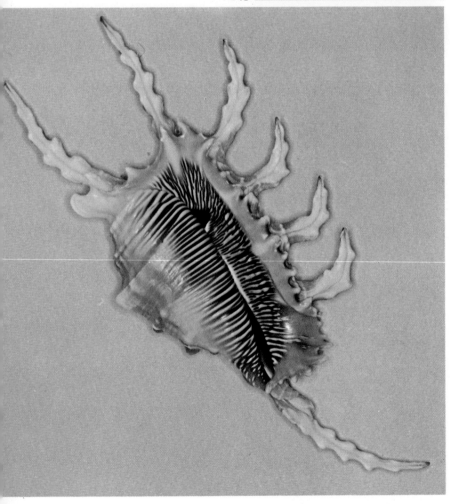

644

64

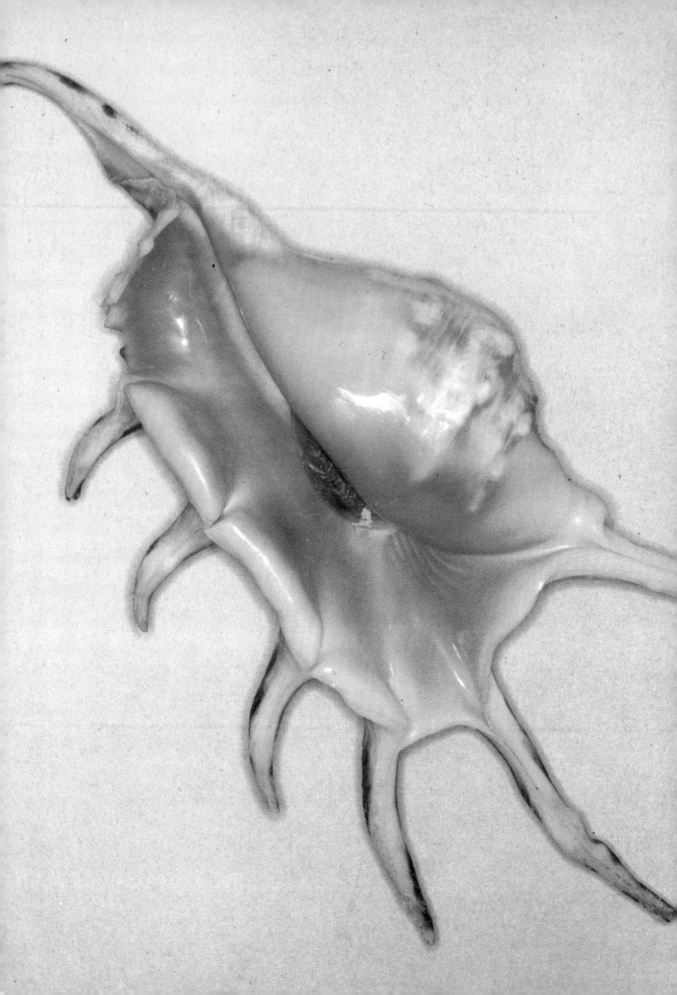

646
STROMBIDAE
Freckled Stromb
Strombus lentiginosus
Linnaeus, 1758

Inhabiting rubble patches on low tide sand banks, this solid, moderately sized shell is fairly well camouflaged in its natural habitat. Although the mouth displays delicate tones of orange, yellow and pinks, etc. the back is usually covered with algae and fine silt. This blends in perfectly with their surrounding environment. At the southern end of the Great Barrier Reef this species can be found at various depths below tide level down to 20 metres. Range: north Qld. to N.T. Size: 82 mm. Common.

647
STROMBIDAE
Red Mouthed Stromb
Strombus luhuanus
Linnaeus, 1758

Extremely prolific in the Qld. Great Barrier Reef areas this species has also been found at Shell Harbour in southern N.S.W. It mostly inhabits areas of intertidal coral rubble although divers have obtained specimens living in sand to 10 metres. The largest and best specimens in Australia are found at Lord Howe Island, off the coast of N.S.W., where large colonies live in the lagoon on rubble and sand at depths of 3 metres. Range: N.S.W., Qld. Size: 76 mm. Common.

648
STROMBIDAE
Flower Stromb
Strombus mutabilis
Swainson, 1821

These little strombs come in a variety of colours. They are found in large colonies on algae covered coral rubble and sand flats usually in sheltered conditions. Range: N.S.W. to southern W.A. Size: 35 mm. Common.

648

649
STROMBIDAE
Beautiful Stromb
Strombus plicatus pulchellus
Reeve, 1851

Figured specimen was the first to be recorded from Australian waters and was taken amongst algae covered rubble at 20 metres off the Whitsunday Group, Qld. in the late 1960s. Since then it has been recorded from W.A. A solid robust little stromb it has an orange and brown animal. Range: Qld., W.A. Size: 30 mm. Rare.

650
STROMBIDAE
Giant Spider Shell
Lambis truncata sebae
Kiener, 1843

This spider shell inhabits the rubble sand patches on the Great Barrier Reef in moderately shallow water. They live in colonies as do most of their relatives. Excellent eating, the majority of adult specimens are useless as cabinet specimens because of eroded shell extensions. Exclusively herbivores they feed on the short soft algae growing on dead coral rubble. The animal has well developed prehensile eyes and a very strong clawed foot. Range: Qld. Size: 304 mm. Common.

49

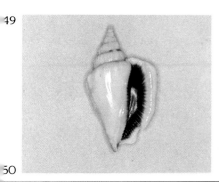

50

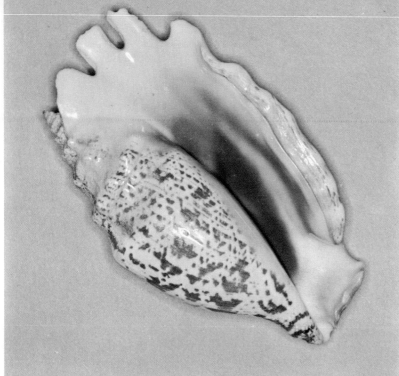

651

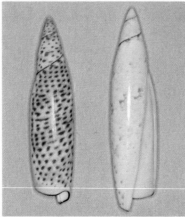

652

653

651
STROMBIDAE
Purple Mouthed Stromb
Strombus sinuatus
Humphrey, 1786

Not often found by collectors in Australia, *S. sinuatus* is nevertheless quite common in other Indo-Pacific and Indian Ocean areas. They have been taken by scuba divers in 13 metres of water off the Great Barrier Reef and living on algae covered rubble. Range: Qld. to northern W.A. Size: 101 mm. Uncommon.

652
STROMBIDAE
Bullet Stromb
Terebellum terebellum
Linnaeus, 1758

Looking more like an auger shell than a stromb, this bullet shaped species lives in coral sand areas. It is a very agile mollusc, disappearing into the sand within seconds of being disturbed. Its colour variations and patterns are extremely variable. Little is known of its habits or egg laying. Range: Qld. to W.A. Size: 51 mm. Common.

653
STROMBIDAE
Ponderous Stromb
Strombus thersites
Swainson, 1823

A rather thick heavy shell for its size, *S. thersites* was extremely rare with doubtful locality data until recent skindiving activities discovered their habitats. The shell lives on sandy algae covered rubble bottoms below tide level to depths of 30 metres. Range: from Lord Howe Island off N.S.W. to reefs off northern Qld. coast. Size: 120 mm. Uncommon.

654
STROMBIDAE
Variable Stromb
Strombus variabilis
Swainson, 1820

A beautifully patterned shell, it lives on algae covered sandy mud banks and is usually found on extreme low, tides. More common in deeper water where it lives in similar habitat. In photograph it is browsing on algae. Range: Qld. to N.T. Size: 60 mm. Common.

655
STRUTHIOLARIIDAE
Ostrich Foot Shell
Tylospira scutulata
Gmelin, 1791

Commonly washed up on southern beaches, the shell lives in subtidal sand at depths of 8 to 30 metres. Readily identifiable by its unusual shape, *T. scutulata* is mostly collected by dredging or diving. Shells of this type are found only in Australia and New Zealand. Range: N.S.W. Size: 50 mm. Common.

655

656
TELLINIDAE
Striped Sunset Shell
Tellinella virgata
Linnaeus, 1758

These shells are found by digging in sandy flats intertidally. They also inhabit shallow water areas and can be taken by dredging. Colours range from white through to deep pink. Range: Qld. to W.A. Size: 50 mm. Common.

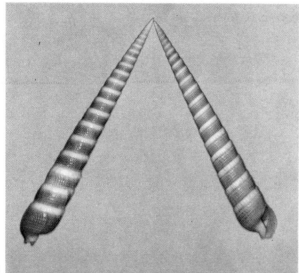

657

657
TEREBRIDAE
White Margined Auger
Terebra amanda
Hinds, 1844

This shell lives in sand subtidally but may also be taken occasionally at low tide. Range: the Great Barrier Reef. Size: 70 mm. Fairly common.

658
TEREBRIDAE
Old Woman Auger
Terebra anilis
Roeding, 1798

Occurring on muddy sand flats in northern Qld., these distinctive little augers can be found in sand tracks intertidally. Although fairly common in some areas most specimens are subject to healed breaks. Range: Qld. Size: 50 mm. Moderately common at certain localities.

659
TEREBRIDAE
Fly Swat Auger
Terebra areolata
Link, 1807

A common auger found in tracks on intertidal sand banks. Shells living in sand pockets on the Great Barrier Reef are usually below tide level down to 20 metres. They are carnivorous and feed on small soft bodied invertebrates. Range: N.S.W. to W.A. Size: 100 mm. Common.

658

659

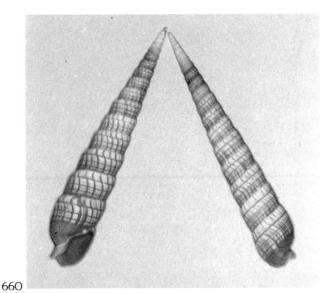

660

660
TEREBRIDAE
Babylon Auger
Terebra babylonia
Lamarck, 1822

T. babylonia lives in sand banks and is relatively easy to distinguish. As with many species, adults are often eroded on the spires. Range: Qld. to W.A. Size: 60 mm. Common.

661
TEREBRIDAE
Crenulate Auger
Terebra crenulata
Linnaeus, 1758

This species occurs intertidally in coral sand patches and sand banks on the Great Barrier Reef. It is not commonly collected, except in the more northern areas off Cairns and Mossman, Qld. Erosion takes place on most spires of the large adult shells making them useless as collectors' items. Range: N.S.W. to W.A. Size: medium sized adults around 95 mm make the best specimens. Moderately common.

661

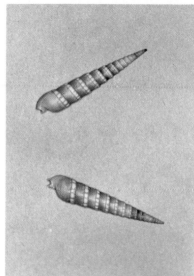

662

662
TEREBRIDAE
Quoygaimard's Auger
Terebra quoygaimardi
Cernohorsky & Bratcher, 1976

Quoygaimard's Auger mostly inhabit subtidal shallow waters and is occasionally found in sandy areas on the islands and cays of the great Barrier Reef. Range: Qld. Size: 40 mm. Uncommon.

663
TEREBRIDAE
Orange-Lined Auger
Terebra dimidiata
Linnaeus, 1758

A spectacular coloured auger, *T. dimidiata* lives on intertidal sand banks from the Great Barrier Reef to W.A. Like other members of its family it has an operculum which fits tightly into the aperture. Range: Qld. to W.A. Size: 114 mm. Common in some areas, rare in others.

663

664
TEREBRIDAE
Duplicate Auger
Duplicaria duplicata
Linnaeus, 1758

Found intertidally on sand banks, *D. duplicata* is very variable in colour. Range: N.T. to W.A. Size: grows to around 65 mm. Common.

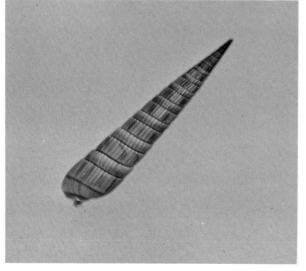

664

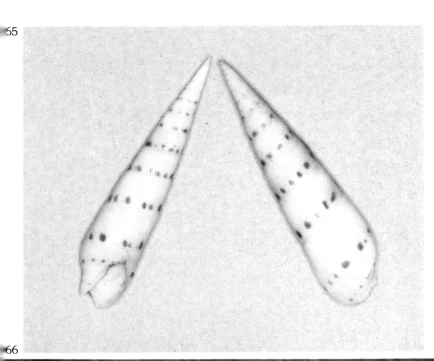

65

66

665
TEREBRIDAE
Cat Auger
Terebra felina
Dillwyn, 1817

These shells inhabit sandy areas of
the Great Barrier Reef and range as
far as W.A. This species seems to be
more prolific below tide level. Range:
Qld. to W.A. Size: 80 mm.
Moderately common.

666
TEREBRIDAE
Chocolate Spotted Auger
Terebra guttata
Roeding, 1798

One of the most sought after species
of the larger auger shells. *T. guttata*
inhabits sandy areas and is more
likely to be found below low tide
level. Larger specimens are subject to
eroded spires. Range: Great Barrier
Reef to N.T. Size: 127 mm.
Uncommon.

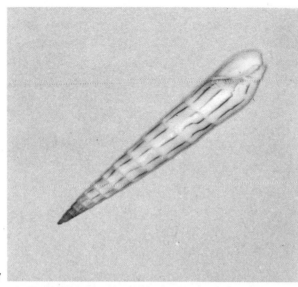

667

667
TEREBRIDAE
Lance Auger
Hastula lanceata
Linnaeus, 1767

Taken at low tide on sand banks or by diving or dredging, this species is found on islands and cays of the Great Barrier Reef. Range: Qld. Size: 60 mm. Uncommon.

668
TEREBRIDAE
Giant Marlin Spike
Terebra maculata
Linnaeus, 1758

This thick heavy shell lives beneath coral sand from the Great Barrier Reef to W.A. Although members of this family sometimes possess a poison apparatus similar to the cone shells, the poison is not harmful to humans. Occasionally found on intertidal sand banks they are much more plentiful below tide level where they leave distinctive tracks in the sand. Range: N.S.W. to W.A. Size: 228 mm. Common.

669
TONNIDAE
Partridge Tun
Tonna perdix
Linnaeus, 1758

A sand dwelling nocturnal species, this shell feeds on molluscs and echinoderms. The animal is brown in colour with white blotches. Although dead shells are often encountered, the living mollusc is not always easy to find. Range: N.S.W. to W.A. Size: 150 mm. Moderately common.

669

670

670
TONNIDAE
Variegated Tun
Tonna variegata
Lamarck, 1822

Found from low tide level down to 200 metres this species is very variable in colour and pattern. Range: it is found only in W.A. Size: 200 mm. Common.

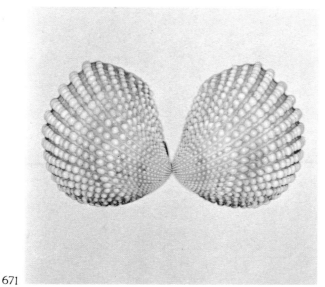

671

671
TRIGONIIDAE
Strange's Trigonia
Neotrigonia strangei
A. Adams, 1854

Peculiar to N.S.W. this rare species has for years been known only from dead valves washed up on beaches or dredged. Once thought to be a very deep water shell specimens have recently been found by the author in 30 metres off southern N.S.W. They live in sandy patches within areas of reef, this accounts for their habitat remaining unknown until the advent of Scuba diving. Range: N.S.W. Size: 37 mm. Rare.

672
TURBINIDAE
Hayne's Turban
Turbo haynesi
Preston, 1914

Although found on tidelines, *T. haynesi* is not often encountered by the collector at low tide. It lives below tide level to depths of 30 metres in areas of algae covered rubble. The animal is red and white and has black tentacles. Range: Qld. Size: 25 mm. Moderately uncommon.

673
TURRIDAE
Formidable Turrid
Inquisitor sterrhus
Watson, 1881

These shells can be found on intertidal sandy mud flats within their range. Like others of their family they kill their prey, worms and other small invertebrates, by means of a poison apparatus connected to their radula. The victims are then swallowed whole. Range: N.S.W. to N.T. Size : 50 mm. Moderately common.

672

673

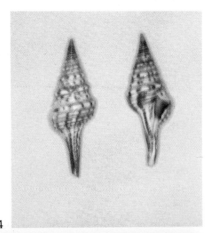

674

674
TURRIDAE
Informer Turrid
Lophiotoma indica
Roeding, 1798

This shell inhabits areas of intertidal sand flats, often amongst weed patches. It is a carnivore and feeds mostly on worms and other small invertebrates, usually injesting them whole. Range: Qld. to W.A. Size: 30 mm. Moderately common.

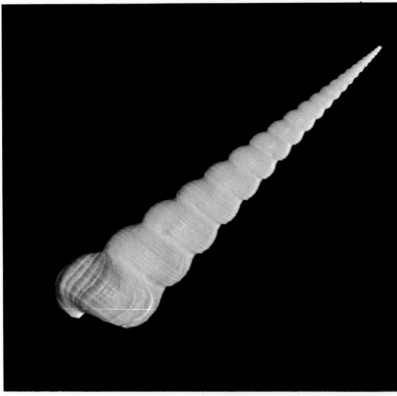

675

675
TURRITELLIDAE
Waxen Screw Shell
Turritella terebra
Linnaeus, 1758

Australia's largest *Turritella, T. terebra* is fairly common amongst shell drift on beaches within its range. Living below tide level in sandy mud they are not often found alive. Range: northern Qld., N.T. Size: 120 mm. Common.

676
VASIDAE
Spiky Vase Shell
Tudicula armigera
A. Adams, 1855

Most vase shells are very thick and heavy in shell formation, but *T. armigera* is an exception. A delicately spinose species it lives on sandy rubble bottom at depths of 20 metres plus. It is carnivorous and feeds mainly on other invertebrates. Range: Qld. Size: 63 mm. Common.

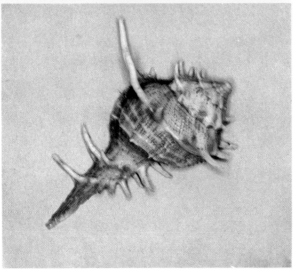

676

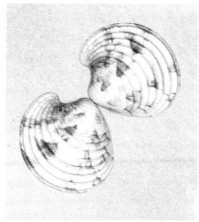

677

677
VENERIDAE
Beaked Venus Shell
Venus embrithes
Melvill & Standen, 1899

A fairly common bivalve which lives subtidally in sandy tropical areas. The external colour pattern tends to vary, over its distribution but specimens display a rose pink blotch internally in the vicinity of the umbos. Range: Qld. to W.A. Size: 30 mm. Common.

678
VENERIDAE
Lamellate Venus Shell
Venus lamellaris
Schumacher, 1817

This shell occurs in sandy or sandy mud areas usually below tide level. Attractively laminated with external frills the internal colouring is bright pink. Figured shell is from Qld. Specimens found in the vicinity of Sydney, N.S.W. are much lighter in colour, smaller and with less extensive ribbing. Range: N.S.W. to W.A. Size: 50 mm. Common.

679
VENERIDAE
Maiden's Purse Shell
Periglypta puerpera
Linnaeus, 1758

Found mostly subtidally in sand patches on the Great Barrier Reef, this shell seems to prefer areas of shallow water. It is fairly large for a subsand dweller. Range: Qld. to N.T. Size: 80 mm. Moderately common.

78

679

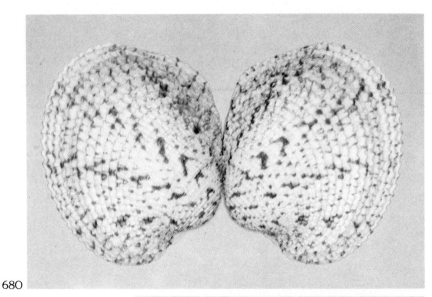

680

680
VENERIDAE
Reticulated Venus Shell
Periglypta reticulata
Linnaeus, 1758

This shell is found in shallow waters along the Great Barrier Reef. It inhabits sandy areas and is taken by dredging or diving. Although venus shells are quite variable and difficult to identify, this species has orange or yellow hinge teeth, which helps to distinguish it. Range: Qld., N.T. Size: 60 mm. Common.

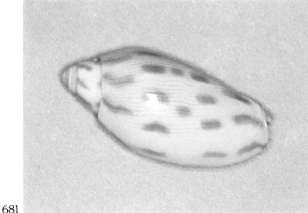

681

681
VOLUTIDAE
Caniculate Volute
Amoria canaliculata
McCoy, 1869

Taken in waters between 4 and 160 metres this shell is found in lagoons and sandy areas on the Great Barrier Reef. The animal has one of the most outstanding colour patterns in the volute family, white, yellow and deep red. Shells are taken by trawling or dredging. Range: Qld. Size: 60 mm. Moderately common.

682
VOLUTIDAE
Damon's Volute
Amoria damonii
Gray, 1864

Quite a common species on intertidal sand flats, various sub-species inhabit particular areas and one of these, *A. d. reevi*, is found to depths of 60 metres. Range: W.A. Size: 120 mm. Common.

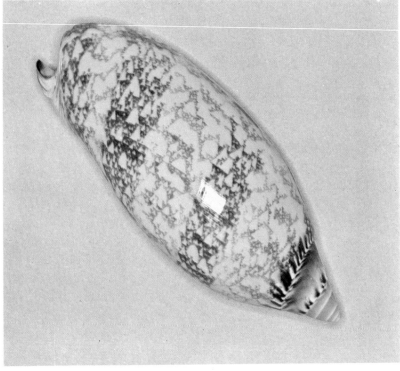

682

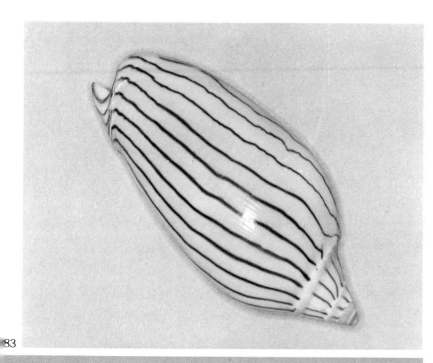

683

683
VOLUTIDAE
Elliot's Volute
Amoria ellioti
Sowerby, 1864

Found only in the vicinity of Port Hedland in W.A. This species lives on sand flats intertidally to 10 metres. It feeds on bivalves and other small molluscs. Range: W.A. (see above). Size: 100 mm. Uncommon.

684
VOLUTIDAE
Much Desired Volute
Amoria exoptanda
Reeve, 1849

It was not until 1965 that specimens of this rare volute became readily available. Skin divers discovered their habitat and although these volutes still command a high price the shells are no longer a rarity. Like most volutes they are voracious carnivores coming out of their sandy retreats at night to prey on other molluscs. Range: S.A. to southern W.A. Size: Large specimens exceed 101 mm in length but these can be very poor specimens and should be left for breeding purposes. Uncommon.

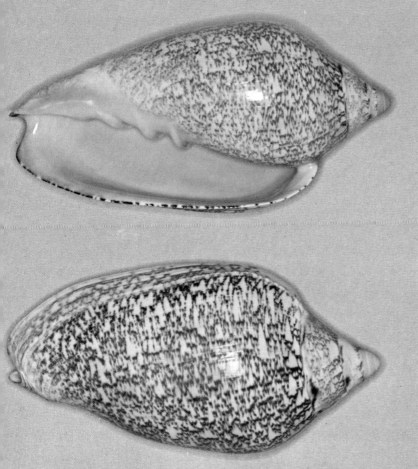

684

685

685
VOLUTIDAE
Lightning Volute
Ericusa fulgetra
Sowerby, 1825

Living below tide level to depths of 260 metres the usual shallow water forms available to collectors are taken by divers working in 5 to 20 metres. The shells seem to be fairly common even though their collecting is restricted to mostly diving or trawling. Very variable in shell patterning. They lay circular egg capsules up to 25 mm in diameter. The capsules are laid singularly and kept within the foot of the mollusc until such times as deposition beneath the sand takes place. *E. fulgetra* feeds specifically on other molluscs which are usually caught on the surface of the sand and taken below to be eaten. Range: S.A. to W.A. Size: 160 mm. Common.

686

VOLUTIDAE
Gray's Volute
Amoria grayi
Ludbrook, 1953

Harbouring a strikingly patterned
animal, *A. grayi* is perhaps the most
common of the medium-sized volutes
in W.A. It lives on low tide sand
banks and subtidally to depths of
beyond 200 metres. Very variable in
colour and design. Range: southern
W.A. to N.T. Size: 96 mm. Common.

686

687

VOLUTIDAE
Lord Howe Lyria
Lyria deliciosa howensis
Iredale, 1937

A small shell, *L. d. howensis* can
be found in the shallow waters
surrounding Lord Howe Island off
the N.S.W. coast. Living below
tide level in sand they are
sometimes found beneath rocks.
Range: N.S.W. to Qld. Size:
25 mm. Uncommon.

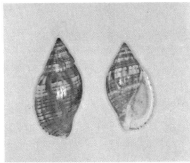

687

688

VOLUTIDAE
Jamrach's Volute
Amoria jamrachi
Gray, 1864

Another of the fairly uncommon
volutes endemic to northern W.A.
A. jamrachi inhabits sand flats in the
intertidal zone and is usually found by
investigating small cracks in the sand
surface. Range: northern W.A. Size:
70 mm. Uncommon.

688

689
VOLUTIDAE
Port Keat's Volute
Amoria damonii keatsiana
Ludbrook, 1953

This sub-species lives intertidally and subtidally in sand. Specimen figured is from Darwin, N.T. where specimens are regarded as fairly uncommon. Range: northern W.A. to Qld. Size: 90 mm. Uncommon.

690
VOLUTIDAE
Kreusler's Volute
Notovoluta kreuslerae
Angas, 1865

One of the rarer species of volutes found in S.A. this species lives in sand and rubble in depths of between 20 to 120 metres. Colonies seem to be fairly isolated with shells coming out of the sand during hours of darkness to feed on other molluscs. Range: S.A. Size: 100 mm. Rare.

689

690

691

691
VOLUTIDAE
Zebra Volute
Amoria zebra
Leach, 1814

Found in large colonies on tidal
sand banks along the coast of Qld.
They have a number of colour
and pattern variations. The golden
form was once a prize collectors
item, but in recent years they have
become reasonably common.
Range: N.S.W. to Qld. Length:
50 mm. Common.

692

692
VOLUTIDAE
MacAndrew's Volute
Amoria macandrewi
Sowerby, 1887

These shells are found on several
islands off Onslow and Dampier in
W.A. Shells are also occasionally
found on the adjacent mainland.
Range: W.A. (see above). Size:
65 mm. Moderately common.

693
VOLUTIDAE
Spotted Volute
Amoria maculata
Swainson, 1822

With a range extending almost the
entire length of the Qld. coast, *A.
maculata* is one of that State's most
widely known volutes. Although the
shell pattern is extremely variable the
molluscs body pattern tends to
remain the same throughout its
geographical distribution. It emerges
from the sand or rubble habitat to
hunt for prey during a flooding tide
or the hours of darkness. Food
consists mainly of other molluscs.
Range: Qld. Size: 80 mm. Common.

693

251

694
VOLUTIDAE
Southern Baler Shell
Melo miltonis
Gray (in) Griffith & Pidgeon, 1834

These beautifully patterned balers inhabit sandy bottom areas throughout the entire south-west of Australia north to Shark's Bay. There is some evidence of this species interbreeding with the northern baler *Melo amphora*, where geographical ranges overlap. They feed mainly on other sand dwelling molluscs but also travel over rocky reefs in search of food. Commercial abalone divers consider them a menace as they consume large numbers of abalone. Range: south-west Australia. Size: grow to at least 508 mm in length.

695
VOLUTIDAE
Mitre Volute
Lyria mitraeformis
Lamarck, 1811

A small well-known southern species, *L. mitraeformis* is common on intertidal sand banks and deeper waters to 10 metres. Very variable in pattern and form. Range: Vic. to W.A. Size: 50 mm. Common.

696
VOLUTIDAE
Blotched Snowflake Volute
Cymbiola nivosa
Lamarck, 1804

Found on intertidal sand banks from N.W. Cape to King Sound, W.A. One of the commoner W.A. volutes it has two main colour variations. The figured specimen is the most prevalent although dark pink specimens are not uncommon. Mating usually takes place in October/November after which several shells may indulge in communal egg laying. Range: W.A. Size: 90 mm. Common.

695

697
VOLUTIDAE
Papillose Volute
Ericusa papillosa
Swainson, 1822

Trawled by prawners from Qld. to
southern W.A. these shells are not as
common as their fairly extensive
range might convey. They live on
sandy or mud bottom sometimes
amongst reef and feed on other
molluscs. Range: Qld. to southern
W.A. Size: 150 mm. Uncommon.

698
VOLUTIDAE
Black Spotted Volute
Cymbiolacca peristicta
McMichael, 1963

Found only at the Swain's Reefs on
the outer Great Barrier Reef, this
shell lives in sand at depths of 4
metres and is usually dredged or
taken by divers. Range: Qld. Size:
70 mm. Fairly common within its
area.

697

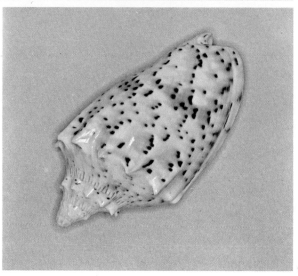

698

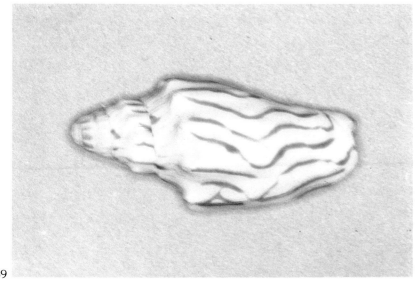

69

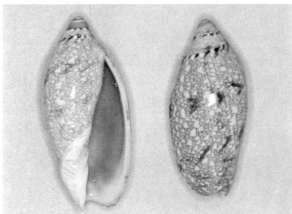

700

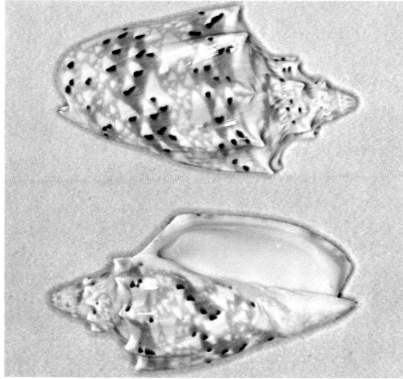

'01

699
VOLUTIDAE
Reticulated Volute
Cymbiolacca perplicata
Hedley, 1902

This shell has been one of the rarest and most sought after species for over 70 years. For the greater part of this century its locality and habitat remained a mystery challenging collectors from all over the world. Large expeditions spent many thousands of dollars searching but without success. Recently the mystery was solved by Mr Tom Nielsen of Yeppoon, Qld., who after searching for the shell for many years dredged specimens from an area in the Coral Sea. Range: Qld. Size: 76 mm. Uncommon.

700
VOLUTIDAE
Juvenile Volute
Amoria praetexta
Reeve, 1849

With its restricted range, this species is not regarded as common. It lives in sand and sandy mud flats at low tide level. Range: northern W.A. Size: 60 mm. Uncommon.

701
VOLUTIDAE
Beautiful Volute
Cymbiolacca pulchra
Sowerby, 1825

Extremely variable in shape and colour, a number of geographical forms have been given the rank of species and sub-species in the past. Found almost the complete length of the Great Barrier Reef, they live from low tide level to 60 metres on sandy bottom. A number of deep water forms have also been trawled off the Qld. coast down to 160 metres. They feed mostly on small bivalves and other molluscs. Range: N.S.W. to Qld. Size: 80 mm. Common.

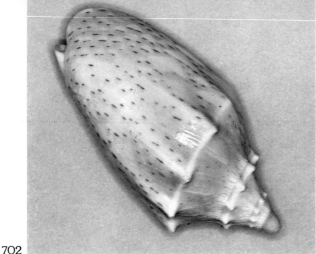

702

702
VOLUTIDAE
Randall's Volute
Cymbiolacca randalli
Stokes, 1961

The original specimens of this volute were dredged from a sandy lagoon approximately 50 kilometres north of Mossman. Qld. Since then numbers of intergrading shells have been found. Range: Qld. Size: 76 mm. Moderately common.

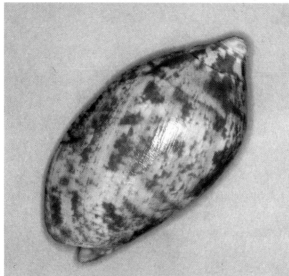

703

703
VOLUTIDAE
Blood Volute
Cymbiola rutila
Broderip, 1826

Restricted to areas off north Qld. These shells live in sandy rubble patches on intertidal reef. Specimens are also taken in deeper water down to 20 metres in sand. Range: Qld. Size: 100 mm. Fairly common.

704
VOLUTIDAE
Thatcher's Volute
Cymbiolacca thatcheri
McCoy, 1868

It is only recently that specimens of this once rare volute became available to collectors. Before 1972 only a few score shells were known and these were held mostly by State museums. Found in several areas along the outer Great Barrier Reef and Coral Sea they live in sand and sandy rubble to depths of 20 metres. Although mostly taken by dredging, the shells have also been collected by divers at night. Range: Qld. Size: 100 mm. Uncommon.

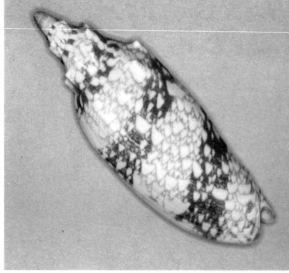

704

705
VOLUTIDAE
Turner's Volute
Amoria turneri
Griffith & Pidgeon, 1834

A. turneri lives in muddy sand from low water to 50 metres. It is fairly variable in pattern and is not a common shell. Range: Qld. to N.T. Size: 54 mm. Uncommon.

705

06

706
VOLUTIDAE
Undulate Volute
Amoria undulata
Lamarck, 1804

A sand dweller, *A. undulata* is taken at low tide, by diving, trawling and dredging to depths of 200 metres. The shell and the animal are extremely variable in colour and pattern over the geographical range. Range: Qld. to S.A. Size: 100 mm. Common.

707
VOLUTIDAE
Verco's Volute
Notovoluta verconis
Tate, 1892

08   707

Dredged at various depths to 40 metres, *N. verconis* lives in sand patches and is not a common species. The animal itself is interesting as the colour of the foot and the colour of the siphon are completely different which is unusual in volutes. Range: S.A. to W.A. Size: 40 mm. Uncommon.

708
VOLUTIDAE
Wiseman's Volute
Cymbiolacca wisemani
Brazier, 1870

This species has a very limited range which extends from Cairns in Qld. to approximately 80 kilometres further north. They are found only on offshore reefs and never on the mainland. Collected at very low spring tides on sand banks or by dredging or diving. Range: Qld. (see above). Size: 76 mm. Uncommon.

709 See 691

709

257

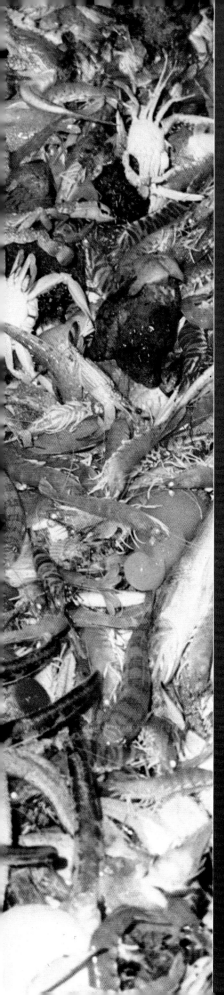

Part 5
Continental shelf

Continental shelf

710

In theory the continental shelf is all the area of land covered by water from low tide to 200 metres. However, for the purpose of this book the species in this section are those which are usually confined to deep water in excess of 40 metres.

These shells are of such beauty and rareness that many are known from only one or two specimens. For it is an unknown world where few may visit and then only for a short time. The hazards of deep diving even for the well trained and healthy, are manyfold, bottom time is negligible and most species live below the subsurface. So, to obtain specimens they must be bought or exchanged from fishermen, trawlermen, prawners, scallopers or crayfishermen who bring up molluscan wonders from the deep.

Many years ago, because of the limited demand, fishermen just shovelled shells over the side with the rubbish from a haul. Some perhaps picked out a few of the prettier ones and sold them for a very low price or often they gave them away. Today, like many other things, the price of shells has risen with the increasing demand. It must be remembered that the fisherman's lot is not always an easy one, their work is hazardous, arduous and in many cases unrewarding. They have bad weather and high overheads to contend with so it is an advantage for them to have a reasonable knowledge of shells and their value in order to supplement their incomes.

A few skippers with an interest in conchology have realized the potential in shells and rigged up dredges which they use in conjunction with their nets. Thus they are contributing greatly to the knowledge of marine fauna on the continental shelf.

The natural histories of these deep water molluscs are almost unknown with only a small proportion of the animals themselves ever having been studied. It can only be assumed that they behave in a way similar to their shallow water relations.

'12

712
PECTINIDAE
Ballot's Saucer Scallop
Amusium balloti
Bernardi, 1861

One of the largest species of saucer
scallops in Australia, these shells
have long been the basis of the
commercial fisheries in Qld. They
live on sandy or muddy bottom
between 18 and 40 metres. Range:
N.S.W., Qld. Size: 115 mm. Common.

713
ARCHITECTONICIDAE
Large Sundial
Architectonica maxima
Philippi, 1848

Usually trawled, this species is also
found occasionally washed up on
beaches. They live on sandy mud and
are fairly common in depths of 20 to
40 metres. Range: N.S.W. to Qld.
Size: 50 mm. Common.

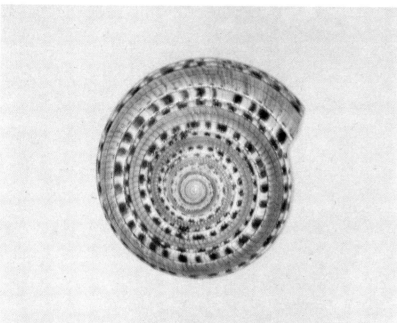

'13

714
BUCCINIDAE
Grand Buccinid
Penion mandarinus
Duclos, 1831

Moderately common along the
southern Australian coast, this
species is collected by trawlers or
brought up in crayfish pots. It is a
carnivore and feeds mostly on other
molluscs. Range: Vic., Tas., S.A, W.A.
Size: 120 mm. Common.

714

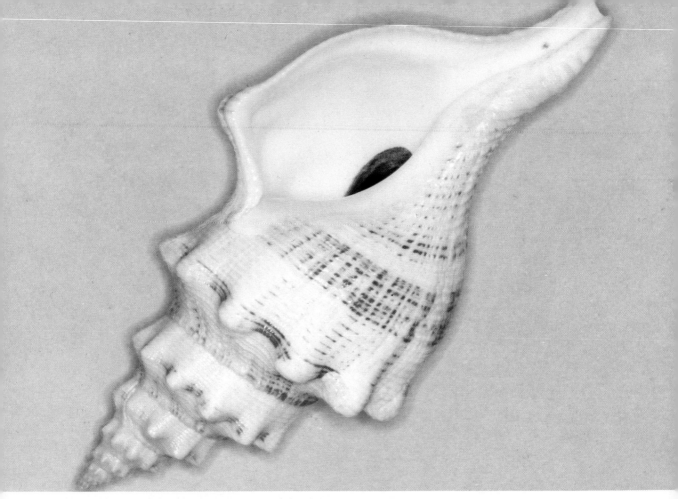

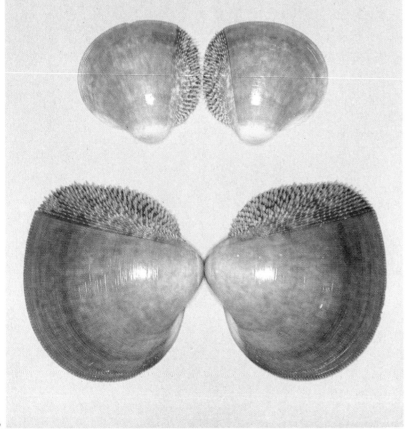

715 See 714

716
CARDIIDAE
Beche's Cockle
Nemocardium bechei
Reeve, 1840

Trawled at various depths along the east coast, this very strikingly coloured shell lives in a muddy sand bottom and has a transparent yellow periostracum. Range: N.S.W. to W.A. Size: 50 mm. Moderately common.

715

716

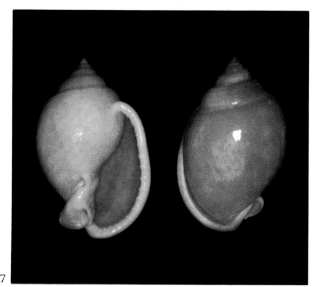

717
CASSIDAE
Angas's Helmet
Phalium glabratum angasi
Iredale, 1927

This almost transparent sub-species is confined to the waters of Australia. Although found in intertidal sand banks off Qld., the shells are much more prevalent in 20 to 40 metres where they are trawled by prawners. Range: N.S.W. to northern W.A. Size: 50 mm. Common.

718
CASSIDAE
Cancellate Helmet
Oniscia cancellata
Sowerby, 1824

Trawled from deep water off the Qld. coast, this unique shell is eagerly sought by collectors. Easily identified, it has a light yellow periostracum over its dorsal surface. Range: Qld. Size: 70 mm. Moderately common.

719
CASSIDAE
Nodulose Helmet
Cassis nana
Tenison-Woods, 1879

Trawled off the Qld. coast, this little helmet shell is of fairly common occurrence. It lives in sandy areas at depths of between 60 and 300 metres. Range: N.S.W. to Qld. Size: 50 mm. Common.

18   717

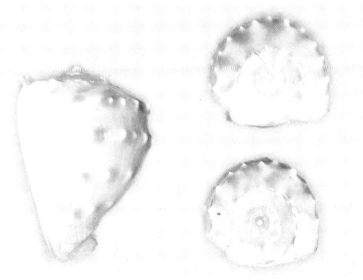

719

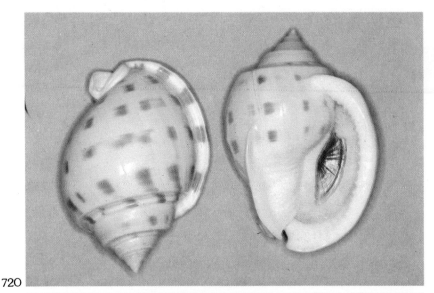

720

720
CASSIDAE
Sophy's Helmet
Phalium sophia
Brazier, 1872

One of the most attractive shells of its genus, *P. sophia* is trawled on a sandy bottom at depths of around 100 metres. Range: N.S.W. to Qld. Size: 80 mm. Not common.

721
CASSIDAE
Thomson's Helmet Shell
Phalium thompsoni
Brazier, 1875

Available to collectors through trawlers, these shells are brought up from deep water along the south-east coast. For a helmet shell they are somewhat fragile. Range: N.S.W. to Vic. Size: 76 mm. Fairly common in some areas.

721

722
COLUMBARIIDAE
Spindle Pagoda
Columbarium spinicinctum
von Martens, 1881

This interesting and exquisitely sculptured species is trawled off the continental shelf of Qld. Specimens seem to be far more prolific dead than alive, although this may be due to a burrowing existence. Range: Qld. Size: 80 mm. Uncommon.

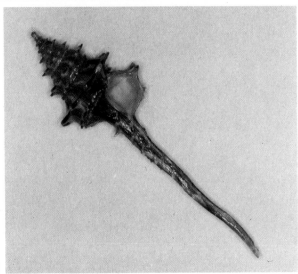

722

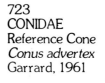

723
CONIDAE
Reference Cone
Conus advertex
Garrard, 1961

First dredged in deep water off
southern Qld. at 160 metres, *C.
advertex* can now be enjoyed by the
majority of collectors. The increase
in deep water prawning boats in
those areas has led to its availability.
Range: N.S.W. to southern Qld. Size:
30 mm. Uncommon.

723

724
CONIDAE
Angas's Cone
Conus angasi
Tryon, 1884

C. angasi can be obtained from
prawn trawlers working out of
southern Qld. areas where they are
brought up from around 100 to 200
metres. Range: Qld. Size: 40 mm.
Moderately common.

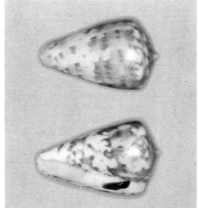

724

725
CONIDAE
Illawarra Cone
Conus illawarra
Garrard, 1961

This species lives at 150 metres on a
muddy bottom in southern N.S.W.,
but is dredged in much shallower
water in northern N.S.W. It has a thin
transparent periostracum. Range:
N.S.W. Size: 30 mm. Uncommon.

726
CONIDAE
Cox's Cone
Conus coxeni
Brazier, 1875

Trawled and dredged at depths of 40
metres. This is an attractive little
cone which has a transparent
periostracum. Range: N.S.W. to Qld.
Size: 20 mm. Uncommon.

725

726

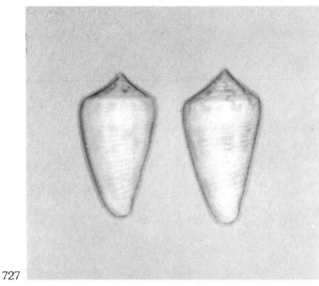

727

727
CONIDAE
Lizard Island Cone
Conus lizardensis
Crosse, 1856

Originally, shells were from the vicinity of Lizard Island, Qld. Since then specimens have been trawled at various localities along the Qld. coast at depths of 60 metres. They have a transparent yellowish periostracum.
Range: Qld. Size: 50 mm.
Uncommon.

728
CONIDAE
Mrs Nielsen's Cone
Conus nielsenae
Marsh, 1962

Mr Tom Nielsen, one of Australia's greatest modern day shell discoverers, first dredged this species in 34 metres of water off Townsville, Qld. It was named in honour of his wife Mollie. The shell lives on a sandy rubble bottom but since its discovery has been found at other localities.
Range: Qld. Size: 48 mm.
Uncommon.

729
CONIDAE
Recluse Cone
Conus recluzianus
Bernardi, 1853

This large, deep water species was first recorded from off the Qld. coast in 1966. Since then specimens have been trawled at other localities. It lives in depths of 120 to 160 metres and nearly always shows signs of healed breaks or growth scars.
Range: Qld. Size: 100 mm.
Uncommon.

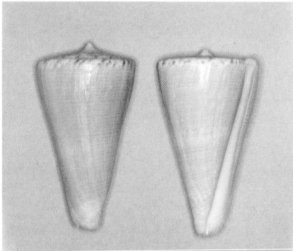

728

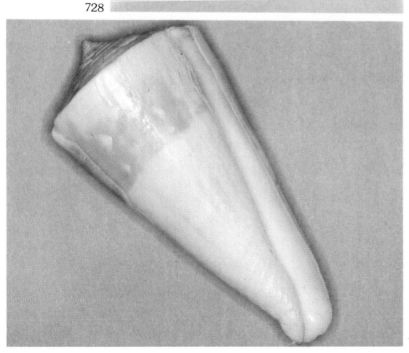

729

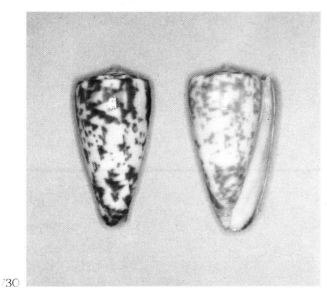

730

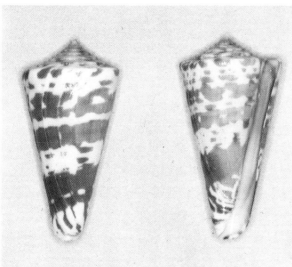

731

732

730
CONIDAE
Red Spotted Cone
Conus rufimaculosus
Macpherson, 1959

Trawled in deep water off N.S.W. and southern Qld., this cone has become more available to collectors during the past few years. Range: N.S.W., Qld. Size: 50 mm. Moderately common.

731
CONIDAE
Scullett's Cone
Conus sculletti
Marsh, 1962

Trawled off the southern coast of Qld. in depths of 200 metres. *C. sculletti* is unique to the area. Range: Qld. Size: 50 mm. Moderately common.

732
CONIDAE
Society Cone
Conus temnes
Iredale, 1930

Trawled off southern Qld. in 30 to 40 metres. These shells display a wide variety of colours and patterns. Beautifully designed, they show an affinity towards *C. ammiralis* and may only be a deep water form of that species. Range: Qld. Size: 80 mm. Moderately common.

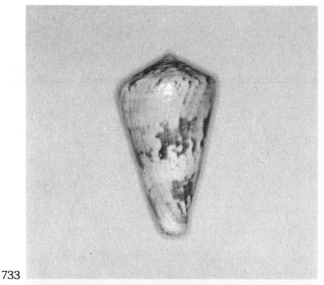

733

733
CONIDAE
Ocean Cone
Conus wallangara
Garrard, 1961

Found in depths of 150 metres, this shell ranges from southern N.S.W. to Qld. and lives on a muddy bottom. It has a very thin brown periostracum. Range: N.S.W. to Qld. Size: 30 mm. Uncommon.

734
CYMATIIDAE
Long Tailed Triton
Ranularia sinensis
Reeve, 1844

Trawled in fairly large quantities on muddy shell grit bottom, these shells live at depths in excess of 20 metres. Live specimens have a brown periostracum of medium density. Range: Qld., N.S.W., W.A. Size: 55 mm. Common.

735
CYMATIIDAE
Girdled Triton
Linatella cingulata
Lamarck, 1822

An unusual species, sometimes trawled at depths of between 60 and 100 metres. This shell lives on a muddy sand bottom, but is not often taken alive. Range: N.S.W. to N.T. Size: 60 mm. Uncommon.

734

735

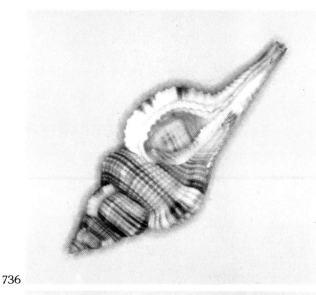

736

737

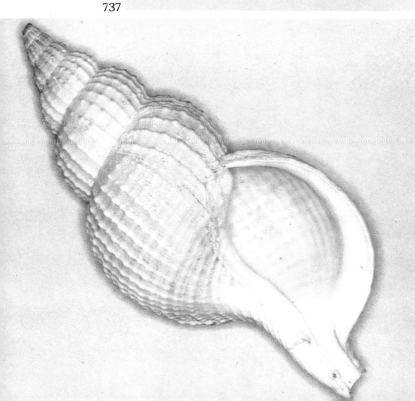

738

736
CYMATIIDAE
Pfeiffer Triton
Septa pfeifferiana
Reeve, 1844

This shell is trawled from 30 to 50 metres off northern Qld. It is found on a sand mud bottom but is still fairly uncommon in Australia. Range: Qld. to N.T. Size: 76 mm. Uncommon.

737
CYMATIIDAE
Reticulate Triton
Distorsio reticulata
Roeding, 1798

Living on muddy sand in deep water off the Qld. coast, this species is taken in small numbers by prawn trawlers. In life it has a thin periostracum with long bristles on the dorsal surface. Shells are usually a delicate pink in colour. Range: Qld. to W.A. Size: 60 mm. Moderately common in some areas.

738
CYMATIIDAE
Netted Triton
Fusitriton magellanicus retiolus
Hedley, 1914

Trawled in 100 to 200 metres off the N.S.W. and Vic. coasts, this species lives on mud. It has a rather thin shell, typical of deep water forms, and an opaque yellowish periostracum. Range: N.S.W., Vic. Size: 120 mm. Uncommon.

739

739
CYMATIIDAE
Smooth Triton
Linatella succincta
Linnaeus, 1771

Mostly taken by trawling or dredging, this shell lives subtidally in medium depths on a muddy sand, rubble bottom. It has a brown sparsely haired periostracum. Range: Qld. Size: 55 mm. Uncommon.

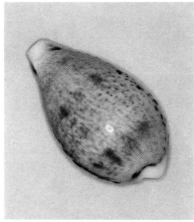

740

740
CYPRAEIDAE
Coucom's Cowry
Cypraea hungerfordi coucomi
Schilder, 1964

This exquisite shell inhabits deep water usually around 160 to 200 metres. It is brought up on rare occasions by trawlers working off southern Qld. The subspecies was named in honour of Mr Cec. Coucom, a well known and very keen member of the molluscan fraternity. Range: Qld. Size: 45 mm. Rare.

741
CYPAEIDAE
Wonder Cowry
Cypraea hesitata
Iredale, 1916

A deep water species trawled in depths of 80 to 100 metres. Two other recognised forms of this shell are also trawled — an albino and a dwarf, but as there are many intergradable shells, these may only be variations and not subspecies. Range: N.S.W., Vic., Tas. Size: 100 mm. Common.

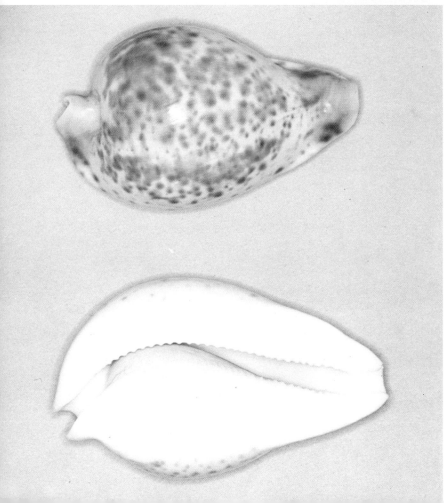

741

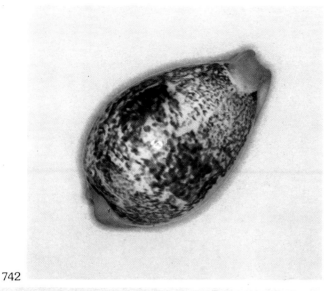

742
CYPRAEIDAE
Cape Moreton Cowry
Cypraea langfordi moretonensis
Schilder, 1965

This Australian subspecies is a rare deep water form trawled off southern Qld. in 200 metres. As yet, nothing is known regarding its natural history. Range: Qld. Size: 65 mm. Rare.

743
DENTALIIDAE
Elephant Tusk Shell
Dentalium elephantinium
Linnaeus, 1758

This distinctive shell is found on and in sand at depths of 30 metres, and can be taken by dredging or diving. It seems to be restricted to northern Qld. waters where shells are found in moderate numbers. Range: Qld. Size: grows to a little over 100 mm. Moderately common.

744
DENTALIIDAE
Erect Tusk Shell
Dentalium erectum
Sowerby, 1860

Fairly common off Sydney, this species lives in a sandy mud bottom at depths in the vicinity of 100 metres. Almost always orange in colour, shells are often marred by healed breaks. Range: N.S.W. Size: 70 mm. Common.

742

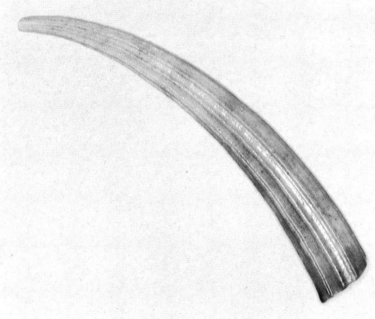

743

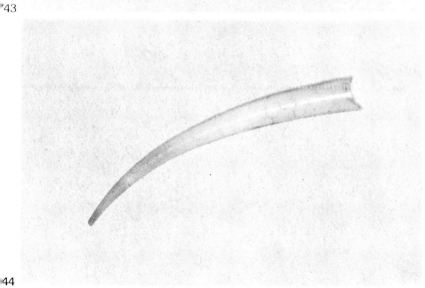

744

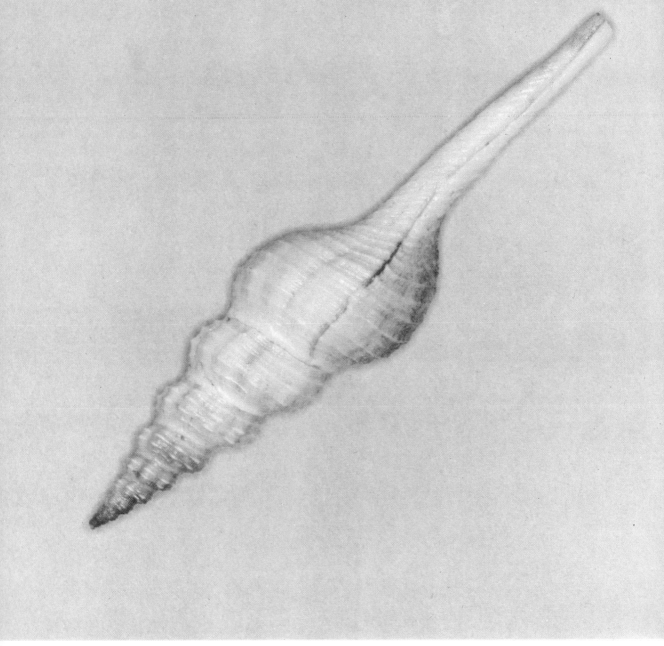

745

745
FASCIOLARIIDAE
New Holland Spindle
Fusinus novaehollandiae
Reeve, 1848

Trawled at depths of over 150
metres. These shells possess a fawn
coloured periostracum and are the
largest of the Australian spindles.
Range: N.S.W., Vic., Tas., S.A. Size:
grow to over 220 mm. Common.

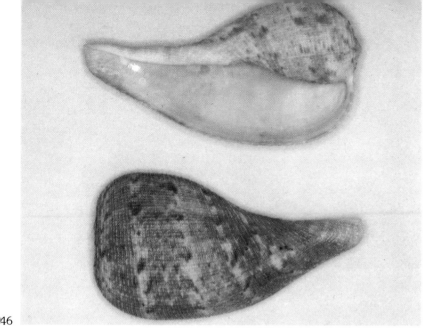

746
FICIDAE
Underlined Fig Shell
Ficus subintermedia
D'Orbigny, 1852

Living beneath sandy mud at depths exceeding 25 metres, it is trawled regularly off Qld. coast. This shell has a pink animal which is dotted all over with red markings and yellowish specks. Range: Qld. to W.A. Size: 80 mm. Common.

747
HARPIDAE
Articulate Harp Shell
Harpa articularis
Lamarck, 1822

Living mostly below tide level, this shell is not collected alive in many numbers. It inhabits areas of sand in depths down to 30 metres. Range: Qld. to W.A. Size: 100 mm. Uncommon.

46

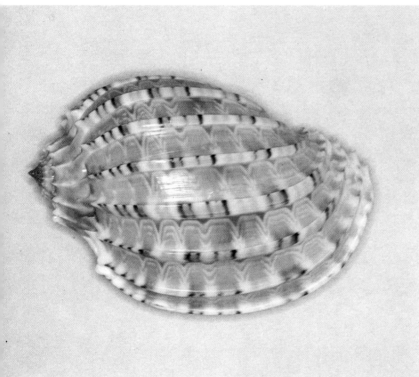

748
HARPIDAE
Exquisite Harp Shell
Austroharpa exquisita
Iredale, 1931

This species occurs between 140 and 200 metres and is trawled or dredged in deep water on a muddy, shell grit bottom. It has a fine, ochre coloured periostracum and a relatively fragile shell. These two features are unknown in the larger more well-known species. Range: N.S.W., Vic., and W.A. Size: 30 mm. Rare.

47

748

749

MAGILIDAE

Australian Coral Shell

Latiaxis australis

Laseron, 1955

Fairly common in prawn trawls to 100 metres off the coast. These beautiful shells are always in great demand. Because of their deep water habitat little is known of their habits. Food consists mainly of small fan shaped solitary corals. Range: N.S.W., Vic. Size: 40 mm. Common.

750

MAGILIDAE

Flat Topped Coral Shell

Latiaxis mawae

Griffith & Pigeon, 1834

Trawled in waters at around 200 metres. These shells feed on solitary corals. It is only in the last few years that this species has been known from Australia. Range: Qld. Size: 70 mm. Uncommon.

751

MITRIDAE

Barred Mitre

Neocancilla clathrus

Gmelin, 1791

N. clathrus occurs in subtidal sand and is taken by dredging or diving off the Great Barrier Reef. The pictured shell was trawled off southern Qld. in 50 metres. Range: Qld. Size: 50 mm. Uncommon.

750

749

751

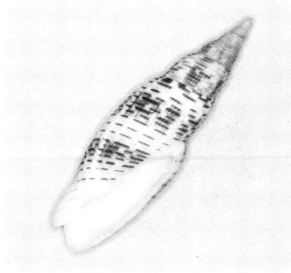

752

752
MITRIDAE
Granulated Mitre
Cancilla granatina
Lamarck, 1811

Found subtidally in sand off the Great Barrier Reef. The figured specimen was trawled in 32 metres off Townsville, Qld. This fairly large species is not often available to collectors. Range: Qld. Size: 60 mm. Uncommon.

753
MITRIDAE
Solid Mitre
Mitra solida
Reeve, 1844

The pictured shells were trawled off southern Qld. in 120 metres. This medium-sized, rather attractive species, has been recorded from the Great Barrier Reef. Range: N.S.W. to Qld. Size: 50 mm. Uncommon.

753

754
MURICIDAE
Coppinger's Murex
Murex coppingeri
E. A. Smith, 1884

A rare shell for many years, *M. coppingeri* is now brought up in small numbers by trawlers working in northern Australia. It lives on a muddy bottom at depths of around 34 metres. The smallest of the *Murex* genus within Australia. Range: Qld. to northern W.A. Size: 55 mm. Uncommon.

754

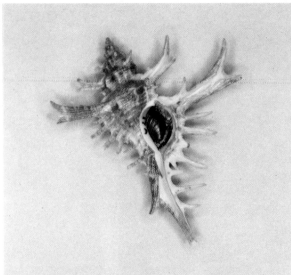

755

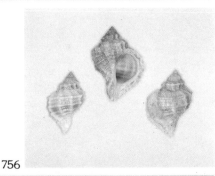

756

755
MURICIDAE
Long Horned Murex
Chicoreus damicornis
Hedley, 1903

The typical long spined form of this
shell is trawled commonly in areas
off N.S.W. on hard or muddy bottom.
These shells can be brown, mauve,
yellow, orange or white and live at
depths of between 60 and 140
metres. This typical form has also
been found in Vic. and S.A. However,
in Qld. another short-spined form
exists which is also commonly
trawled at depths of around 160
metres on hard bottom. Several
other consistent shell forms also exist
in areas within the known range, all
forms feed on bivalves. Range: Qld.
to S.A. Size: 60 mm. Common.

756
MAGILIDAE
Broad Emozamia
Emozamia licinus
Hedley & Petterd, 1906

A rare deep water shell, *E. licinus*
lives on muddy bottom from 200 to
500 metres. It has a thin brown
periostracum. Range: N.S.W. to Tas.
Size: 16 mm. Rare.

757
MURICIDAE
Black Tipped Murex
Murex aduncospinosus
Sowerby, 1841

Taken by dredging or trawling off the
Qld. coast this species inhabits sandy
bottom in depths of between 20 and
40 metres. Although it has dark
tipped spines this is not always a
good identification characteristic as
there are several species of this
genus which have similar darkened
varice extensions. Food consists
mainly of bivalves. Eggs are laid in
the sand, usually attached to a shell
or other small solid object. Range:
Qld. Size: 90 mm. Fairly uncommon.

757

758

758
MURICIDAE
Bordered Murex
Pterynotus patagiatus
Hedley, 1912

Trawled or dredged in 50 to 70 metres off the Qld. coast this species lives on hard rubble bottom. Shells are subject to marine growths and attacks by boring organisms. A perfect specimen, heavily frilled, is difficult to obtain but certainly well worth the effort for a specialist. Range: N.S.W. to Qld. Size: 60 mm. Uncommon.

759

759
MURICIDAE
Dancing Lady
Siphonochelus pavlova
Iredale, 1936

First discovered by a trawler skipper, Captain Moller, the original shell came from 220 metres off Sydney, N.S.W. Since then small numbers of shells have been dredged in 140 to 200 metres off Moreton Bay, Qld. It lives in a muddy shellgrit bottom and is one of the most attractive Australian typhids. Range: N.S.W. to Qld. Size: 22 mm. Uncommon.

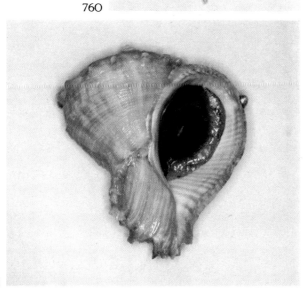

760

760
MURICIDAE
Short-Spined Typhis
Typhis philippensis
Watson, 1886

Dredged in mud at depths of between 30 and 70 metres, this shell is somewhat slimmer and more delicate than *T. yatesi*. Range: N.S.W., Vic., Tas. Size: 25 mm. Moderately common.

761
MURICIDAE
Turnip Shell
Rapana rapiformis
Born, 1778

Quite a common shell brought up in prawn trawls of the Qld. coast. This shell is not closely related to *Rapa rapa* although the shells resemble each other superficially. Range: Qld. Size: 70 mm. Common.

761

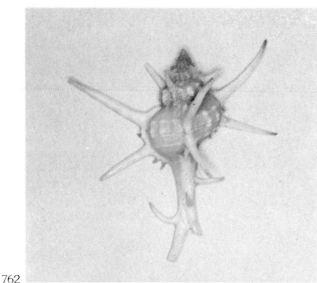

762

762
MURICIDAE
Straight-Spined Murex
Chicoreus longicornis
Dunker, 1864

A moderately common, deep water
species, this shell is trawled in depths
of 160 metres off Cape Moreton in
Qld. It lives on a hard coral sand
bottom and feeds on small bivalves.
Trawler-men dislike the species as it
is difficult to remove from the nets
and its sharp dorsal spine easily
penetrates footwear. Range: Qld.
Size: 60 mm. Common.

763
MURICIDAE
Triple-Spined Murex
Murex tribulus
Linnaeus, 1758

A variable species, trawled on muddy
sand bottom in depths of 30 to 50
metres off the Qld. coast. So far it
seems to be restricted to the east
coast. Range: Qld. Size: 100 mm.
Uncommon.

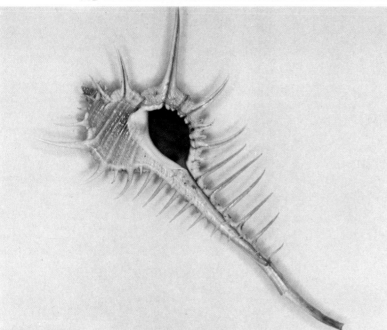

763

764
MURICIDAE
Tweed Heads Murex
Haustellum tweedianum
Macpherson, 1962

A rather prettily marked species that
is trawled off southern Qld. at depths
ranging from 20 to 120 metres.
Although mostly taken on a muddy
bottom the shells also live in sand on
the Great Barrier Reef. They have a
white animal. Range: N.S.W. to Qld.
Size: 60 mm. Fairly common.

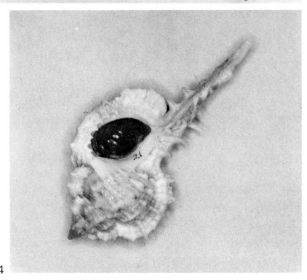

764

765

765
MURICIDAE
Yate's Typhis
Typhis yatesi
Crosse, 1865

A rather robust shell taken in 10 to 100 metres on muddy or coarse bottom. Not considered to be common. Range: N.S.W., Vic., S.A. Size: grows to around 25 mm.

766
OLIVIDAE
Three Waters Zemira
Zemira bodalla
Garrard, 1966

Z. bodalla is trawled on a muddy bottom off southern Qld. at depths of 160 metres. It has a thin yellowish periostracum and a distinct tooth or spur towards the anterior end of the apertural lip. Range: Qld. Size: 25 mm. Moderately common.

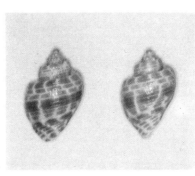

766

767
OLIVIDAE
Girdled Ancilla
Ancillista cingulata
Sowerby, 1830

One of the largest Australian species within the family Olividae, *A. cingulata* ranges from Qld. to W.A. where it is commonly brought up in prawn trawls. The animal is quite large and cannot withdraw into the shell for protection. Living mostly under sandy mud it ventures out in the hours of darkness in search of food in the form of other small molluscs. Range: Qld. to W.A. Size: 60 mm. Common.

767

768
OLIVIDAE
Aggressive Ancilla
Ancillista velesiana
Iredale, 1936

Trawled extensively from N.S.W. to Qld. and N.T. at depths of 22 to 40 metres. The animal of *A. velesiana* is very large in comparison to the shell. Like most ancillas the body cannot be drawn back into the shell for protection. The mollusc's foot is flat and oval — perfectly shaped for burrowing under the sand where it spends a great part of its existence. The wide expanse of foot also comes in handy for swimming which is accomplished by flapping the anterior and posterior extensions backward and forward in a similar fashion to the sea slugs. Range: N.S.W., Qld., N.T. Size: 89 mm. Common.

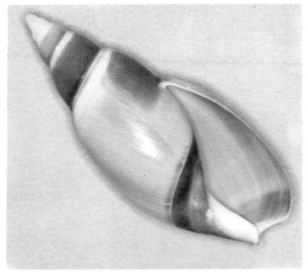

768

769

769 See 267

770
PECTINIDAE
Windowed Fan Shell
Semipallium fenestratum
Hedley, 1901

This beautiful little species is trawled or dredged at depths of between 100 and 200 metres. Range: N.S.W. and Vic. coasts. Size: 50 mm. Uncommon.

771
PECTINIDAE
Glory Scallop
Chlamys gloriosa
Reeve, 1853

Valves of this shell are often found on beaches in N.S.W. and Qld. Live shells live subtidally to depths of 40 metres and most specimens are taken by dredging or trawling. A number of different colours may be encountered, some being quite spectacular. Range: N.S.W. to Qld. Size: 50 mm. Common.

770

771

772
STROMBIDAE
Powis's Tibia
Tibia powisi
Petit, 1842

Trawled in depths of 160 to 200 metres on a mud bottom, *T. powisi* is only a recent addition to the Australian molluscian fauna. Still fairly uncommon, it is a distinctive shell and easily identified. Range: Qld. Size: 76 mm. uncommon.

773
TEREBRIDAE
Lime Auger Shell
Terebra lima
Deshayes, 1859

A deep water species, *T. lima* is trawled at depths of 40 to 60 metres off northern N.S.W. and Qld. on a muddy sand bottom. Range: N.S.W., Qld. Size: 90 mm. Moderately common.

774
TEREBRIDAE
Three-Girdled Auger
Terebra triseriata
Gray, 1834

Usually dredged or trawled in deep water it is not often this shell is taken in a perfect condition. It lives in sandy mud and has a yellow translucent animal. Range: Qld. to W.A. Size: 100 mm. Uncommon.

72

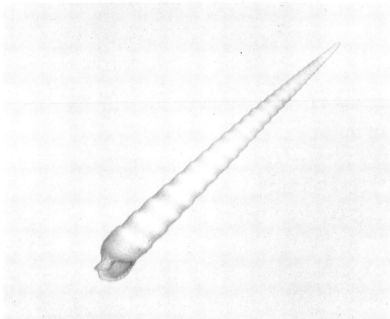

73

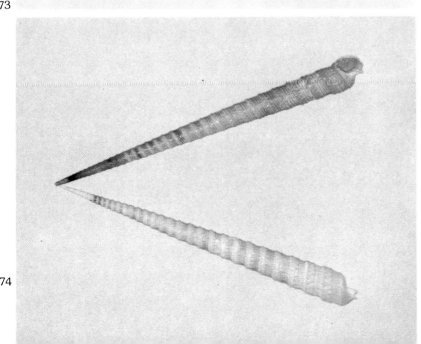

74

775
TONNIDAE
Beer Barrel Tun
Tonna cerevisina
Hedley, 1919

Trawled regularly off the N.S.W. and
Qld. coasts, these large gastropods
live on a sand or sandy mud bottom
from 30 to 200 metres. They have a
thick brown periostracum and many
different colour variations. Mostly
nocturnal, they feed on molluscs and
echinoderms, particularly
holothurians (sea cucumbers). Range:
N.S.W. to Qld. Size: 250 mm.
Common.

776
TONNIDAE
Deep Water Tun
Tonna tetracotula
Hedley, 1919

Growing almost as large as the giant
bear barrel tun, *T. tetracotula* is
usually restricted to deep water
where it is trawled in moderate
quantities. Found on sandy mud
bottom from 20 to 160 metres.
Range: N.S.W. to Qld. Size: 120 mm.
Moderately common.

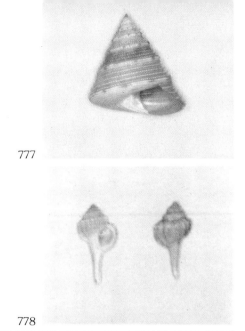

777

778

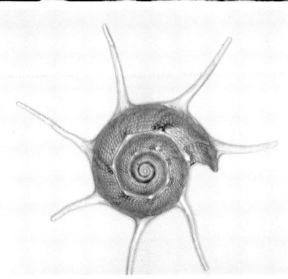

779

780

777
TROCHIDAE
Many-Waters Trochid
Astele bularra
Garrard, 1961

This shell is quite common on muddy shellgrit bottom off Cape Moreton, Qld. around depths of 200 metres. Several specimens have been recorded from other localities in Qld. as far south as Broken Bay, N.S.W. Range: N.S.W., Qld. Size: 28 mm. Common.

778
TROPHONIDAE
Graceful Trophon
Xenotrophon euschema
Iredale, 1929

First named from specimens found off southern N.S.W. in 120 metres. Most shells available today are brought up in dredges from deep water off Moreton Bay, Qld. They live on a muddy shellgrit bottom and are carnivorous. Range: N.S.W. to Qld. Size: 20 mm. Uncommon.

779
TURBINIDAE
Golden Turbo Shell
Bolma aureola
Hedley, 1907

B. aureola lives along the northern N.S.W. coast to southern Qld. Once considered a very rare species, the results of commercial prawning in that area have since revealed extensive colonies. Specimens have also been found on the Great Barrier Reef. Range: N.S.W. to Qld. Size: 76 mm in diameter. Moderately common.

780
TURBINIDAE
Yoca Turban
Guildfordia yoca
Jousseaume, 1899

Still a rare species in Australia, this shell is fairly common in countries to the north, particularly Japan. Several specimens have been trawled in depths of 160 to 200 metres off southern Qld. recently and it is assumed that others also will be found in due course. Range: Qld., N.T. Size: 70 mm. Uncommon.

781

781
TURBINELLIDAE
Polished Vase Shell
Tudicula rasilistoma
Abbott, 1959

This shell mostly inhabits areas of hard bottom, and is trawled at depths of 120 metres. It is an easy shell to identify. Range: N.S.W. to Qld. Size: 80 mm. Moderately uncommon.

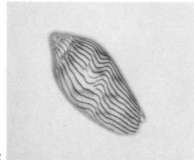

782

782
VOLUTIDAE
Benthic Volute
Amoria benthalis
McMichael, 1964

A small shell, *A. benthalis* is either dredged or trawled at depths of 200 metres off Cape Moreton in Qld. As yet this species has not been recorded from other parts of Australia. Range: Qld. Size: 35 mm. Uncommon.

783

783
VOLUTIDAE
Red Volute
Cymbiolacca cracenta
McMichael, 1963

Trawled or dredged off the coast of Qld. to 40 metres, these shells are not considered to be common. As with many shells of this type future workers may conclude that they are only forms of other well-known species. Range: Qld. Size: 80 mm. Uncommon.

784
VOLUTIDAE
Tin Can Bay Volute
Volutoconus grossi
Iredale, 1927

Not always obtainable, *V. grossi* lives below tide level to depths of over 200 metres. Most shells live in patches of sand near hard bottom and rubble. Range: N.S.W. to Qld. Size: 100 mm. Reasonably uncommon.

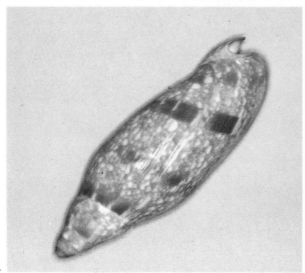

784

785

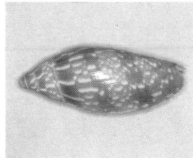

786

785
VOLUTIDAE
Gunther's Volute
Paramoria guntheri
Smith, 1886

Once considerably rare, this little shell has recently become a little more available to the collector. Trawled or dredged in 40 to 60 metres on sand and rubble bottom off S.A., the species is also recorded from W.A. Range: S.A., W.A. Size: 50 mm. Uncommon.

786
VOLUTIDAE
Blushing Volute
Amoria guttata
McMichael, 1964

Trawled and dredged off the Qld. coast, this very beautiful volute lives on sandy bottom at 40 to 120 metres. Range: Qld. Size: 50 mm. Uncommon.

787
VOLUTIDAE
Hunter's Volute
Cymbiolista hunteri
Iredale, 1931

A very distinct and beautiful volute which lives on a sandy mud bottom and is trawled off the N.S.W. and Qld. coasts in depths of between 20 and 160 metres. Many variations in colour and form exist, with shells from deeper water displaying extremely enhancing patterns. Animal is white with red stripes. Range: N.S.W., Qld. Size: 170 mm. Common.

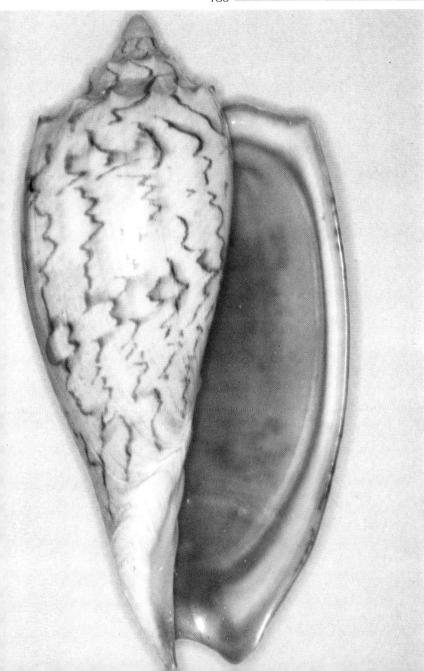

787

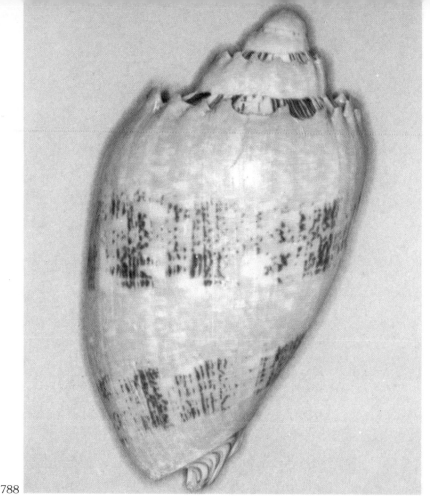

788

789

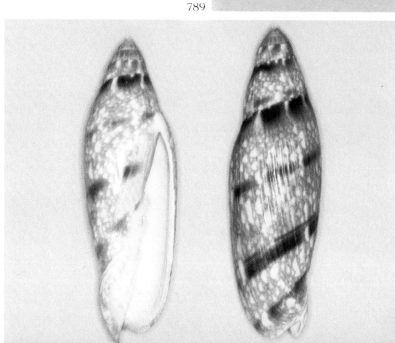

790

788
VOLUTIDAE
Irvin's Volute
Cymbiola irvinae
Smith, 1909

As yet the living animal of *C. irvinae* has not been studied. The shells, usually inhabited by hermit crabs, are brought up in craypots off W.A. in depths of 20 to 170 metres. Range: W.A. Size: 120 mm. Uncommon.

789
VOLUTIDAE
Laseron's Lyria
Lyria laseroni
Iredale, 1937

Still to be found alive, dead specimens of this little shell are found irregularly on beaches and by trawling and dredging off the central N.S.W. coast. It lives around reefy areas and it may well have a similar habitat to other lyrias, in sand pockets on the reef itself. This would explain why live specimens have not shown up by the aforementioned methods of collecting. Range: N.S.W. Size: 25 mm. Uncommon.

790
VOLUTIDAE
McMichael's Volute
Volutoconus grossi mcmichaeli
Habe & Kosuge, 1966

Much smaller and slimmer than *V. grossi* this sub-species is readily recognised by its dark brown or black bands. Range: Found only off Townsville, Qld. Size: 80 mm. Uncommon:

791
VOLUTIDAE
Magnificent Volute
Cymbiola magnifica
Gebauer, 1802

Trawlermen often bring up large numbers of these shells when working in depths down to 100 metres off the coast. A few have been picked up on sand banks at low tide and a number taken by divers in depths of 10 to 50 metres. They are carnivorous and are occasionally found crawling on reef looking for smaller molluscs upon which they prey. Range: Vic., N.S.W., southern Qld. Size: 300 mm. Common.

791

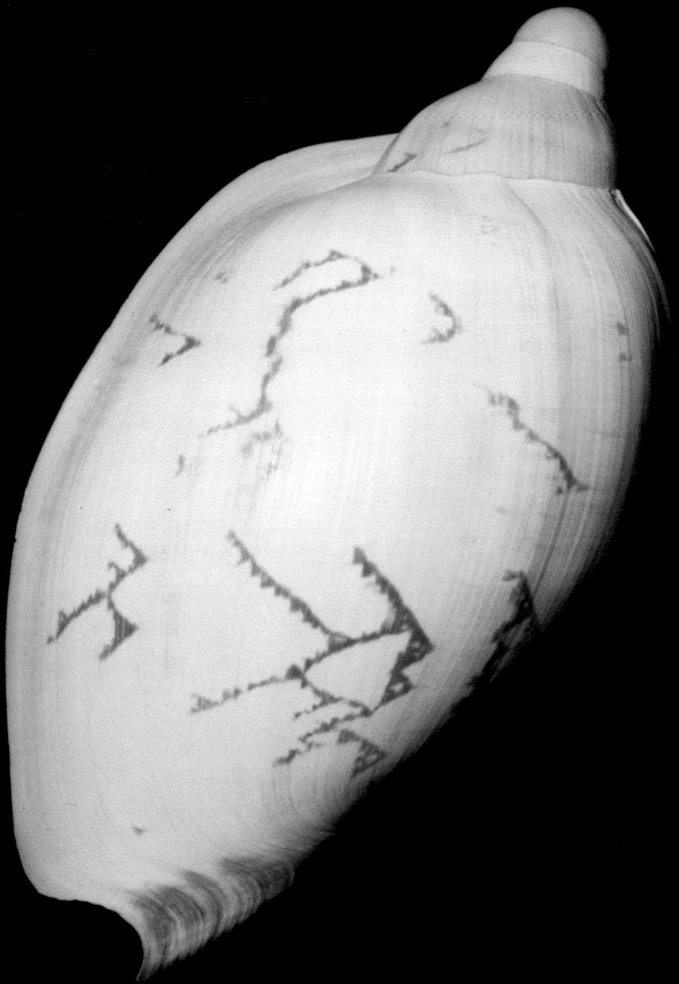

93

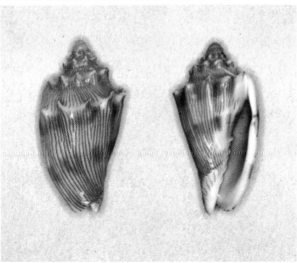

794

792
VOLUTIDAE
False Melon Shell
Livonia mammilla
Sowerby, 1844

One of the largest Australian volutes, these shells live on sandy or muddy bottom and are trawled to depths of 180 metres. The animal is orange in colour and is carnivorous. Often old adult shells are encrusted with barnacles and marred by boring organisms. Range: Qld. to Tas. Size: 300 mm. Common.

793
VOLUTIDAE
Moller's Volute
Amoria molleri
Iredale, 1936

Exclusive to deep water, A. *molleri* is trawled regularly off the central east coast at depths akin to 200 metres, on a mud bottom. Specimens have also been taken off southern N.S.W. but these are fairly rare. Range: N.S.W. to Qld. Size: 100 mm. Common.

794
VOLUTIDAE
New Moon Volute
Nannamoria parabola
Garrard, 1960

This unique species is dredged and sometimes trawled at depths below 200 metres on a mud bottom off Qld. Range: N.S.W. to Qld. Size: 40 mm. Uncommon.

792

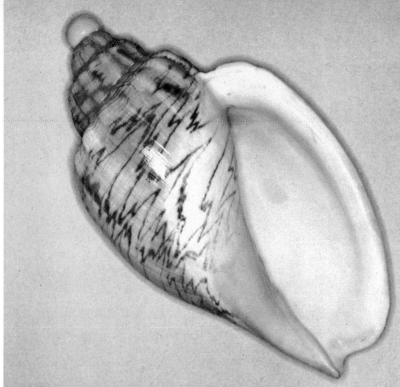

795

795
VOLUTIDAE
Roadnight's Volute
Livonia roadnightae
McCoy, 1881

Very rare in a live condition, shells of this species are trawled and also brought up in craypots from deep water. They live on a sandy mud bottom, at depths of around 200 metres. Range: N.S.W. to W.A. Size: 160 mm. Uncommon.

796
VOLUTIDAE
Silky Volute
Ericusa sericata
Thornley, 1951

A magnificent salmon coloured shell, *E. sericata* remained unknown until the early 1950s. It was first found off Pt. Stevens in N.S.W. and is now constantly trawled in deep water within its area. Range: N.S.W. to Qld. Size: 115 mm. Fairly common.

797
VOLUTIDAE
Sophia's Volute
Cymbiola sophia
Gray, 1846

A. sophia is usually trawled or dredged on a mud bottom between 20 to 40 metres. They have similar characteristics to *C. nivosa*. Range: Qld. to N.T. Size: 80 mm. Uncommon.

796

797

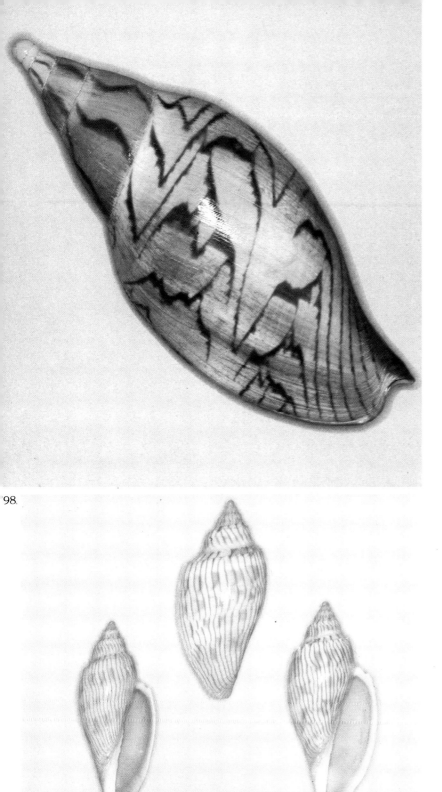

798
VOLUTIDAE
Sowerby's Volute
Ericusa sowerbyi
Kiener, 1839

Trawled in moderate quantities in depths ranging between 20 and 160 metres on sand or mud. They are very variable in colour, pattern and size. There is enough evidence to suggest a certain amount of sexual dimorphism exists within the species. Range: Qld. to Tas. Size: 220 mm. Common.

799
VOLUTIDAE
Studer's Volute
Ternivoluta studeri
von Martens, 1897

This species lives on muddy bottom from 140 to 200 metres. It is fairly common and is trawled regularly by prawners. Range: N.S.W. to Qld. Size: 55 mm. Common.

800
XENOPHORIDAE
Adorned Carrier Shell
Xenophora peroniana
Iredale, 1929

The habit of incorporating shells and other debris into their shells makes it difficult for normal predators to find this species. However, man does not have this problem and can distinguish specimens in natural habitat by the circular pattern of camouflage on the shells back. Not often taken by hand, this species is usually dredged or trawled. Range: Qld. Size: 35 mm. Fairly common.

798

799

800

Part 6
Ocean pelagics

Ocean pelagics

This final section contains only a few species in comparison with other sections. Perhaps it could be said that all molluscs with drifting veligers are ocean pelagics, for a small part of their lives is spent drifting with the currents.

Nevertheless true ocean pelagics are molluscs which spend their whole lives on the surface of the ocean or between the surface and the sea floor coming to rest on the bottom only after death. Amongst these are the giant squids which grow to over 15 metres in length and pelagic octopods with fine webbing between their arms similar to a parachute. This webbing enables the mollusc to remain almost stationary in midwater at any depth it prefers. It is not likely that the collector or naturalist will encounter these molluscs although several of their relations — the paper nautilus group — are frequently found on southern hemisphere beaches.

There are beautiful blue janthina snails and millions of small translucent sea butterflies, delicate little beings that live in the depths, their buoyant shells washing ashore periodically on beaches. Australian seas probably contain several score of pelagic molluscs but most of the smaller forms are relatively unknown. The figured specimens are those which are most likely to be found by people fossicking on beaches after storms.

Taking Care

The shells available to the collector or naturalist in Australia today are without equal. It is a simple enough thing to become an efficient human predator and amass vast collections of beauteous objects. But it is so much more fulfilling to try and learn their secrets, to keep records and to study their way of life, to contribute a little to the overall knowledge of our bountiful shores. At the very least it doesn't hurt to pause sometimes and give thought to those fascinating creatures whose external skeletons convey so much pleasure to so many, the molluscs. Their future generations, are in your hands.

802
ARGONAUTIDAE
Argo Paper Nautilus
Argonauta argo
Linnaeus, 1758

A. argo is a much slimmer shell than *A. nodosa* and with many more smaller ribs. The shell, like all paper nautilus, is secreted by paddle-like membranes situated at extremities of the female's dorsal arms. The little female begins construction as soon as she leaves her egg capsule and it grows as she does until she becomes adult and mates. This happens only once and soon after her eggs hatch the female dies. Range: Qld. to W.A. Size: grows to 250 mm. Uncommon.

803

803
ARGONAUTIDAE
Hian's Paper Nautilus
Argonauta hians
Lightfoot, 1786

803
ARGONAUTIDAE
Hian's Paper Nautilus
Argonauta hians
Lightfoot, 1786

A small brown shell, this species is found on beaches only on very rare occasions. Live specimens have been seen off Lord Howe Island, N.S.W. Range: Qld. to W.A. Size: 50 mm. Rare.

804
ARGONAUTIDAE
Paper Nautilus
Argonauta nodosa
Solander, 1786

This shell is found in fairly large numbers washed up on southern beaches. Because of their delicate texture and unique shape, they are always in demand. The argonauts are pelagic relations of the octopus and the females construct these shells to house their eggs. Range: N.S.W., Vic., S.A. Size: specimens each 250 mm. Uncommon.

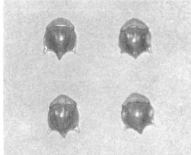

805

805
CAVOLINIDAE
Three Spined Sea Butterfly
Cavolina telemus
Linnaeus, 1758

A globular pinkish shell, sometimes found in thousands at the high tide mark washed up by the sea. These little shells are inhabited by small delicate molluscs which live suspended at very great depths, over 1,600 metres. When they die some shells float to the surface and are washed ashore. Range: Qld. to W.A. Size: 9 mm. Common on beach.

806

806
GLAUCIDAE
Margined Sea Lizard
Glaucus marginata
Bergh, 1868

G. marginata is a nudibranch, but unlike the majority of nudibranchs which inhabit the sea floor, it floats on the surface of the ocean, upside down. Here it lives amongst the colonies of 'Portuguese-men-of-war' or blue bottles upon which it feeds. When there is a prevalence of onshore winds hundreds of these little molluscs get swept ashore to die on the beaches. Range: Australia-wide. Size: 50 mm. Common.

80

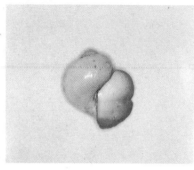

807

808

809

811

807
JANTHINIDAE
Prolongate Violet Snail
Janthina prolongata
Blainville, 1825

This species is pelagic and although a little smaller than *J. janthina*, is easily distinguished by the deep vee-like niche in the outer lip of the aperture. Washed up intermittently on all south coastal shores, usually in the summer months. Range: N.S.W., Vic., Tas., S.A., southern W.A. Size: 15 mm. Uncommon.

808
JANTHINIDAE
Globose Violet Snail
Janthina globosa
Swainson, 1826

The smallest of the violet snails, this species seems to be restricted to the waters of southern Australia. Infrequently washed up on beaches, this shell spends its entire life cycle on the open seas. Range: N.S.W. to W.A. Size: 10 mm. Uncommon.

809
JANTHINIDAE
Large Violet Snail
Janthina janthina
Linnaeus, 1758

Living its entire life cycle on the surface waters of the ocean, *J. janthina* is at the mercy of the wind and tides. Their presence on beaches is usually only a result of strong winds or storms at sea. They do not swim but secrete gelatinous substance which hardens on contact with the water and acts as a raft. This species is the largest and most commonly found on Australian beaches. Range: Australia-wide. Size: 30 mm. Common.

810
NAUTILIDAE
Pearly Nautilus
Nautilus pompilius
Linnaeus, 1758

This species so far has only been found in an uninhabited condition washed up on east coast beaches. When alive the mollusc resembles an octopus but is beautifully striped and has many more arms. Unlike the paper nautilus, *N. pompilius* is attached to its shell by a siphonal tube which extends through a small central hole in the coils. The chambers in the nautilus shell are filled with gas and by means of this tube it can adjust the amount of gas in each chamber allowing the animal to rise or sink at will. Mostly a deep water dweller it bumps along across the bottom in depths below 60 metres. It feeds on fish, crabs and other invertebrates and is caught in modified fish traps off the deep water reefs of New Caledonia. Range: Qld. to N.T. Size: 200 mm. Fairly common.

811
SPIRULIDAE
Ram's Horn Shell
Spirula spirula
Linnaeus, 1758

This is an internal shell which comes from a small rarely observed species of Cephalopod. Called a tail-light squid because of a light producing organ situated at the anterior end of the body, this species inhabits the deep ocean waters in many parts of the world. No doubt the light has a specific purpose but as yet scientists have not agreed on it. Very common on most Australian beaches the shell assists the animal's buoyancy. Range: Australia-wide. Size: 25 mm. Common.

81

Glossary

ADDUCTOR MUSCLES
Muscles attached to the shells of bivalves which are used to open and close the valves.

ANTERIOR CANAL
A hollow extension at the front of a univalve through which the siphon protrudes.

APERTURE
Entrance or mouth of a univalve shell.

BIVALVE
A shell having two valves, e.g. scallop.

BODY WHORL
Largest coiled tube of a univalve, usually the last.

BYSSUS
Fibres with which some bivalves attach themselves to objects.

CALCAREOUS
Made of lime.

CEPHALOPOD
Meaning 'head footed', it refers to molluscs of the octopus and nautilus

COLUMELLAR PLAITS
The folds or teeth on the inner lip or axis of a univalve.

DORSAL SURFACE
Upper surface of a shell.

ENDEMIC
Restricted in range to one area.

FOOT
Muscular extension of a mollusc's body used for locomotion.

GASTROPOD
Meaning 'stomach footed', and relates to all univalve shells.

GENUS
The name given to a number of related shells at genetic level.

GREGARIOUS
Found together in groups.

HINGE
Interlocking tooth found in bivalves.

LITHOTHAMNIAN
Coraline algae.

LITTORAL
Between high and low tide (intertidal).

MANTLE
The membraneous shell forming organ of a mollusc.

MOLLUSC
Soft fleshy invertebrate usually covered by a shell.

NACREOUS
Pearly.

OPERCULUM
The apertural lid or door found in many univalves.

OUTER LIP
Outer edge of the aperture.

PELAGIC
Open ocean dwellers.

PERIOSTRACUM
External skin covering or epidermis.

PLANKTON
Drifting or floating animals and plants relying on wind and currents for distribution.

POSTERIOR
Towards the rear or bottom end.

PROTOCONCH
The part a mollusc is born with.

RADULA
A ribbon of serrated teeth with which the mollusc reduces food to digestible particles.

SIPHON
The organ through which water enters the mantle cavity.

SPECIES
A group of organisms which through isolation, environment or interbreeding have formed their own genetic race, and in theory, will not produce offspring when mated with another such race.

SUB-LITTORAL
Below low tide level.

SUB-SPECIES
A geographical varient of a species which is sufficiently different to be recognised as such.

SUTURE
The continuous line between the whorls of a univalve.

UNIVALVE
Singular coiled shell.

UMBO
The opposing beaks of a bivalve shell situated near the hinge.

VENTRAL
Under side.

ZOOXANTHELLAE
Microscopic algae found in the mantle tissues of clams.

Bibliography

Australian Shells J. Allan (1959). Georgian House Melbourne, Vic.

Australian Shells B. Wilson & K. Gillett (1971). A. H. & A. W. Reed, N.S.W.

Australian Seashores W. Dakin, I. Bennett & E. Pope (1960). Angus & Robertson, N.S.W.

An Illustrated Index of Tasmanian Shells W. L. May (1958), as revised by J. H. MacPherson. Government Printer, Hobart, Tas.

Marine Molluscs of Victoria J. H. MacPherson & C. J. Gabriel (1962) Melbourne University Press, Vic.

Marine Shells of the Pacific Vol. 1. W. O. Cernohorsky (1967). Vol. 2. W. O. Cernohorsky (1973). Vol. 3. W. O. Cernohorsky (1978). Pacific Publications, N.S.W.

Shell Collecting in Australia Neville Coleman (1976) A. H. & A. W. Reed, N.S.W.

Shells in Australia Neville Coleman (1978). A. H. & A. W. Reed, N.S.W.

Shells of the Western Pacific in Colour Vol. 1. T. Kira (1962). Vol. 2. T. Habe (1964). Hoikusha Publishing Co. Osaka, Japan.

Shells of New Guinea and the Central Indo Pacific A. Hinton (1972). Jacaranda Press, Qld.

The Great Barrier Reef and Adjacent Isles K. Gillett & F. McNeill (1959). Coral Press, N.S.W.

Index by scientific names

Index by popular names